MISFIT TO MAVEN

From 'ARGH' to 'AHHH'

Dear Stephanie,

Stay Wild
Stay True,
Always Be You!
Always
You ROCK
xoxo
Ebonie

MISFIT TO MAVEN

From 'ARGH' to 'AHHH'

EBONIE ALLARD

First published in Great Britain by Practical Inspiration Publishing, 2015

Copyright © Ebonie Allard, 2015

The moral rights of the author have been asserted

ISBN (print): 978-1-910056-32-5

ISBN (ebook): 978-1-910056-33-2

For more information, see *www.ebonieallard.com*

 **Practical Inspiration** PUBLISHING

CONTENTS

THE RIDDLE 7
STAY WILD, STAY TRUE 9
INTRODUCTION 13
MISFIT/MAVEN 19

Part 1: MYSTERY   21

LET'S START AT THE BEGINNING 23
NOT NORMAL AND THE QUEST FOR NORMALITY 29
ALWAYS TOO MUCH, NEVER ENOUGH 43
SHAME AND SHADOWS 65
DARK NIGHT OF THE SOUL 73

Part 2: MASTERY   83

THE NEXT CHAPTER 85
OVER, ROUND, OR THROUGH 127
DARKEST DAYS 139
CHOOSE LOVE, CHOSE LIFE, CHOOSE JOY 159

Part 3: MYSTERY   171

MYSTERY MASTERY MYSTERY 173
FROM ARGH TO AHHH 177
MORE 183

Part 4 : FROM ARGH TO AHHH!

STEP 1: FROM NUMBNESS TO AWARENESS 187

STEP 2: FROM APATHY TO ASPIRATION 211

STEP 3: JUDGMENT AND ACCEPTANCE (DISCERNMENT) 231

STEP 4: FROM INERTIA TO ACTION 253

STEP 5: FROM BLAME TO ACCOUNTABILITY 273

STEP 6: FROM IGNOR-ANCE TO ACKNOWLEDGEMENT 285

STEP 7: FROM CRITICISM TO APPRECIATION 293

STEP 8: AD INFINITUM 301

THE RIDDLE

It's all very simple.

Which doesn't mean it's easy.

You were born curious…..

…..and you have access to all the answers to all your questions.

You know how to love you. You know how to feel. You know how to think.

You also know how to process, to connect, to engage or to numb and to run away.

It is all here for you.

Everything you have ever had the notion to desire or want or not want for yourself, others and the world is all here for you.

There has also been a misunderstanding, and that common and widespread misunderstanding has led you to believe that all of this is somehow outside of you. It is not. It is inside of you.

You are constant. No matter what, there is always you.

You are born alone, you fear alone, love alone, joy alone, share alone, connect alone, live alone, die alone. And you are constantly changing. For some of you this is a scary truth. But it is not as scary as you think.

You have been given yourself as a wonderful riddle. Once you figure this riddle out, you are no longer alone, but part of the universe, and from this place of *being* not *doing* you can experience all that this adventure playground called life has to offer, from a place of wonder.

Don't misunderstand me when I say this; you will still experience anger, sadness, and feelings of all varieties, but without suffering them. A life of AHHH is not about living in BLISS or about some kind of spiritual bypassing of human feelings. It is about experiencing it all with reverence.

You have been given a guide to help you understand the riddle that is you. It is an inner voice, a gut feeling, a sense of knowing. Learning to listen to it is all there is to 'do', everything else is 'being'.

And actually, you are not entirely alone. Actually there are all the other people in the world who are part of the big riddle too. We all entangle and entwine and mix and meet and muddle, acting as mirrors and triggers and carers and preoccupations for one another.

Isn't it fantastic?

Isn't it frustrating?

Breathe.

Have you ever noticed what happens when you breathe? Everything calms down. Everything makes sense again. Nothing is urgent. Inside and outside become one. Breath is the link between inside and out.[1]

---

1.   Our autonomic nervous system regulates primarily involuntary activity such as heart rate, breathing, blood pressure, and digestion. Although these activities are considered involuntary, they can be altered either through specific events or through changing our perceptions about a specific experience. The system is broken down further into two complementary systems: sympathetic and parasympathetic nervous systems. The sympathetic nervous system controls 'fight or flight' responses. In situations we perceive as threatening our sympathetic nervous system kicks in to prepare our bodies: our heart rate quickens to get more blood to the muscles, our breathing becomes faster and deeper to increase oxygen, blood flow is diverted from the organs so digestion is reduced and our pupils dilate for better vision. In an instant, our body is prepared to either defend or flee.

However once the threat has passed the relief we feel may be instant, but our body takes longer to adjust, the parasympathetic nervous system kicks in and returns everything to normal. This system is slower acting, and may take several minutes or even longer to get your body back to where it was before the scare.

Regulating your breath, making it smooth, slow and even, activates your parasympathetic nervous system and therefore calms down your entire body. In this information age so many things trigger our 'fight or flight' responses, we can often be in a state of high alert for prolonged periods, which is not how we were designed. Consciously focusing on and slowing down your breath really does calm you down.

STAY WILD, STAY TRUE

Dear Mum, dear Dad, dear siblings, dear ex-lovers, friends, clients, colleagues, readers; teachers both knowingly or unknowingly, please know this:

I love you.

Forgive me.

I'm sorry.

Writing this book has been one of the most joyful and most terrifying experiences of my life! I have lived the hell out of my life, and yet this – sharing my truth – has been tougher than anything else I've done yet.

Fear that I may hurt feelings, fear of being misunderstood almost stopped me. However it is because this is a truth for so many of us that I want to share my story with open-heartedness and transparency, hopefully in some small way setting a precedent and giving you all permission and desire to share yours too.

So many of us carry secrets and shame and are reluctant to share these with our closest friends, and this saddens me. I hope that somehow this book enables you to open a window and let in some air and some light to the closed dark spaces that we are all afraid to look at more closely. I hope that through personal growth and awareness we get better at discerning who is trustworthy and upon finding those people trust them; sharing our vulnerabilities and allowing them to do the same, so that we may all experience the honour and connection of this kind of intimacy.

The story I am about to tell is my truth, and it may not be the same as yours. Both can exist, just because you remember it one way and I another doesn't mean that one is right and the other wrong. The truth is that each minute of each day, each of us gives meaning to our experience differently, and so many times it is not the event itself but our reaction to it that colours our perception of a situation. Reading through the diaries and journals that made this book possible, it became really clear to me just how much our perceptions and memories change as we move through our lives. Please know this: I take responsibility for my life and I wouldn't change a moment of it, for it has brought me to where I am now. If you have played a part in the tale so far, whatever that might have been, I am truly grateful.

The way I see it; life is a series of soul lessons, and as my father[2] once told me:

> 'You sat up in the sky as a star looking down on earth and picked us, you picked all the players in your life and they picked you. You chose those souls to experience the interactions of life with, you chose the heartache and the joy, the frustrations and the ease, all of it.'

Thank you for picking me, I'm so glad I picked you.

To every single person who has supported me in writing this book, from the 50 or so people who generously crowdfunded it to those friends and coaches who listened while I wept in sadness, frustration and fear – Thank you. I particularly want to thank Alison Jones, without whom I may very well have given up when it got tough, all my clients who have shared with me their stories and offered me their encouragement – often explaining to me using my own words back at me why it is that I do what I do, and what the point of the book is – and in memory of Freya Marylin Moonbeam Murphy (I love you sis! You are in my heart always)

---

2.   These are probably not his exact words: I was young, 7 or so when he explained how it all worked and where we came from, and 14 when he reminded me of it as I slammed the door in his face. Later as I read Caroline Myss's *Sacred Contracts* I more fully understood what he had said and honed my beliefs about this.

and Claire Louise Hose (you were a huge inspiration to me and I often ask myself, what would Claire do?).

So, to YOU, the misfits and the mavens, I hold my hands up in reverence:

Let's live our lives NOW, not waiting for a retirement, or for skinny, or for richer, or for permission.

The happiness we seek can only be granted to us, by us. The happiness we seek is also seeking us.

Each of us is unique and it is that uniqueness that is our gift to the world. In your weirdness is your wonder! Every one of you sees problems to be solved; it is not your job to bemoan them but instead to be a part of the solution. It is your duty to shine, to creatively bring your gifts to the world, and to encourage others to do the same.

I hope this book inspires you to do just that.

STAY WILD, STAY TRUE,
XOXO EBONIE

'Faith means living with uncertainty — feeling your way through life, letting your heart guide you like a lantern in the dark.'

— Dan Millman

INTRODUCTION

This book is not for you if you are looking to find *the* answers to your questions...

By which I mean that each of us has the exact right answers to OUR own exact right questions. The tone, context, and language you use to ask your questions are personal to you and so are your interpretation and understanding of them – the same is true of the answers. *The* person who has all of the answers to *your* questions is you. I am a big fan of talking it out and a big fan of getting a different perspective than my own but ultimately, I am responsible for me, and you are responsible for you.

It is far more powerful to figure it out for yourself, and self-governance is in my opinion the key to it all. When I talk about self-governance, I mean learning to listen to yourself and govern yourself responsibly. Discovering self-awareness and self-acceptance is perhaps the absolute point of everything. In this book and in my work I intend to give you a set of principles, guidelines and theories which when applied to your life will enable you to uncover your reality and your truth for yourself.

At this point, it is also necessary to understand that I am making assumptions about you. I assume that you aren't as happy or as satisfied as you would like to be. I am assuming that you have begun some sort of process of self awareness and self discovery and that you have moments (long ones or short ones) where you can't see the fucking point in any of it.

Ouch.

I really know that. Trust me, I've been there.

I am also assuming that there are some bits of life that fascinate the hell out of you, and that you have touched or tasted or smelt some *bliss* or *contentment* and want to find more.

Think of this book as a handy way to remind yourself about what is important, and give us both some pointers on those days where the point has seemingly vanished.

You can start at the beginning and read through to the end – I would probably do that the first time – and then you can open it on any of the workbook chapters and read it as a standalone. The exercises and the questions are there to help you on your journey of self-discovery and awareness, and the lists and suggestions are not exhaustive or compulsory. I want for you to take what works and leave the rest. Walk to the beat of your own drum and be comfortable and confident doing so.

I am a fan of making notes as I read. I tend to write in books but if that's not OK with you, get a notebook to accompany you on this journey as I will at times invite you to make notes or answer questions.

Why should I write it down and not just think about it?

Well, there are now plenty of studies which indicate that the physical act of writing really does boost learning and goal achievement. Dr Gail Matthews, a psychology professor at Dominican University of California, found that people who wrote down their goals, shared them with others, and maintained accountability were 33% more likely to achieve them, versus those who just formulated goals.[3]

Writing stimulates a bunch of cells at the base of the brain called the reticular activating system (RAS). The RAS acts as a filter for everything your brain needs to process, giving more importance to the stuff that you're actively focusing on at the moment—something that the physical act of writing brings to the fore. As Anne Klauser[4] says, 'Writing triggers the RAS, which in turn sends a signal to the cerebral cortex. Once you write down a goal, your brain will be working overtime to see you get it, and

---

3. *http://www.dominican.edu/dominicannews/study-backs-up-strategies-for-achieving-goals.html*
4. *Write It Down, Make It Happen*, by Henriette Klauser *http://www.henrietteklauser.com/_books/_writeitdown/index.htm*

will alert you to signs, signals and evidence to let you know that you are on track.'

That said, it's just an invitation, you are the boss of you: do what you find works…. ☺

This book, like the work I do out in the world, is about living a 360-degree, self-governed life.

I've talked a little about what I mean by self-governed, so what do I mean by *life*? Well for the purposes of explanation I divide life into three main sections:

Work – the thing you do in the world, to solve a problem and make a living.

Ideally, this should be something you are good at and enjoy and people will pay for. Whatever this is for you, don't let yourself do anything for money that you wouldn't do for free, but don't do it for free – charge the most you comfortably can, knowing that you are providing value.

Relationships – with clients, colleagues, friends, lovers, family – with everyone.

There is something that happens in our belly, a flicker of uncertainty, when someone else enters our space. Other people are our best teachers, our mirrors; we love them, they can be a source of great joy, *and* they challenge us immensely. People buy from people, so learning about attraction, being self aware and honouring boundaries brings great quality relationships and better business. As does giving yourself what you need rather than waiting for someone else to, and asking for what you need – learning to communicate effectively.

EGO / Enlightenment – this is about the relationship you have with your Self and your God. When I talk about Self I mean your reflection, your individuation, your mortality, this incarnation. It's about how you value you, and that which is greater than you (than all of us). I am not here to talk about organised religion or one set of spiritual beliefs over another, I'm talking about how important I am in my own life and you are in yours. Things belong to you and are YOURS, this is your individuation.

Then there is the fact that we are both just specks of stardust in the grand scheme of it all and nothing belongs to anyone; we are all one. For me this section of our lives is about combining the studies of quantum physics with our intuition, and other 'feely' magic. Whatever you believe, whether it be GOD, or The Divine, The Universe or just plain Physics, whatever words work for you; I'm talking about when you feel at home, like you belong in your own body and you *get* your relationship to 'God'. If you don't know what I am talking about, then maybe this is not the right book for you. If you are at all curious – then stick around with an open mind. If you have been internally nodding, then great, because we will explore this further. When you have this bit sorted, everything else falls into place.

This book is about the whole gamut of life: living it, learning it, playing it, surviving it, thriving it. It's about how to enjoy experimenting, having fun and doing 'good'...

This book is not your standard business book – because for you business isn't just about making a living, it's about making a life. This book has more drugs, sex and eating disorders than most business books I've read and far less business, but if it was just the mechanics of business that were important to you, you'd buy a different book. If you have or want to have your own way of making a living and a life, that is as extra-ordinary as you are, you are in the right place. For too long there has been a notion that to be spiritual means to give away your gifts and live a life without financial gain and material reward. I am proud to be living in an age that is redefining the status quo. It is your duty to make money and to create value and to recognise your own worth and the worth of others. It is your duty to look after yourself first and foremost and then to look after those who cannot look after themselves. We are in the midst of a paradigm shift, the new matrix is one of heart and love, or honesty and transparency, of value and information. The world of work is changing, relationships are changing – we are moving from an overtly masculine modality into one that marries both masculine and feminine energies and ways of being.

If I haven't yet scared you off, I actively encourage you to tweet me with any questions you might have, or any gems that really resonate with you or even bits that you just don't get. I love a conversation. Let's chat.

Use #misfit2maven and @ebonieallard.

MISFIT/MAVEN

MISFIT: A PERSON NOT SUITED IN BEHAVIOUR OR ATTITUDE TO A PARTICULAR SOCIAL ENVIRONMENT - SOMETHING THAT DOES NOT FIT OR FITS BADLY.

A person who is too innovative, too creative, too geeky and/or too full of heart to clock in and clock out of a job and/or life.[5]

A person who doesn't naturally conform, who is awake enough to not want to be a sheep, but not completely accepting of or able to embrace, surrender to and trust their uniqueness, difference and vulnerabilities.

A person who feels like they don't belong.

MAVEN: A TRUSTED EXPERT IN A PARTICULAR FIELD, WHO SEEKS TO PASS KNOWLEDGE ON TO OTHERS.

The word maven comes from Hebrew, meaning 'one who understands', based on an accumulation of knowledge.

A person who is innovative, creative, geeky and full of heart.[6]

A person who walks to the beat of their own drum, who is awake and accepting of themselves and others.

---

5. This is my definition, not necessarily a recognized and shared definition
6. This is my definition, not necessarily a recognized and shared definition.

A person who makes daily practice of embracing, surrendering to and trusting their uniqueness, difference and vulnerabilities and those of others.

Part One:
MYSTERY

LET'S START AT THE BEGINNING

Before I was seven years old I had lived in a house truck, on a commune, in France, in New Zealand, in Ireland, and in several homes in England. I had been bathed in a sink, had a pet goose called Lucy, and had police in two different countries looking for me – I think it would be fair to say that my parents gifted me with a curiosity for the world.

I was born in France on 23rd July 1980. I was supposed to be born at the end of that September but I arrived early – a trait that has for the most part remained with me.

My parents, both British, were living in Hyères in the South of France in a place I only really know as The Cabanon. At the time of my birth the place had no electricity, running water or roof… I think the plan was to finish up before I arrived.

But I arrived before they were ready for me. 12 weeks before.

I weighed 3lbs and my head was the size of a small orange. I was put into an incubator in a hospital in Toulouse and cared for by French nurses. Money was tight and the 60km distance was too great; they couldn't afford the petrol to come and see me. For the first 6 weeks of my life I was pretty much alone in my little glass box; a place I have returned to many times metaphorically.

Although medically there is no rhyme or reason why babies are born so prematurely, for most of my childhood I believed that it was my desire for drama and attention that led to my early arrival rather than perhaps the circumstances or any number of other factors. In those days 28 weeks was really very early, and I was lucky to be so healthy.

For a while, like many children, I was convinced that I was adopted or that my parents married because my mum was pregnant with me. Neither assumption was founded on anything other than my feelings of difference and disconnect. (In fact I remember my dad enjoying trying to tell a young and easily embarrassed me with passion and conviction about the night I was conceived. I ran out the room with my fingers in my ears yelling 'La la la – I can't hear you!')

I'd like to tell you about both of my parents in detail as they are both hugely fascinating people for whom I have so much respect and who have impacted me significantly. However, if I am honest there is so much about their lives before me that I don't know and cannot share with the accuracy that they deserve. What I do know is that they are both very private people who, whilst respecting what I am trying to do with this book, would be happier to remain anonymous. Their lineage, the secrets and patterns of their past form a part of my story, but it is also part of theirs and so in respect for them I have chosen carefully what I share.

Every family has stories and patterns and secrets. Stories from either side of mine were not always handed down with pride, instead I got snippets here and there and as I grew up I got the sense that there were important reasons for the secrets being kept. So I stopped asking. There were often hints of dramatic events and emotional scars on both sides but very little detail was given. The events were always referred to in a very matter-of-fact way, no drama, no great and entertaining stories. I am a storyteller, it is my predisposition to make everything into an entertaining tale. I love the phrase 'never let the facts get in the way of a good story'. But in our house the bare facts were what I got if I asked a question about the past. From a very early age I felt that there were things one shouldn't talk about. I felt a pressure of required secrecy that, because it was unnatural for me, left me feeling suffocated and fearful that I may upset someone accidently by sharing a story.

I feel strongly that emotional DNA is a thing; that the wounds of the elders are passed on to be healed. I think that the study of epigenetics will eventually find that emotional trauma impacts and is stored in our cells. I believe that in families there are patterns and histories that repeat themselves over and over, passed on not just by nurture, but also by nature. Passed on with or without the explicit telling of the stories. I share this because I wonder about the stories our DNA would tell.

In 1980, when I was born, my father was 23 and my mother 21. I was the first grandchild in both their families. After I was well enough to be released from the hospital we travelled by car first to Paris to visit my dad's aunt, then on to Switzerland to his grandmother. I was still so small that they bathed me in the sink and dressed me in dolls' clothes. After Switzerland we came back to England and I was shown off to both my grandmothers.

Between 18 months and five years old the hippocampus is developing our sense of self. This tiny horseshoe-shaped part of the brain forms part of the limbic system and is primarily associated with memory and spatial navigation. It is the hippocampus's job to create meaning out of memory.

At three years old it is at its peak point of creating your narrative sense of self; giving you an identity and determining how you fit into the story.

There will have been many things that were happening when you were learning about who you are, recognising your body and distinguishing where you end and where the universe begins. Those things – your family, culture, traditions, and surroundings – were filtered and you began to form beliefs[7] and perceive your reality.

The things that happen when we are very young inform how we perceive reality, how we understand love, and what levels of physical touch and intimacy feel good and come naturally. Whether we were smacked, how often we were held, the level of conflict or love demonstrated in our home environment at that age, all of this impacts us hugely.

I was two and a half when my brother was born. By then we had lived in Ireland on a vegan commune where I had a goose called Lucy. We had been to Italy, and lived in Scotland in a tiny house up a very big hill. In 1983 we lived in Thame, near Oxford, where my brother was born at home on a Sunday morning after brunch. My dad's mum came over to look after me and I remember being excited.

I loved my brother immediately.

In fact my first real techni-colour and ever-so-happy memory is pushing him in a toy pram across a field of grass and flowers, under the biggest, bluest sky, in New Zealand. The sun made everything sparkle and refract tiny little rainbows, the world was huge, expansive and I was wild and free. In that memory I must have been three and he about six or seven months. My belief about life then was that it was truly magical.

For a year we lived in a house-truck in New Zealand and it was an adventure. I loved it. In every picture I am smiling and naked and having the time of my life. We lived in a community of other young hippies and my dad was my hero. I remember all the important stuff that happened during the year we were there; firstly my parents got the local police out looking for us because they thought we'd run away, only to find us three hours later tucked up in our beds. A local boy stuck his middle finger

---

7.   I talk more on beliefs in the workbook section, Step 3: Judgment and Acceptance.

up at me and I didn't know what it meant but did like the reaction it caused. I went over the handlebars of my tricycle and landed at the foot of a fountain.[8] And, my dad shaved off his moustache.[9]

In 1984 we moved back to London. We moved into my grandma's house in Hackney, where I had a makeshift bed of wooden boxes on wheels on the landing at the top of the stairs. It was all mine, and I loved it. I loved that I could hear everything that was going on downstairs. I loved staying awake and listening to the adults talking and I loved that the night I had my first nightmare (about a red dinosaur trying to eat me) my dad came and tucked me in so tightly that nothing in any dream could get me.

Shortly after that we moved into our own house. It was just around the corner from my grandma's and it was a real grown-up house. I was four when we moved in and we stayed there until I was seven. It was the longest we'd ever lived anywhere. I remember people commenting on it. I remember helping my dad lift the paving stones and lay turf in the garden. I remember the day we got a climbing frame, with a trapeze that hung down in the middle. I remember the green gym mats that lined the floor underneath and smelled of rubber. I remember swinging and making up songs, singing as I swung. I remember having a playroom and I remember having Victorian telephones rigged up between our playroom and our bedroom. We were happy. Life was good.

From four to six I felt pretty normal, I'm not sure that I knew what normal was, but I knew when I stopped feeling it.

---

8.   I still have the scar on my forehead, even though my wonderfully clever mum did an amazing job at putting me back together with butterfly stiches.

9.   I was mortified and went looking for it. I remember climbing up onto the sinks in the men's portacabin honeywagon. I knew it was naughty to be in there on my own, but I felt sure I'd find his facial hair in a little strip in the sink and get him to put it back on... I did not.

NOT NORMAL AND THE QUEST FOR NORMALITY

'NOW I AM SIX I AM CLEVER AS CLEVER,
I THINK I'LL STAY SIX FOR EVER AND EVER.'
– AA MILNE

The year I turned seven things changed for me.

One day, while I was still six, we were driving to a place we'd not been before. We were going to visit an old friend of my mum's. I was super excited because she had told me that he had fairies at the bottom of his garden, that she'd seen them and maybe I would see them too. On the way there in the car my parents fought; she was a fucking-awful-map-reading-passenger, he was a shouty-aggressive-impatient-driver, and I was an annoying are-we-nearly-there-yet child, who got shouted at by them in unison for trying to make them stop. My grandma and my brother were also in the car. At one point I remember my dad saying, 'Well if you don't fucking know, let's just follow that car, he seems to know where he's going.'

Pretty normal family car journey, right?

When we finally arrived I snuck off to the end of the garden and sure enough, right down at the bottom, past the lawn, in the long grass, hanging out by an overgrown Christmas tree, there *were* fairies. They were awesome.

No one else could see them, but I didn't mind – the adults believed I could and so that made it OK. I was special, I could see fairies and it was magical. That was when I was still six.

When I was seven it was no longer OK to be psychic or intuitive or magical. Up until then I thought it was, because people believed me, but then one day no one believed me anymore.

Not long after my seventh birthday I was walking home with my mum, excited because my grandma was making me a skirt. She'd not told me anything about it, just that it was almost done. We didn't get new things all that often and I could not wait. My grandma's house was about a ten-minute walk from ours. I asked if we could go via her house and get it. I was told no.

'She might not be in.' My mum tried to hurry me along and get us home.

All I could think about was the skirt. I'd imagined it in my head over and over. And then I saw it lying on the street.

'That's my skirt!' I trilled, skipping over and picking it up.

'No it's not. Leave it alone. Put it back.'

'But I KNOW it's my skirt. I promise it's my skirt. It must have fallen out of Granny's handbag. Please can we take it home!'

How did I know it was my skirt? I just knew. I love how the French have two words for 'knowing': *savoir* and *connaître*. There are proper definitions of when to use which, but in my mind one is for the stuff you just know, and the other is for the things you learn to know. I *just knew* all sorts of things as a child. Before I was seven I think I was 100% in tune with who I was; my wild uninhibited intuitive nature was as yet untarnished and in that moment, standing on the street with my mother, it changed. I could no longer trust what I *knew* because my mum, who knew everything as far as I was concerned, was MORE sure than I was that this was not my skirt.

When we got to our house Grandma was there, having a cup of tea with my dad and brother.

'Hello darling,' she said, 'go and fetch me my handbag, I've got your skirt for you.'

I felt like saying *'No you don't it's down the street, on the wall where I left it, waiting for some other little girl to call it hers.'*

But she was excited and so I was too. I fetched her handbag, gave it to her and watched as she pulled everything out. She pulled out tissues, then Polo mints, then keys and the coin purse she used to give us elevenses money, but no skirt.

'Was it pink and blue with little flowers on it and a stretchy elasticated waist?' I piped.

'Yes!' she exclaimed.[10] 'How do you know that? Did you sneak a look?' She wagged her finger at me.

'NO,' I shouted. 'I know because it fell out of your handbag and it's down the road!' I was off, I had already swung open the front door and I flew as fast as my legs would allow back to where I'd seen MY skirt.

That day was the first time I had an inkling of 'not normal'. It began to register that KNOWING, the kind that comes from deep inside, isn't *normal*. I didn't like how it felt to be different. I wanted to be loved and trusted unconditionally. I began to be curious about 'normal'.

And it wasn't long before I encountered an opportunity to make a trade for normality.

I need to set the scene a little more… My parents did the very best they could for us; I guess I'd describe them as innovative 'now' age hippies, way ahead of their time. They fed us organic and whole foods; we didn't have sugar until we were at least three. Unnecessary vaccinations and medicines were a no-no and in education we were gifted to Steiner

---

10. You might think that no one 'exclaims' but my grandma did, she often exclaimed with all her might and vigorous gesticulation.

Schools[11] as much as they could afford. Steiner school was great for me at Kindergarten; there were stories and large colourful wax crayons and yoga. It was only later, after I was seven, that it was another thing that I decided made me weird and not normal.

Steiner School meant no television and no plastic toys. Our toys were animals carved out of wood or handmade dolls. It was beautiful, *but* it was not 'normal'. One day, I took my handmade doll to the park. The sort of park you got next to every housing estate in England in the eighties: a strip of grass with a swing-set, a slide with puddles on it, a sandbox full of cigarette ends and a couple of ride-on animals on big metal springs. We were at the park with our au pair, a young French girl who sat on a bench and read her book. While she read, we played. For my brother that meant interacting with the equipment and for me it meant interacting with other kids. I chatted to a girl from the estate. She spoke differently to us. She said 'waughtar', we said 'water'. She was normal. She had a television at home and she had Star Wars figures with her in the park and I had a handmade doll. We switched. My mum was furious.

---

11. Steiner (Waldorf) education is a humanistic approach based on the educational philosophy of the Austrian philosopher Rudolf Steiner. Steiner distinguished three broad stages in child development. His early years education focuses on providing practical, hands-on activities and environments that encourage creative play. The emphasis in junior school is on developing pupils' artistic expression and social capacities, fostering both creative and analytical modes of understanding. The secondary education focuses on developing both critical and empathetic understandings of the world through the study of mathematics, arts, sciences, humanities and world languages. Throughout, the approach stresses the role of the imagination in learning and places a strong value on integrating intellectual, practical, and artistic activities across the curriculum rather than learning each academic discipline as a separate concern. The educational philosophy's overarching goal is to develop free, morally responsible, and integrated individuals equipped with a high degree of social competence. Teaching is intended to emphasize qualitative over quantitative assessment methods. Each school has a high degree of autonomy to decide how best to construct its curriculum and govern itself.

This experience reinforced what I believed to be true. We really weren't normal.

The next BIG thing that happened when I was seven is that two girls I didn't know died from anorexia. My dad was reading the newspaper and when he got to the story about these young girls he called me over and we had a conversation about it. Before that day I hadn't really thought anything about my body. It just was. I can see now that the relationship I developed over the years with food has been for the most part about control and certainty. When I needed to find and gain control, 'anorexia' and later bulimic behaviour was what I pulled out of my toolbox. Later I moved on to other things too, but restricting and then rebelling and binging on food has most often been my addictive and numbing technique of choice. I am not an expert on, nor have I studied eating disorders or addiction; I have learned a great deal about food and nutrition over the years but what I recount throughout this book is only my experience and what I believe about my on-going relationship with 'Self and God'. (One of the best books I have ever read on this subject is *Women, Food and God – An Unexpected Path to Almost Everything* by Geneen Roth. I highly recommend it to anyone who finds themselves restricting or bingeing on food.)

Three months after I turned seven we moved to the south coast, to Brighton. Brighton is my *spiritual home*. I have lived here on and off ever since. Even when I live somewhere else, Brighton is still my 'home'.

We arrived the weekend of the hurricane in 1987 and whilst my brother slept soundly through it, I got into bed with my mum and dad and began to realise that the world could be a pretty scary place. While my mum lit tea lights and placed them all around, I crept over to the sash windows and carefully looked outside. Dustbin lids flew up the street, trees had fallen onto cars. It was fierce. It was not normal.

Wild weather like that probably makes everyone think about God. Or the Universe, or the Divine, or whatever. As I lay in bed I really began, probably for the first time, to think in this way. Something MUCH bigger, greater than me, could crumple cars and blow over trees.

As a child I knew a little about Judaism and that our families had been Jewish but the teachings were not passed on to us. Neither of my parents practised any sort of organised faith. Being Jewish is passed through one's mother and my mum wasn't Jewish because her mum wasn't. Both our fathers were, so I saw myself as three quarters Jewish. I felt and still feel that our ancestry is a very important part of my identity. Whilst the faith and teachings weren't of so much interest to me, the rituals, the story and history was. We didn't really celebrate the Jewish holidays (apart from the occasional Seder at Pesach with my paternal grandmother.) My mum got us involved with the more pagan holidays – Solstice, Mayday, and Equinox and we sort of celebrated Christmas and Easter like everyone else. I mean we did, but not the religious part. I was fascinated by my friends who went to Midnight Mass on Christmas Eve. I had another friend who went to church every Sunday and if I stayed the night at hers I wasn't allowed to come up and take communion with them so instead I remained alone in the pews eating her penny sweets, contemplating why anyone would want to eat the body of Christ. Our Jewishness or non-Jewishness confused me. It added to an array of things that confused me. I had so many questions. I was so curious. I needed answers and Google hadn't been invented yet. So I went to my dad. Sometimes when I asked a question he would answer and other times, he would throw the question back to me and I would say: 'I don't know.'

'I don't know is a lazy answer.' He sent me off to look in an encyclopaedia.

Encyclopaedias are enormous and these days you can't give them away, but back then owning a complete set of Encyclopaedia Britannicas was a big deal. They were huge and they had no pictures; they were boring. So often, after what felt like forever of trying to find the right book and the right section, I would just make something up.

In my adult life this is something that I am thankful I learned, I am now proud of my ability to find out or blag it. I believe that saying YES and finding out how to execute something afterwards is one of the most commonly shared attributes of entrepreneurs.

My childhood – the liberalism, the organic and wholefood diet, yoga, open mindedness, lack of TV and encouragement of creativity in both thinking and expression – were fantastic. NOW I am hugely grateful and thankful for the attention, consideration and energy my parents gave us, but in the 1990s? Not so much. I wanted NORMAL. I wanted a normal name. I wanted a TV. I wanted plastic toys. I wanted a hairdresser or someone qualified to cut my hair. Being the hippy child with hand-me-down clothes and hedge-like frizzy hair who made up answers about things she didn't know was not cool and it was not normal.

Being normal meant belonging, and I didn't feel as though I belonged. I didn't belong anywhere. We were a sort of nothing, in between everything and everybody else. We weren't council-estate poor. We weren't rich enough to eat whatever we wanted out of the fridge. We weren't real Jews but we weren't atheists. We didn't believe strongly in politics. There wasn't a family motto, or a football team. We didn't have a band that we were publicly in support of. In fact we didn't do anything publicly. We kept ourselves to ourselves, but we weren't a team either. I constantly felt like I had something to be ashamed of, but I wasn't sure what. I felt like we had to hide, but I wasn't sure why.

Take Halloween. In most people's houses it was a fun time, for dressing up all spooky, having fun, and eating sweets. In our house it was an evening when we stayed in, at the back of the house, with all the lights turned off. There was no jack-o-lantern outside our house, no answering of the door if it was knocked on. I didn't understand what we were ashamed of, or why we couldn't interact. I felt like a misfit.

As soon as I was old enough to sleep over at other people's houses I did. As soon as I could eat TV dinners, or watch Neighbours and study *normal* at someone else's house, I did. I was really good at fitting in. I discovered that I could be a wonderful chameleon. Other people's parents loved me. I was polite, I offered to help out. I created rapport. I mirrored and matched them way before I had any idea about NLP[12] or what it was I was doing. I just wanted to be part of something, and feel like I belonged.

My beautiful little sister was born in February 1990. She was not the kitten I had asked for, and I didn't know what we needed another family

---

12. Neuro Linguistic Programming.

member for, but my parents seemed excited.[13] The upside of my sister's arrival for me as an independent nine-and-a-half-year-old was that I could get away with being out more often.

I spent most of my time with the kids up the street. They were SO normal. The kind of normal I wanted to be. They were my first surrogate family. We watched TV. We started 'the babysitters club' like in a book we had read. We recorded our very own radio show on the boombox my grandmother gave me. (My brother joined in too sometimes.) We made up dance routines and sang tunelessly to Madonna and New Kids on the Block. I had my first crush (Joey McIntyre – he was only 16 and I figured that wasn't much of an age gap). I knew every single word to every single song on Hanging Tough, Step by Step and The Immaculate Collection.

Sometime in 1991 it was time to wean my sister off breast milk and so my mum and I went on a holiday. It was a whole weekend in France, and it was just the two of us: I was so excited! Spending time just my mum and me was so rare. This and one other weekend that we went to Monkton Wyld Court[14] are the two memories I have from my childhood and teens where it was just the two of us and we weren't seething or screaming at one another. That weekend was lovely. It was also the next time that I had a profound (and life-saving) intuitive and unexplainably magic moment. The place we visited was a commune of creative people who were seeking to bring a version of Tipi Valley[15] to France.

I remember a tiny fluffy black kitten who followed me everywhere, I felt honoured. Organically grown tomatoes that I picked myself, which tasted amazing. Fresh duck eggs, with the largest and most golden yolks I had ever seen, and Wolfy. Wolfy was a four-year-old girl who was also there with her mum. She was awesome, we went exploring the epic grounds together. We were the only kids, except for a local boy called Jay. Jay was about my age and he spoke a little English but he was a boy, so we hung

---

13. I love my sister to pieces and I am SO happy she was born. But in 1990 I was nine and a half and I was fucked off. I wanted a kitten. My brother had a rabbit, and it all felt very unfair.

14. *http://www.monktonwyldcourt.co.uk/About_the_Court/index.html* I think we went so that she could research EO (Education Otherwise). There was a brief period where they thought about educating us at home.

15. Tipi Valley is the daddy of all UK Eco communities. Founded in 1976, it's a 200-acre expanse of rolling countryside bought piece by piece from local farmers by its 200 or so residents (100 during the winter). The community includes families, singletons, activists, hippies, many 'originals', festival junkies, environmentalists, astrologers, artists, musicians and the like. The majority live in low-impact dwellings – tipis, yurts, caravans, huts, round houses – scattered across the idyllic valley. Source: *http://www.huckmagazine.com/*. For more information about communal living and eco-communities see *http://www.diggersanddreamers.org.uk/*.

out for a while and then we went off on our own. In the grounds there was a forest and we walked in it, we walked and walked and walked. We found a stream and moss and made totems out of rocks. It was magical. At some point I realised that I was the 'adult' and that it was probably time to go home. We began walking back the way we'd come. After a while I realised we were lost. Really lost. The kind of lost where you try to find, but can't see, the sun to make a guess at your bearings. I was eleven and I had a four year old with me and it would start getting dark soon. Fuck. I don't know why I did what I did next, but remembering the fairies in the garden that the adults couldn't see, I instructed Wolfy to sit down cross-legged opposite me. I explained that we were lost, and that we needed help.

'Do you remember Jay?'

'Yep.' She nodded her little dreadlocked head back at me.

'OK, good. I need you to think about him. Think really hard. We're going to send him a message. We're going to tell him with our minds that we need him, and we're going to tell him where we are.'

She didn't even flinch at this bizarre request. She closed her eyes and did it.

I did too. I concentrated with all my might on telling Jay how important it was that he listened and that we needed him.

'How long do we wait?' a little voice broke my thoughts.

'As long as it takes. He won't be long. He's just got to find us.'

It was about twenty minutes I think. He appeared with a smile on his face.

'Bonjour. Ça va?'

I actually have no idea what he said, but he took us home. When I asked him how he knew we needed him and where to come, he told me he just knew. Something came to him and told him we needed his help. I mentally noted that some other kids could connect to *the knowing* too, and then promptly forgot as soon as we were back in England and our old lives again.

I had a good childhood – I was loved and cared for – but I also always had an angst inside me waiting to get out and explore. Some of you will really be able to relate. I wanted to go and discover the whole world, right now! I felt too big for our little life. I felt destined for grandeur and at the same time I felt a duty of care to my family. I was torn between running away to be the curious wild child, and staying put to look after my tribe. *My family.*

When I was seven I tried to run away to the fair.

I didn't get very far.

I was out with my Grandma and my brother. We were walking along the promenade of Brighton sea front. I wanted to go on the rides, hear the voices of other children and spend some time soaking in 'normal'… I wanted to have FUN!

'No. It's time to go home.'

'I've got pocket money.' I pleaded

'No. I'll leave you here, come on.'

'Go home without me then!' I stomped my foot and stood my ground.

A battle of wills ensued.

My Grandma took my brother by the hand and walked away, along the boardwalk to the stairs that went down towards the way home.

I waited.

I wanted to call her bluff. I knew this game. They weren't really going to leave me here. I waited as long as I could bear (I was seven, it couldn't have been more than five minutes). I ran towards the next set of stairs, thinking they would only have gotten that far. I gathered pace and whizzed down to the bottom, scanning around for them as best I could while still moving and not tripping.

They had gone.

In that split second I felt two things:

1. *Contraction/Fear:* They left me - I am alone in the big dangerous world!!!!!!

2. *Expansion/Autonomy:* I'm FREEEEEEE and I can go to the fair!!

I looked around for them again, and I couldn't see them. I felt sure that the world was conspiring to allow me to go to the pier and go on the rides. *WOOHOO!* My little entrepreneurial brain kicked in, creatively solving the problem. I walked along the roadside where the cars were parked and found the parking payment machine.

Maybe someone dropped some change and then I can go on the rides!

The first one had nothing. I carried on carefully walking along the road-side by the parked cars. I reached the next pay station. I reached up into the change slot and wiggled my little fingers around. Still nothing.

Nee Naw, Nee Naw...

Startled by the siren pulling up right next to me I jumped.

My memory of what happened next is awash with shame as my joy turned to guilt watching my grandma crying and my brother distraught.

The policeman shouted. His attempt to frighten me into not running away again, or to see the severity of the situation, was lost on me, I just felt BAD.

I felt misunderstood. I didn't mean to upset anyone. I wasn't hurting anyone. I just wanted to have some fun!

'You are so irresponsible. Look how upset you've made your grandmother.'

I felt horrible.

The things our brain picks out to remember and give meaning to are weird and random. Last year I was at T. Harv Eker's MMI[16] in London and Marcus DeMaria led us through a visualisation process to uncover an early emotional incident involving money that had impacted our money blueprint, and this story is the little gem that appeared in my

---

16. *http://www.millionaireminduk.com/* A 3-day seminar created by T. Harv Eker on money and mindset.

mind. As I relived the memory consciously for the first time in years I realised that my brain had hung on to an emotional memory and given it meaning: 'Look how upset you've made your grandma and brother – you are irresponsible and money is not for having fun. You don't deserve to have fun with money!' or something like that.[17]

When I was nine I tried to run away again. My brother and I packed some rice cakes and tools into the largest of my dad's handkerchiefs we could find, and after tying it to a stick, Dick Whittington-style, we attempted to run away on a skateboard. We walked to the top of the hill by our house and with him at the front and me at the back, one arm holding him and the other our supplies, we attempted to abscond on his large white deck with its eighties neon wheels. We didn't get very far. We veered off the pavement into a parked car and I hurt my arm so we went home.

Outside of my family life there was school. At this point I was at Brighton Steiner School. The class I was in was made up of ten boys and ten girls. We were all pretty weird and I liked that. It normalised things. It was like having a whole class of siblings. I got picked on but I didn't mind it all that much; it felt like the kind of thing brothers and sisters say to each other so I let it go. I saw the name calling as affectionate. I figured that it was harmless fun. I liked school for a while. I really enjoyed learning in such a narrative way.

When my teacher picked on me it felt different, it didn't feel like a nick-name or like kids playing, it felt personal. One day I came into school with a piece of indigo dyed silk tied into my hair and bright turquoise dangly dolphin earrings on. I had just had dyed the silk with my mum and was so proud of what we had done. The earrings were new, my newly pierced ears had just healed, and I felt like a 'lady'. I almost skipped into class. I felt beautiful. I was happy to share who I was with the world. As I entered the room my teacher stopped me.

'Ebonie Allard, this is not a fashion parade, take that ridiculous garb off now.'

I could hear everyone laughing.

---

17. To identify your money memories and reframe them go to *www.misfit2maven.com/bonuses*

I was so embarrassed.

I felt ashamed. After that I retreated, believing somewhere that it was shameful to be expressive and free and beautiful.

A new girl joined our class. She had a birthday party. She was allowed to invite 10 boys and 10 girls to her party. She invited everyone but me.

On Monday at school everyone else was laughing and joking together.

I remember feeling like I didn't belong there anymore. I wasn't part of anything.

I had felt OK at school but now I didn't fit in anywhere. I started to spend a lot of time alone. I liked being alone, but I also hated it. I wanted to fit in and I wanted to belong. I felt more and more like a misfit and less and less like I belonged anywhere. And that was before my parents separated, and the hormones of adolescence kicked in.

ALWAYS TOO MUCH, NEVER ENOUGH

I moved to a proper high school in the spring of 1992. Big school. Fucking HUGE school. I went from a class of 21 children and 8 classes in the whole school to a class of 35, 10 classes in a year and 5 years in one campus. Mind BLOWN.

It was scary, but it was also exciting; the ultimate chameleon test.

The lessons were boring, the teachers were boring and most of the people were boring, but this was normality and I had arrived. Some of these kids were *cool* and I wanted to be like them.

I wanted to engage, I wanted to make friends and be a part of their world, but I'd joined in the spring term and everyone already had a best friend and a group that they hung with. I didn't know how to act in this environment, I hadn't worked out the rules yet. So I just loitered in between the groups, flitting from one to another and trying to figure it all out. I desperately wanted to belong, but I didn't fit anywhere. I saw this move into normality as an opportunity and I was determined to make the most of it.

Why won't you like me? What are the rules? How do I play?

Outside of school I had festivals, not the big music festivals you might know of, but smaller camps organised by peace-loving, art-making eco warriors. Some I went to with my family, some I went to alone or with festival friends and their parents. At these festivals there was always a space especially for teenagers like us and I could relax and be myself there. I didn't feel like I fully belonged, most of the other juves[18] knew each other outside of these camps, their families and lives were intertwined beyond the time we spent in a field and in my mind this was their space. I wasn't the same as them either. They didn't seem to have the kind of ambition I did. They weren't interested in things and stuff like I was. I wanted consumerism. I wanted the status a job title gave. I longed for the badge a fancy car provided. I ached for external validation and proof that I belonged. They belonged *here*, and I was an inbetweener, I wasn't quite one of them and I wasn't quite a normal person.

However these people were kind and inclusive and so I was accepted as one of them, and with them was the one place I felt most like myself. I am grateful for every single one of those people in their fields of tents and yurts and tipis for what they taught and instilled in me.

I lived for the summers and half-term holidays. There was always a gathering or festival to go to and I got to feel briefly that I was somewhat part of something. The people at these festivals have huge open hearts, it was always a big extended surrogate family, and they were kind enough to include and love me. I got to be out in nature and I could be all of myself there, I was just really unsure who that was.

Back in term time I still just could not figure out how to get the normal kids to like me. I tried my best to blend in, but I just didn't get it. They didn't get me and I so desperately wanted to get them. I felt sure that if I figured them out I could work out how to fit in. I could bend and sculpt myself to be one of them.

---

18. Juves = juveniles. A nickname we were given that I loved because it made me feel like part of something. I still love having and giving nicknames. I had a lot of nicknames growing up, that was something my family did really well and I am still really fond of my nicknames and all that they mean to me.

ME?
WHEN I THINK, WELL WHO AM I?
I TAKE MY TIME AND PONDER HARD,
I REALLY CANNOT SAY IN WORDS...
I'M FAT AND SHORT AND FUNNY AND PROUD!
I STAND UP TALL AND WATCH THE CROWD.
I LIKE TO LOVE, AND LOVE TO BE LIKED.
I JUMP, I HOP AND LEAP AND SKIP,
(AND WISH THAT I COULD BACKFLIP)
BUT MOST OF ALL I SLEEP AT NIGHT, AND DREAM...
AND HOPE...
THAT ONE DAY I'LL FIND A PLACE I FIT.

- EXTRACT FROM MY DIARY IN THE SUMMER
OF 1993 AGED 12, NEARLY 13.

One day a group of girls invited me to come to the fairground with them.

Oh my God they like me!

So I went. As we dawdled at a snail's pace along the pavement, dragging our heels and sprawling across the entire walkway, completely unaware of anyone trying to get past, one of the girls pulled out a packet of cigarettes.

'I stole these from my mum. Who'll smoke one with me?'

And I was in, I belonged.

I decided that the goal was to be normal enough to blend in, but edgy enough to be *cool* and hide the fact that I was not really at all normal. This meant pushing the boundaries in every direction but not drawing attention to my rebellion or recklessness in a way that would alert my parents or teachers who might raise the alarm.

During the years that followed I did many things to prove that I belonged, including but not limited to:

- Skiving off school, particularly maths lessons
- Shoplifting – I used police cars as taxis for a while, and tried to steal only from large corporations and not independent storeowners.

- Hitching from the countryside into town to drink in pubs
- Clubbing from the age of 14
- Kissing doormen and men about 20 years older than me who might buy me drinks and pay my cab fare home
- Drinking and drug taking
- Sex
- Starving myself, binge eating followed by throwing up, and a whole host of other creative ways to try and be skinny.

I wasn't the only one playing this 'how the fuck do I stop being a misfit and fit in' game. I had a great friend who also went from a Steiner School and a 'weird' family to a 'normal' school. She and I went to different 'normal' schools, and in discovering each other's secret we formed our own little gang. We smoked cannabis together, hitched rides together, snuck into clubs together and ran away from men together.

We looked out for each other. We took risks, knowing that we had each other's back. One time I found her being assaulted by a guy 20 years older than us in a car park stairwell. One minute they were just behind me as we walked to find a taxi rank. The next they were gone. By the time I found them he already had his hand up her skirt and she was trying but failing to wriggle free. I screamed at him, kicked him and grabbed her hand – pulling her away from him with all my might. We ran away as fast as our drunken teenage legs would carry us and jumped into a taxi, laughing.

One time we jumped out of a moving car because the guy we were hitching a lift from started to lock the doors and was freaking me out. I was in the front, she was in the back. I got a bad feeling about the guy so I made eye contact with her in the mirrors and signalled with my hands and then we jumped, hitting the grassy verge with a teenage bounce and a giggle.

Another time I tried to stop a guy flirting with an uninterested friend in a bar and ended up being hit by him; I don't really remember very much of what happened, only that I came to outside afterwards surrounded by a doorman and my friends. Up until that moment I didn't think a man would hit a woman in public. Shocked and shaken, I was taken and lifted by a group of celebratory friends to sit high up on a red letterbox. All bloodied and eating chips I felt the familiar mix of significance and shame.

By the time I got to sixth-form college in 1996 I was snorting speed in the common rooms and giving boys blow jobs in bathrooms. I was so cool.

NOT.

It seemed that whatever I did I was still not cool enough.

Inside I just wanted to be seen for being me, but I was so scared of being rejected as myself that I perfected playing the role of 'cool girl'[19] instead. When people fell for my creation I secretly dismissed them. Every time someone made friends with, employed or fell in love with *her*, a piece of the real me got stuffed further down and away.

Looking back now, I realise that I even though I decided that I had become an adult at 14, I was still so young. So self-absorbed. Not in a good way or a bad way, just still learning who I was and how I fitted into everything. Somehow believing that there was a definitive answer. Fourteen was a big year for me; my parents separated and began divorce proceedings, I dyed my hair black, and I began numbing my feelings with drugs, sex and food.

My parents' separation meant that on the one hand I got a whole heap of freedom and on the other, a whole heap of responsibility. Initially they tried splitting custody half a week each. Within six months we had moved to one week on, one week off, which was slightly better, but not much. The leap from year 9 to year 10 at school and the start of my GCSEs was also a big deal. My life suddenly got much more complex than it ever had been before and my hormones were all over the place. I got a stepmum and a stepbrother and sister, whom I now consider to be as much family to me as the rest of them, but who were then an added complexity to my ever more unpredictable life. I started having periods, often ones that would knock me over in complete agony for two to three days. I also started to feel feelings as if they were going to swallow me whole. My

---

19.   A role that Gillian Flynn captures the essence of so well in *Gone Girl. http://gillian-flynn.com/gone-girl/*

mum and I were at each other's throats A LOT. By November of that year I was going to live with my Dad full time because my Mum and I were not finding it easy to live together. As with so many mothers and daughters, as with her own earlier relationship with her mother, the relationship between me and my mum was complex. I understand it a lot better now, I love her and have learned so much about myself and life because of the way that we push each other's buttons. But then, when I was 14, I didn't understand it or appreciate it as I do now. I was rebellious; I had fire in my belly and passion in my heart. I was free spirited and dynamic but I was not dangerous or out of control. Or at least I didn't think I was. One of the many strategies I had for coping with the ever-growing uncertainty in my life was to snoop through stuff; somehow knowing what was in people's pockets, or mail or handbags meant that I felt more in control. One day when I was snooping, I found correspondence from a mental health clinic, which led me to believe that there was a possibility of my being sectioned.[20] Like the time on the street when I was seven, and no longer sure that I could trust myself, this letter reinforced that belief and added a layer of evidence which had me questioning my sanity, telling me that I was 'crazy' or out of control.

---

20. *http://www.thesite.org/mental-health/depression-mental-health/being-sectioned-5844.html*

ANGRY
ANGRY, YOU MAKE ME MAD,
I CLENCH MY FISTS AND GRIT MY TEETH,
MY HEAD BEGINS TO TIGHTEN,
MY EYES GLAZE OVER,
THE LUMP IN MY THROAT INCREASES BY MORE NUMBERS THAN
IMAGINABLE,
I PERSPIRE RAPIDLY,
MY MIND RACES,
MY FLESH CRAWLS WITH ADRENALIN,
I SMELL FEAR! I LOVE IT!
MY ANGER SWELLS.
SLOWLY EACH ASPECT SHARPENS, I AM AWARE OF ALL…
I FIGHT VERBALLY
I KNOW WHAT I AM SAYING IS CRAP, BUT I PURSUE
I KNOW THAT SOME (AND ONLY SOME MIND YOU) OF WHAT
SHE'S MUTTERING IS TRUE, BUT I PURSUE.
MY FINGERNAILS DIG DEEP INTO MY PALM,
I AM DESTROYING THE FORT, IT IS WEAKENED,
MY EYES CAN TAKE THE STRAIN NO LONGER,
THE BOUGHS BREAK,
THE SHIP SINKS,
THE ANGRY SEAS FALL AWAITING THE NEXT STORM.

HUH?
SCARED, SO SCARED,
AFRAID TO SPEAK FREE,
ASHAMED TO BE ME,
WORRIED ABOUT THE PAST,
WHAT MY FUTURE BRINGS,
THIS AND LOTS OF OTHER THINGS.
WELLING UP INSIDE,
THE TEARS BEING TO POUR,
SILVERY DROPLETS, MORE AND MORE,
LAMENTING OLD SORROWS,
WHAT I'VE DONE WRONG,
HOPING THE EVIDENCE WON'T LAST LONG,
MY SHELL SHOWS HAPPINESS,

INSIDE IS WEAK,
AM I A FREAK?
HOPING TO COPE,
SITUATIONS OCCUR,
ALL SEEMS A BLUR...
HEAD IN VERTIGO,
SENSELESS TALKING,
BRAIN IS WALKING,
I WISH IT WAS JUST ME,
PLAYING WITH FOAM,
I WANT TO GO HOME.

- EXTRACTS FROM MY POEM JOURNAL
DECEMBER 1995, AGED 14 AND A HALF.

I didn't feel that I had anyone to talk to about what was going on for me and I was trying to process a lot. Sometimes I would come home and accidently slam all the doors, just trying to get to my room to cry. I had no idea what an empath[21] was then, but I did know that often times I would be filled with all sorts of crazy feelings and just have to cry into my pillow until I could breathe again.

Sometimes I would lie on my bed and write in my journal for hours; reams and reams of stuff I felt angry and sad and overwhelmed by. Most of it didn't feel like mine. Sometimes I would write and cry for the starving children in Africa, or the girl I heard crying in the toilets at school. My belief about life was that it was messy. You couldn't trust people. I found ways to stop it all feeling too overwhelming. At the time I thought I was doing great. I felt pretty unaffected by my family life. I felt sure that I was holding things together. I dyed my hair a different colour every week and began to find a style that was somewhere between punk rock and flower girl. Looking back I can see that I was incredibly ferocious and angry but putting on a mask of sugar and spice and all things nice. The only time I really felt good was when I climbed out of my bedroom window and sat

---

21. Empaths have highly attuned mirror neurons. They are able to feel what others are feeling physically, emotionally and spiritually. Often called overly sensitive or cry-babies, empaths take on the feelings or emotions of those around them – it is a skill to distinguish which are your own and which are coming from your environment, a skill which most empaths develop over time through a process of discernment – for many often feeling like they are going insane. Wanting to or choosing to numb feelings is not uncommon, and can be part of the process. It is a gift, but can initially feel like a curse. By the time I was at college I had become aware that not all of what I felt was mine.

alone, quietly gazing out over the rooftops and down to the sea, at the horizon and all its possibilities, while smoking a Lucky Strike cigarette.

Most of the time I felt vulnerable and scared and alone, and I didn't know what to do with those feelings so they blurted out sideways and I acted out. I escaped from home as often as I could. I made myself a home from home. From 14 to 17 I had the perfect best friend. We met at a camp in Wales, but lived just a few streets from one another. She was cool. In my eyes she was the real deal while I was just an imposter. I wanted to be just like her. In term time she went to a grammar school and hung out with attractive, wealthy boys and in the holidays she hung out at the camps with all the attractive hippie boys. Everyone fancied her and I wanted them to like me as much as they liked her! Her mum was liberal and lenient and let me stay over all the time. For a while I practically lived at their house. My friend and I were alike in many ways, but also very different. I aspired to be just like her. I decided that she had the perfect blend of normal and unique. I felt sure that she was more popular than me and my belief was that it was because she was skinnier. I figured that if I could get skinny, then everyone would like me more.

Looking back over my diary entries while writing this book was both interesting and saddening. It became really clear, written there in black and white, that from the age of 14 until really relatively recently I thought and wrote really horrible things about myself over and over. It became habitual to put myself down, to call myself fat and ugly and stupid.

Knowing what I know now about how powerful writing down our beliefs can be for manifesting and creating, it is no wonder that I spent so many years at war with myself.

31ST JANUARY 1996

NEW YEAR'S RESOLUTIONS:
I'VE DECIDED TO BECOME ANOREXIC OR SUCH LIKE.
NO FOOD… IT'S ONLY BEEN TWO DAYS SO FAR, BUT
HEY - LET'S SEE HOW LONG I CAN LAST…

1ST FEB 1996
TODAY I ATE:
AN APPLE, 4 MOUTHFULS OF SPAGHETTI BOLOGNAISE.

2ND FEB
HALF A CHEESE SANDWICH. 2 RICE CAKES.
A YOGHURT AND AN APPLE.
TEN AND A HALF STONE. FUCK

3RD FEB
CHEESE AND MARMITE SANDWICH, PIECE OF TOAST,
A PIECE OF FUDGE, A PIECE OF PIZZA.

4TH FEB
GOT STONED. BINGED. 2 PACKETS OF SPACE RAIDERS.
CRÈME EGG. PACKET OF BISCUITS.

5TH FEB
I'M JUST A FATTY WHO CAN'T CONTROL HERSELF.
I CAN'T EVEN BE ANOREXIC!
I HATE MYSELF AND I WANT TO DIE.

The conversation I'd had with my dad all those years before about those two anorexic girls swirled around in my head and even though I was smart enough to know starving myself was not a good idea, I so badly wanted to look like I fit in. During the holidays I did my best to make excuses about meals and skipped as many as I could. After the first week I weighed myself at my grandma's house and saw that I'd lost half a stone. Momentarily I was so proud. Then the hunger for better results kicked in. For those of you who have been lucky enough to escape addictive behaviour, I want you to think about when you get an alert on your phone, or a text message from someone you like. You get a little 'hit' – an endorphin rush. You want more. Have you ever messaged someone a question just to get a response? That's how addictions start, curiosity.

What happens if I say this? What happens if I do this? Searching for a rush, connection and a boundary.

When we went back to school I kept at it, cutting apples into pieces and sucking on them in class. Careful to never eat them, just suck the juice out. One day it was announced by one of our teachers that a girl from our class would not be coming back this term as she had been admitted to a special clinic for her eating disorder. Instead of being sad for her and her family like those around me, I was jealous. *I can't even do this as well as the other girls!* The belief I had about myself was that I was failing at everything I cared about.

Later that term a well-meaning friend caught me not eating and told my parents. I promised it was just a phase and that I would start eating again. With everyone watching and a new-found emphasis on eating as a family or at the table I made the strategic decision to move on to bulimic behaviour. I wasn't about to stop – I needed to get a body that would make my life better, and I also wanted to smoke a lot of weed.

The two were not congruent and the obvious solution was to make myself sick. I ate normally, and then ran off to the bathroom and stuck my fingers down my throat. Over time the rules were relaxed again and I was allowed out to see my friend. At hers we smoked pot and got high, binged on pizza and then drank pints of salt water to make ourselves sick. Sometimes we did this together, sometimes I did it alone. It made me feel closer to her to share this secret 'naughty' behaviour. I felt like we had found a glitch in the system and that we were tricking life. It felt good to have someone to share secrets with. It felt good to have someone who got me. It felt good to have someone to talk about boys with, to plan parties and fun times with. It felt good to belong.

But juggling school, family, friends, smoking, boys, fashion, hair dye and secrets got very complicated – so much was out of my control.

As the everyday stresses of my adolescent life increased, all I wanted was to escape in a puff of smoke and control. More and more I needed to feel like I had some sort of control over my life. I felt like my entire existence was a charade of trying to fit into a life that I wasn't meant for. I became convinced that I should have died when I was a baby. I wasn't meant for this world. I got more and more stressed out. My body began manifesting severe stress symptoms; first I got ringworm and eczema and then I got a really nasty ear infection.

I was born with something called a preauricular sinus,[22] which is a hereditary and reasonably common congenital malformation. It appears just as a little hole like a piercing up on the top part of the ear. Most preauricular sinuses are asymptomatic and can remain untreated unless they become infected too often. Most people have one on one side. My dad does, my brother does. I had two. One on each side. Mine both got infected a couple of times as a child and my parents were offered surgery but opted not to put me through it. Which was a good decision and they remained fine until I was fifteen. Just before my Year 10 mock exams and GCSE coursework deadline one got really badly infected and I was off school for ages. I missed school, but more importantly for me at the time I missed parties and a Prodigy gig. It felt very unfair. I was at my mum's. The infection got so bad that she took me to casualty. They sent me home with painkillers and gave her instructions on how to drain my ear. I was in a lot of pain and it was not an easy task. She couldn't do it, so she called my dad. Over the course of what felt like FOREVER but was in fact a matter of weeks we went to casualty again, often, and the ENT specialist. Eventually they took us to a room on the ward, gave me a local anaesthetic in my ear and lanced the cyst.

FUCK. I still remember exactly how much that hurt.

I squeezed my dad's hand so hard he visibly sweated and tears rolled down his face. A week later my glands were still up, I had a huge scab in my ear and I was still off school, but it looked like it was healing. Then it flared up again, so we went back to the hospital, where I was told that they were going to try one more thing without using 'knives' but if that didn't work then it would need lancing again. The 'one more thing' was a different course of antibiotics, with a warning that if it didn't get better they would have to give me an internal dressing under general aesthetic. The recommended course of action was to wait until the infection was healed

22. https://www.facebook.com/pages/People-with-Preauricular-Sinus-Their-Abilities
http://en.wikipedia.org/wiki/Preauricular_sinus_and_cyst

before attempting surgery. So I prayed to a God I wasn't sure I believed in that it would heal. Because of their close proximity to the facial nerves, the removal of preauricular sinuses is performed by an otolaryngologist, requires a lengthy and scary consent form, and isn't usually performed whilst there is an infection. The consent form basically said that I could end up with a paralysed face. The doctors and my parents let me read all the information and make my own decision about consent. It was a really big moment for me. A self-responsibility and acceptance moment. A surrender and uncertainty moment. A 'how much do I value my life?' moment. It was another '*FUCK I must be a grown up now*' moment!

MY DIARY ENTRY READS:

SO FAR I'VE MISSED A HALF TERM OF FUN, TWO COOL PARTIES, FOUR WEEKS OF SCHOOL, AND I AM STILL IN SO MUCH PAIN. WHY DON'T I HAVE A BOYFRIEND? OH I KNOW BECAUSE I AM TEN AND HALF STONE. MUST DO BETTER. TARGET 9 STONE.

Even in these circumstances, my focus was the FAT and the lack of boyfriend. The lens through which I viewed the world was completely blinkered. I wanted a boyfriend so I would feel less alone. I fantasised that he would be the person I talked to and made these sorts of decisions with, but the reality is that I wouldn't have shared any of what I was actually going through with a boyfriend even if there had been one. In reality I didn't trust anyone, not even myself. I had a limited set of resources at 15 and I used what was readily available to me. I was sure that the solution to my discomfort was outside of me. I projected all my hopes and fantasies onto an imaginary, idealised boyfriend. I numbed all my uncomfortable feelings with food, drugs and sex. Food became my friend; a silent, non-confronting, comforting friend. Smoking became a way of meditating; taking a moment to just be, notice and breathe. And sex? Well, sex was my path to significance and some very loose sort of connection. If the guys that everyone else fancied wanted me, then I must be *worth something*.

I signed the consent forms, got the surgery and luckily the doctor didn't hit my facial nerves so I still have full use of my face!

During that time I was hugely sociable and rarely spent any time alone. I didn't like what happened in my head when I was alone and the only place I shared my feelings or inner world was in my little book of poetry, usually when stoned.

DEATH, DENIAL, SELF HATE, DO THESE THINGS BRING US TO
HELL'S GATE?
OR IS IT THINGS LIKE LUST, LOVE AND SEX?
THE THINGS WHICH ARE FUN AND I ENJOY BEST?
DOES EVERYBODY FEEL THE WAY I DO NOW?
OR AM I JUST A SAD AND MISERABLE COW?
DOES GOD LOVE ME, AND OTHER SINNERS TOO?
OR WILL I ROT IN HELL? IS THIS TRUE?
SHOULD I BE DADDY'S GOLDEN GIRL?
BEAUTIFUL AND SPLENDID, A SHINING PEARL?
WILL I BE A PAUPER LIVING OFF THE LAND,
OR WILL I BE RICH AND LEND OUT MY HAND?
SHOULD I WORRY DEEPLY AND LAY
AWAKE AT NIGHT?
SHOULD I WORK HARD AND HOLD UP THE FIGHT?
I KNOW THE THINGS THAT SOUND RIGHT
I KNOW WHAT HE WOULD DO….
BUT THAT DOESN'T HELP ME!
WON'T SOMEONE GIVE ME A CLUE!?!

Out in the world I was hard and edgy and fierce. I skived off school, smoked cannabis and tried to numb the *feelings* that snuck their way into everywhere. The anger and grief inside me was huge and inescapable. I remember feeling the opposite of happy. Smoking helped numb some of the overwhelming feelings I would get when in crowds, in school or at parties. I knew that it wasn't good for me to keep pushing these feelings down but I didn't know what else to do. *My diary entry from Easter Sunday 1996 pretty much sums up what I believed about life at that point:*

EASTER SUNDAY 1996

I WORRY THAT I HAVEN'T STUDIED ENOUGH AND THAT I'VE BEEN SMOKING TOO MUCH WEED. I THINK I SHOULD PROBABLY GIVE UP. PEOPLE KEEP TELLING ME I'M DEPRESSED, BUT LIFE'S JUST CRAP AND I'M FAT.

In April 1996 I went to see Leftfield at a club in Brighton. I really wanted one night where I was just me, without any of the stuff that was going on at home. I just wanted to dance. My friends and I did a gram of speed and just as I was coming up and feeling whizzy, I turned around and bumped into my dad and his girlfriend. It was one of those I'm-not-sure-how-to-process-this moments: I was 15 and had just swallowed a cigarette paper full of drugs, he was out with another woman that wasn't my mum. I spent the evening hiding over one side of the club trying to pretend he wasn't there. I remember feeling that everyone had someone or some-place they could go and that I had nowhere. My world was becoming more and more claustrophobic.

At some point in the mid nineties my dad retrained as a psychotherapist and began practising. He and his new partner, now wife, discovered, studied and brought home information and insights into many new and interesting modalities of alternative health, wellbeing, philosophy and spirituality. I took it all in, the work that he was doing, the way that he was changing, the man, the leader, the teacher he was becoming. He has always followed his own path in a way that inspired me and although he'd probably never think it of himself he is a trailblazer and a thought leader to me and to many. I ask many entrepreneurs about who their inspirations are, and many of them cite their families. Mine have been hugely inspirational to me.

In June 1996, aged just fifteen, I got my first tattoo. My first tattoo was not about the artwork or the artist. It wasn't about collaboration or beauty. It wasn't because everyone else had them. (They didn't. No one I knew had tattoos.) It was to mark a time in my life. It was to prove that no one but me had control over my body, it was my way of having a piece of life that was just for me – strange as that might sound. Mostly my tattoos are bookends marking chapters of my life, or they're totems with a meaning known only to me. As I've got older they have also become a celebration of collaboration with an artist, and about beauty for the sake of beauty, but mostly they are about the relationship I have with myself.

That first one wasn't designed or really thought out, it was just a random design from a flash sheet on the wall, and has since been covered up.[23] It hurt. Less than I was expecting, but it still hurt and it bled a lot. I went to the tattoo shop by myself and picked the tattoo by myself then afterwards I went back to the bedsit of the guy I was sort-of dating and stared at the ceiling in pain while he slept after he'd hit me on it because I had my period and wouldn't have sex with him.

Aged 15

I think it's fair and accurate to say that I was not doing a great job of looking after myself. I can now see clearly how little I valued myself and how emotionally immature I still was. At the time, though, I genuinely thought I was doing a good job of being an independent and mature woman. I was proud of myself. I was living the dream. I felt that I was more in control of my life than not. I did what I wanted when I wanted, and no one and nothing scared me. I felt that I was doing a great job of projecting

---

23. I actually had that first one redone in 2006, and then covered over with something much bigger in 2012.

an image of someone who was fearless, fierce and unemotional. Nothing could faze me.

Until I got my GCSE results. The day I opened the envelope with my grades in it, I sat on the doorstep of my dad's rented house and cried. I got an A, four Bs, three Cs and a D. I cried and cried and cried. My dad asked me what I expected if I was going to go out partying every night and not study? He had a point but I was so disappointed in myself. The way I saw it, it was more reinforcement that I couldn't do anything well enough. It wasn't about the grades. They're not even that bad. They were more than I needed to get into sixth form. The point, the thing that triggered the emotion, was that I knew that I could have done better.

In the summer of 1996, after school finished and before I started at college, I worked as much as I could – in clothes shops, in cafés and babysitting – and I used my money to go to festivals. It was the first year I was allowed to go on my own. I loved the independence and freedom. That summer was THE BEST!

I partied hard, met great people, danced a lot and had all sorts of mischievous and marvellous adventures!

That September I started college and I was happy. It was completely different from school and whilst I wasn't dealing with any of my feelings I loved the autonomy and freedom I was being given. Finally I could wear what I wanted, do the classes I wanted and, because it was in a new town and no one from my school had come to this college, I could *be* whomever I wanted. I could start again. Reinvent myself. I have always loved reinvention and prided myself on being a chameleon.

1997 — aged 17, just started college

At the very first college party I got off with[24] eight guys and ended up on the bouncy castle straddling Kevin. Everyone else had gone inside by this point, and someone thought they'd save some power and turn the generator off. Neither Kevin nor I realised we were about to have a tonne of bouncy castle collapse on us until it was nearly too late. Luckily, someone heard my screams and turned the generator back on. Greeting my new peers topless kinda set the tone for the next two years at college. To be fair on me I was not the worst behaved person at that party by a long way. But, however outwardly proud I was of my behaviour, inside I was miserable. I hated that guy after guy would happily spend the night with me but no one would be my boyfriend. I fixated on what I had decided was the reason for all of my unhappiness: fat. But in my teens I was not fat. I wasn't skinny, but I was not fat.

What I see now is that I have spent years disassociating from and disrespecting my body. Treating something with disdain doesn't make you more connected to it. I craved connection, but I never let anyone get close, not intimate, not with the real me. Not even myself. It was safer to scapegoat the fat.

---

24. That's English for 'made out with'

That first year of college I misbehaved and I tried to have as much fun as I could. I smoked a lot of weed and partied hard. I went to a lot of gigs and hung out with bands. I did my college work, but I wasn't engaged in it. At the end of my first year a wonderful art teacher of mine took me aside and had a word with me.

'Ebonie, you are so talented, so full of creative potential and so much more capable than the work you are submitting demonstrates. What's going on?'

'Nothing's going on. I'm passing everything, aren't I?'

'You are, but this term there has been a big dip in the quality of your work. I don't want to tell you how to live your life, and I don't want to be the teacher that gets your parents involved, but if you don't stop smoking your life away you could end up failing your Art A-level and that would be a huge waste.'

I gave him a daggers look and opened my mouth.

'Don't even start.' His tone was stern but fair, catching me as I was about to interject. 'Listen kiddo, you and I hang out at all the same gigs, and I'm not saying stop going out and having fun! Just watch yourself.'

'OK.'

'You're bright, I'm not going to patronise you. I'm going to give you a chance to sort yourself out. I'm not going to involve your parents or the college. Yet. OK?'

'Thank you.'

'What do you want to do with your life?'

'I dunno.'

'OK, what would make you more excited about your art?'

I thought about it.

'There's this artist called Yves Kline[25] who I think is awesome.'

---

25. http://www.yveskleinarchives.org/works/works1_us.html

He nodded at me and so I continued.

'Laura and I would love to recreate his work.'

I believe that the people we have interactions with in our lifetime can come in for a reason, a season or a lifetime. I was hugely lucky to have that teacher. He came and had that conversation with me at a really important time in my life and he worked hard to get us the permission we needed. He was the right person to talk to me. I respected him. I listened. He believed in me when I didn't believe in myself and he showed me who I was again. I was doing a project about mermaids; I took black and white photos of fish and topless photos of my friend Laura and weaved them together in the dark room. That teacher then worked magic to get us permission to get naked and covered in paint in college! The plan was for Laura and I to paint ourselves with blue paint, artfully roll around on paper and create merwomen in the style of Yves Kline. The day before we were set to do so at lunchtime, in a roped off classroom, Laura got ill and we had to postpone. It turned out that Laura had meningitis. Her illness gave me the wake-up call I needed. I decided to live the hell out of my life but to get my act together and get through school. I was passionate about my art and gave it everything I had. Laura lost the use of her right hand,[26] and so I helped her with her coursework too. I got all mine done and we got hers done too. We both got As for our art A levels. I also got a distinction for the 4 units at GNVQ art and design, and an A for the photography GCSE I was doing. We were featured in the local paper as an example of good grades and a touching story. It wasn't about that, it was about values – my values were beginning to show themselves. Freedom. Loyalty. Friendship. Expression. Creativity. Passion.

The day we got our grades I went and got a tattoo. My tribal tramp-stamp may be incredibly nineties, but it reminds me of a good day. It was my second tattoo. I was 17 and loved how hanging out in a tattoo shop made me feel. I loved the smell. The buzzing of the machinery. The permanence of the work. I was aware that this subculture excited me, and at the same time I could see that there was a prejudice against people with tattoos and

---

26. It was only temporary, she got it back eventually, but had to learn to write and draw and paint all over again.

I was mindful that I didn't yet know what I wanted to be when I grew up, so whilst I knew that I wanted more tattoos, I decided to wait a while.[27]

At the end of my first year of college my art studies were going well, but my Sociology A Level was not. This subject that had initially excited me because it was new and about people and ways of thinking was now really difficult and I was getting 3/25 for my essays. I went and saw the teacher and asked if he would sign a piece of paper that would allow me to quit. Again I was gifted with one of the best teachers ever. This incredible man also saw potential in me and told me to wait until one week into the next term. If at the end of that week I was still sure I wanted out, he would sign my piece of paper. I didn't study that summer, but by the time we had our next papers returned to us I was scoring 23/25.

I am a huge advocate for stopping, for taking time out to digest. When we are learning a lot of new information it takes a while for it to embed. In my second year I became passionate about sociology, I loved how I was now able to think and argue with conviction for each of the opposing schools of thought. I believe that I have always been an empath but now with these new skills I had a way of understanding and articulating what other people, with a different mindset or view from my own, might think about something. I had started to be able to translate the feelings I was receiving with a system of articulation. When I did my exam at the end of that year I got an A and I also got a letter telling me that my work was outstanding. I have never forgotten the power of encouragement, how powerful someone else's belief in us can be and how someone outside often has a clearer perspective than we do.

---

27. I did end up having one more done that year, and then no more until I was 25.

SHAME AND SHADOWS

In October 1998 it was socially acceptable and legitimately possible for me to leave home.

Finally, real independence and freedom!

Right?

I needed to decide what was next.

The thing is that there were two parts of me: the 'make it happen' part and the 'let it happen' part. I was unclear on who I really was and what I *should do.*

What we focus on is what we get AND when we don't like aspects of ourselves we stuff them away, where they fester. Every single one of us has qualities that are pleasing to us and qualities that we don't like so much. We shine a light on the ones we are proud of and which have been useful in getting our needs met. We drop into the shadows the ones that we are ashamed of or which we have learned are not so 'good'. There were a lot of qualities in me that I didn't yet understand, which I was ashamed of or saw as 'bad.' A lot of these were issues of femininity and my associations with things like 'softness', 'ease', 'vulnerability', 'emotions', 'sensitivity', and 'uncertainty.'

Although I felt at the time like I had a high level of emotional intelligence, there were huge gaps. Whilst I was headstrong, passionate, mature and determined in some areas, in others I was just a kid. As I left home and embarked on my next adventure, one of individuation and development, I didn't really have any idea of what I wanted next for myself.

The 'make it happen' part of me was running the show, and she won.

Regardless of how quick I am to process cognitively and logically, creating solutions and seeing links quickly, there are other areas where I am much slower. I've often listened to my head and not my heart. Ignored my intuition and been the last one to know how I am feeling. Whilst wearing my feelings on my face and my heart on my sleeve, plain for others to see, I still find it less easy to see my own stuff.

Making decisions about what to study at school had been easy, but now things were getting serious. I felt like I had been at school forever and I wanted a break. I wanted to go and travel the world. I wanted to explore. I was curious and eager for more but I didn't know what I wanted more of. I didn't really want to go and get a degree, but it felt like the next logical step. I can see now that the traits that make me a coach, an entrepreneur, a creative consultant were already there, but at that time I didn't have a clue.

I enjoyed art and was good at it, but I didn't want to be an artist – there was no money in it. I enjoyed sociology, but again I couldn't see how I could make a living from it. I enjoyed painting, and I liked being given a brief. I loved the history and narrative of theatre and the phenomenal storytelling capabilities and technology of film and TV so the logical argument won and I applied to three universities to study courses in Theatre and Film design.

Going on to study felt safer and more responsible than just doing whatever I felt like and drifting.

Once I saw how much the train fare to Nottingham was I decided it was too far; I still wanted to be able to come home to Brighton at weekends. When Rose Bruford wanted me to pay a fee to come to for an interview, – I spent it on new shoes and decided that they weren't for me. When Central School of Speech and Drama in London said that they only took on four or five students a year for Scenic Art on their Theatre Practice course – I was sold. Either I'd be in, or I'd take a gap year and go and live somewhere exotic. Having never been, knowing no one else who had ever been, and not having Googled it (since Google still didn't exist) I decided that if I didn't get in, I wanted to go to Bali[28] or go and live in a tipi somewhere and smoke pot.

I got into CSSD with an unconditional offer based on my portfolio and interview, so I moved to London and embarked on adulthood.

Two distinct parts of me arrived in London: the gypsy artist hippy girl, and the ambitious scenester.

When I left home I felt like I had a chance to reinvent myself. Again. In the big city I could be anyone I wanted. I could have trusted my intuition and learned to love my misfit-self but the truth is I was not confident enough in my weirdness then. I wasn't there internally, I wasn't ready. You can't make yourself be ready. I hadn't learned to value myself at all. Externally it may have looked like I appreciated my weirdness and had self-confidence: I had pink hair, wore whacky clothes, and was really OK with being 'different'. But inside I wasn't content or confident. I was OK with living a caricature of the real me, but not OK with looking at anything about myself that made me feel discomfort.

I really believed that things were one way or another. I hadn't identified, let alone accepted or made peace with, my idiosyncrasies and paradoxes. I got how we all present different faces in different situations, but I was incredibly controlled about what I showed the world and had very clear ideas about what parts of me other people would be OK with and what they would reject. I made huge assumptions. I had never really tested my theories out but I was very sure of what *people* would and wouldn't accept and love about me.

---

28. I have often wondered, what if I had gone to Bali in 1998 instead of 2011? Would I have discovered my purpose then? Did I need the lessons that CSSD, TV land and My Girl Friday taught me? I like to think so. I like to think that my trials, tribulations, tests and triumphs are what make me who I am now, and enable me to empathise in real world terms with other misfit entrepreneurs.

I was consciously never vulnerable. I projected strength as best I could at all times. I wouldn't even allow myself to be privately vulnerable.

I found it much easier to compartmentalise the different 'me's and play the roles rather than ever just be. I'm sure that some of you can relate. I took the things I felt others might tease or make fun of and I would do it first.

My time at Central School of Speech and Drama was incredible. It set me on a path for a fantastic career in the film industry by providing me with skills I still use to this day. I met some amazing people. I forged friendships, pushed boundaries, explored my creativity and playfulness. Theatre and film and being self-employed were all huge unknowns and I had no idea who to ask for help. I had no idea what a mentor was. There was no one in my family or sphere who had ever done anything quite like this before and as I set out on my dream of having a career in the TV and film industry, my only real objective was never to get a real job and to make enough money to have fun and keep a roof over my head.

As far at the relationship part of my life was concerned, I saw romantic relationships as a way of achieving social kudos. I was clear I was never going to fall in love and let my feelings control or rule me. I was never going to be a romantic fool. I was going to be independent and look after myself. I was determined never to be a weak and needy woman. Unconsciously, unsatisfied with the female role models in my life, I looked around me for women to admire and model myself on. I chose Madonna, Marilyn Monroe, Shirley Manson and Skunk Anansie.

I slept with men as if they were trophies. I collected ones that other people would think were an accomplishment. I rejected all whispers from my innate feminine wisdom. I made myself as 'sexy' as I could, but not soft or yielding. I wanted connection, but not love. Falling in love would mean letting go and that was never going to happen. My worth and value were determined by external things – what I looked like, what size I was, who I was with, what shoes I was wearing, what I had collected and achieved. On the outside it may have looked like I was a risk taker, but inside I was all about playing it safe.

On a scale of 1–10 my physical, intellectual, emotional and spiritual health[29] was a two. I was using food again in a way that I hadn't since I was 15. The jump from college to university was HUGE academically. I remember hearing an urban myth that they expected to lose 20 per cent of us in the first year and I remember being determined not to be one of them. Whilst other people I knew were enjoying one or two lectures a week at their university, I was on campus five or six days a week from 8:30 to 5:30 every day. The adrenalin buzz of being part of a theatre *family* was immense. It ticked a whole load of boxes for me, but I still felt that everyone else was sharing some 'in joke' and I had blagged my way into somewhere I didn't really belong.[30]

The stress triggered my need to be in control and I started to binge and throw up again. There was always a part of me that wanted to be healthy and happy, and I knew that this obsessive behaviour was no good for me, but I felt that if I just achieved a little weight loss, everything would be better. I also wanted to ask someone for help but I didn't know how. That might sound silly but I genuinely just didn't have the vocabulary. I didn't know who to go to, I felt if I told anyone what was going on inside my head they would think I was insane and lock me up.

---

29.   PIES – see explanation and exercise in the workbook section, Step 1: from Numbness to Awareness.

30.   I talk about imposter syndrome in the workbook section, Step 3: Judgment and Acceptance

When we need help, it shows up. Not necessarily how we think it will. I was introduced to a guy about my age who was struggling with a gambling addiction and I heard that he was finding attending GA meetings really useful. One day not long after my encounter with him I found a leaflet for OA[31] and decided that it wouldn't hurt to go to one meeting. I went to my first meeting alone and sat at the back. I didn't speak to anyone or join in, I just listened. I genuinely felt that my weight and size were the root of all my problems. I felt sure that if I could just control myself more I would be a better person. I also knew that something that felt so bad couldn't be the answer. Attending OA was great for me at that time. It gave me a structure, it gave me the words to begin to share what I was going through and it allowed me to see that I wasn't alone.

I also saw how OA and all the Anonymous meetings were often used by addicts as a replacement for their addiction. I didn't feel that I had an addiction, and I certainly didn't want attending meetings to become a part of my identity. I was lucky; I also had a great group of housemates. The four of us all started out at university in shitty accommodation and by chance in our first term we found each other and decided to get a house together. They were fun and kind and supportive – we made our own little family unit. When I was diagnosed with a stomach ulcer they were the very best people I could possibly have had around. I don't think I would even have gone to the doctor or felt that anything was wrong enough with me to warrant asking for help unless one of them had dragged me. It was only when I had been glued to a toilet bowl for four days in a row and my stomach was gnawing in agony that I agreed to be taken to the doctor in my pyjamas and duvet. After being prodded, poked, diagnosed and told I needed to start taking care of myself I began to take it slightly more seriously.

Up until that point, in some weird way I had been pleased that I had been throwing up constantly; it meant that I would lose some weight without trying. Although there was no denying the pain I was in, I was happy to ignore it if it would make me skinny. Having my housemate intervene and help me see that my health was at stake was another wake-up call.

---

31. I answered yes to all these questions and felt I needed help: *http://www.oagb.org.uk/do-i-have-a-problem-with-food/*. I went in secret at first, but eventually shared with my housemates where I was going when I needed to go to meetings.

Ultimately, getting the stomach ulcer forced me to stop partying with a different crowd each night and take stock of my health. For the first time I started looking at my diet and the way I was eating, and I made some lifestyle changes in an attempt to heal myself and cure my ulcer. I gave up alcohol, cocaine, cannabis, spicy, fatty foods and smoking for six months. (Actually I don't think I totally gave up smoking completely, but I definitely cut down.)

I took herbs and tinctures. I read up on and ate a low GI and low GL diet.[32] I learned about being more alkaline, reducing inflammation, and food combining. I started to go to yoga classes and to eat well. I was determined to get better. I gave my system the break it needed and through eating mindfully I cured my ulcer. My interest and pursuit of good health was short lived; I was 20 and convinced that I would always bounce back. I did it to be able to party again, not because I loved myself.

---

32. Patrick Holford and Fiona McDonald's *The Holdford Low GL Diet Cookbook* and *Low GI Cookbook* by Louise Blair were especially helpful.

DARK NIGHT OF THE SOUL

In this book I am sharing my 'warts and all' – things which at the outset I really didn't think would end up being important to share and which I certainly didn't feel had a place in a 'business' book have now made it to the fore and centre. As I talked with my clients and peers about what I might include it became clear to me that I 'need' to share it all with you. Don't misinterpret that as meaning it's easy for me to do so, doing so scares me immensely. But, my focus and intention in writing this book has always been to encourage connection and trust via truth, honesty and vulnerability.

Emails like this from clients enabled me to take the risk and feel good about doing so:

> *'[I have been] thinking about something that you asked me when we first spoke. You asked me about why I got in touch with you and what made me feel like I could work with you.*
>
> *Looking back now, I understand that at least part of the answer to that question is the fact that you are clearly an able and passionate coach, but importantly for me you also talk in a really frank and 'un-coach-like' manner. It goes back to that article[33] that said you don't necessarily share a traditional coach's vocabulary. I realise that your style of coaching is one that really works for me. The*

---

33. *http://hrville.co.uk/coach-trip/*

bold and rebellious edge means I don't feel like I'm getting talked at by a corporate suit.

Another part of the answer to that question is precisely the fact that you are courageous yourself, and express your own vulnerabilities and things that concern you, and that you are working on and developing. And I realise that's important for me, too, because it gives me a sense that you can fully understand and relate, and are coming from a place of knowledge and experience.

So... I wanted to let you know that your openness and vulnerability, and the way in which you uniquely communicate that, is a large part of why I dig what you do.'

Graeme Blackwell

Here's the thing – It took me 20 years to learn some of these lessons, and my hope for you is that you don't spend as long repeating the same things over and over. If someone had shared his or her story as frankly with me, maybe I would have wised up sooner. Maybe hearing someone I liked, knew and trusted tell me their story would have enabled me to reflect on my own and maybe it would have normalised some of what I was going through for me.

I am about to share with you some very personal things, things that our society tells me I shouldn't talk about without being ashamed. The thing is that our shame is a part of us and needs to be addressed.

SHAME: A FEELING OF GUILT, REGRET, OR SADNESS THAT YOU HAVE BECAUSE YOU KNOW YOU HAVE DONE SOMETHING WRONG, ABILITY TO FEEL GUILT, REGRET, OR EMBARRASSMENT, DISHONOUR OR DISGRACE.

I have spent years feeling ashamed of some of the choices I've made, but the truth is that it's all just a part of my story. The decisions we make are based on what we deem to be right in the moment we are making them. Being diagnosed with a stomach ulcer did get me to start taking a bit more care of myself, but not as much as you might think.

When I was 21 I found myself naked from the waist down, legs in stirrups, in a room full of medical students. I had been in pain again, not the same stomach pain as before, very similar but lower down. This wasn't in my abdomen, this was in my womb. I didn't want to think about it, so I ignored it. Which it turns out was not a good idea. I had gotten Chlamydia, which led to PID.[34] The shame of having to ring exes and tell them was excruciating but I got over it. What was harder to get over was being told I wouldn't be able to conceive, or that in the unlikely event that I did, it would very likely be ectopic.

I hadn't realised how much I wanted kids until I was told I couldn't have them.

I didn't realise how much other stuff was lurking under the surface either:

I'LL BE THE SAME AGE AS MUM WAS WHEN SHE HAD ME IN A COUPLE OF MONTHS. THIS WHOLE THING HAS BROUGHT UP MY MOTHER ISSUES, I WOULD GIVE ANYTHING TO BE ABLE TO TALK ABOUT THIS WITH MY MUM. (PAUSE TO CRY).[35] BUT NOT HER BECAUSE I DON'T TRUST HER.

Trust.

Trust is a tricky one.

How do we learn to trust?[36]

> 'THE BEST WAY TO FIND OUT IF YOU CAN TRUST SOMEBODY IS TO TRUST THEM.'
> – ERNEST HEMINGWAY

My reaction to being told this news was to go out and have more sex with strangers.

---

34. *http://www.nhs.uk/Conditions/Pelvic-inflammatory-disease/Pages/Introduction.aspx*

35. Yes it really says that in my diary, I have always narrated my life in my journals.

36. A regular mindfulness practice can help. Elisha Goldstein, Ph.D. explains why here: *http://blogs.psychcentral.com/mindfulness/2013/04/the-neuroscience-of-learning-to-trust-yourself*

I was hurting. I was hurting a lot and feeling lonely. I sought to combat that loneliness. I sought out connection in the form of sex. Sex wasn't just about connection; if I am honest it was also numbing my feelings. Connection/love is one of our six humans needs[37] and it is a really fucking tough need to get met if you are not willing to be vulnerable, trust or relinquish control. Mastin Kipp[38] recently told me that the difference between the two is down to certainty. Connection is certain and love is uncertain, and so it makes sense then that when I was unwilling or unable to be vulnerable, I was unable to allow love in.

Inside I felt sad. I felt huge grief, for the children I was told I wouldn't be able to have. For a future that seemed like it had been taken away. For not having a mother I felt able to share this with; who would hold me while I cried and stroke my hair. I wasn't very good at *being* with my feelings. I wasn't engaging in bulimic behaviour anymore, instead I was bottling up and then vomiting my feelings all over my friends, not waiting for their compassion or empathy, but spewing out my unprocessed bile-like feelings and then running away (literally and metaphorically). My behavioural go-to patterns found new ways to manifest.

For a long time my diary entries, journalling or Morning Pages[39] were just lists of baby names and tear smudges. I didn't know how to be with or process my feelings. They scared me, so I numbed them out until they exploded in a way that meant I had to face them.

Fast forward to November 2002, when I packed up my job in a Brighton call centre and flew over to France for my first ski season. I'll let you imagine what it was like. I learned to snowboard a little. I drank a lot. I got pregnant. I came home. On 14th April 2003 at 9:15am under general anaesthetic at 10 weeks pregnant I had an abortion. Making the decision to do so was one of the most difficult decisions I've ever had to make.

I've struggled with whether or not to share this part of my story with you, but it is important to me that I keep it real. It's vital that every person

---

37. I refer to the six human needs throughout the book and in my work A LOT! When we are able to identify what need is not being fulfilled in ourselves or in another we can find a way to satiate it. They are: Certainty, Uncertainty/Variety, Significance, Connection/Love, Growth and Contribution. They determine what and why we do what we do. Find out more here: *http://training.tonyrobbins.com/the-6-human-needs-why-we-do-what-we-do/*

38. Founder of *The Daily Love. http://thedailylove.com*

39. *http://juliacameronlive.com/basic-tools/morning-pages/*

reading this book realises that we are all just human beings struggling with the decisions of our lives. We all have shame. We all have tough decisions to make. We all do things we never thought we'd do until the situation happens to us. None of us know how we will react until we are in our own set of shitty circumstances. I stick by the decision I made and I don't regret what I did, but that doesn't mean I don't still think about it a lot and feel sad.

My dad and step mum were amazingly unjudgmental and supportive. I came home from France and they made a place for me in their home. I spent time ruminating over the decision I faced. I wanted a baby so badly and yet I felt like I had so little to offer a child. The father was not a man I wanted in my life for one week let alone a lifetime. The realness of the life growing inside me awoke something else in me too. The whole experience shook me up, the sickness, the hormones, the reality check jolted me from my numbness and I made the first step into awareness. I began to acknowledge that I was fucking around and refusing to let my heart enter my relationships. I had been convinced that I could remain immune to love and to *feelings* as long as I remained in control. Getting pregnant, being pregnant, having to make a life-altering decision whilst high on hormones is a big deal at any age, and for someone who doesn't like themselves very much it is a fucking great wake-up call. The lessons weren't lost on me. I realised that however much 'control' I thought I had, there was something way bigger than me out there calling the shots. However much I thought I was able to control what I felt and when, facing the full gamut of feelings is a requirement of being alive.

I began to see just how much about life I didn't yet know. I began to see just how much there still was to learn. I made my decision based on what I felt had to offer a child and how much being in between my parents had affected me. I felt sure that I wasn't equipped to be a parent yet and vowed to sort my shit out and become a better person.

When we start out at anything, we don't know what we don't know. The next step is Aspiration – seeing what it is that we don't know, and deciding what we want instead. The next is Acceptance, and then Action: getting ready to learn all this new stuff.

Whilst getting pregnant and making the decision to have a termination gave me an 'aha' moment, I wasn't ready for any more at that point. I learned a lot, I really did. The whole experience was a HUGE eye opener and game changer for my emotional intelligence and personal growth BUT it wasn't as simple as learn my lesson and move on. I wasn't able to grow instantly into a healthy, well rounded human being fully capable of loving myself and others. The experience for me was very much more a case of *'OUCH that hurt a hell of a lot, I know I need to make some changes in my beliefs and behaviour – but not yet, I'm going to concentrate on other areas of my life until I hurt less.'*

It wasn't that conscious, but it took time for me to digest what I had been through and learned. I threw myself into work. I didn't really have a career yet, but I was pretty sure I should have. I wanted to 'make it' in the TV world but I also wanted to be sure I was ready. I wanted to have some money saved. I wanted to try a whole range of other things too. I wasn't ready to leave Brighton. I knew I needed to move to London in order to pursue my dream job, but I wasn't ready yet. I needed to take action. I needed to be busy. So I signed up as a temp and I worked in all kinds of places.

Two that stand out particularly because they challenged my perceptions were both for the police: first in the HR department, and then in the Coroner's Office.

Working for the police is something I would never have considered for myself. I was a pot-smoking, anti-rules liberal – I had a very set perception of what the police service would be like.

I was so wrong. Being in the HR department gave me access to a wide range of departments and allowed me to gain insight into much of the infrastructure involved in running the police force. The people I worked with were incredible, doing amazing work. I learned to challenge my perceptions of people and situations. I learned a load of administrative and organisational skills that I still use today. I learned a lot about discretion. I signed the Official Secrets Act for the first time.

Once I had been temping with them for nearly two months a position at the Coroner's Office became available. Again, it wasn't something I'd ever thought I'd do, but 'never say never', right? What I had learned by that point was that you never know where something will lead and if it isn't a no, then it might be a yes – so I said yes and I am so glad I did. My time with the Coroner's Office was an experience I'll never forget, but a job I decided I could not do full time. The emotion I felt in the couple of weeks I was working with that incredible team was overwhelming. Feeling all my own emotions was overwhelming enough, but I was still unaware of how much of an empath and emotionally sensitive person I am, and dealing with so much residual emotion left me exhausted and confused. I didn't know how to process it all. The recurring belief that maybe I was crazy resurfaced. All my demons buzzed under the surface. I told myself that if I were to stay on in the job I would have to normalise feelings and behaviour that I wasn't willing to make normal. The truth is that I didn't want to deal with any of what I was feeling and if I had stayed, I would have had to. I dealt with it by leaving and ignoring it.

I carried on temping from one place to the next; learning systems, meeting people, side stepping office politics and enjoying being the brilliant new girl. Then I got offered a job as recruitment consultant for the agency I had been temping with. It felt grown up and I felt sure I should be a grown up by now, so I said yes. So convinced was I that I was ready to be a grown up that I took my tongue piercing out and wore a suit! For six months I worked the temps' desk in clip-cloppy heels and a cheap Topshop suit. I enjoyed helping people. I loved my new role, pretending to be a career woman. For a while the pace of it and learning about different businesses and industries kept me amused. I liked the commission I was earning. I liked the regular pay cheque, but once the novelty wore off, I was just playing a role, and not one that excited or stimulated me. I got really bored and when I let it slip that I was considering doing another ski season they fired me.

For my second ski season I was the assistant manager of a large hotel in the French Alps. I didn't make it the whole way through that season either, not for any big dramatic reasons this time though - it just turned out that way. A lot of my staff broke bones and after four months I had only been out boarding four times. I did a lot of night shifts, followed by day shifts, followed by nights. I trained new staff; I gave warnings and had to fire friends. It was tough. I was sleeping with one of the chefs, and having to fire the guy you fancy for taking the piss and not showing up to work is horrible. Being a good manager when you desperately need everyone to like you is impossible. I only ever asked people to do things I would do myself. I wanted my staff and my bosses to like me. I tried to manage in a way that I would be receptive to whilst hitting targets and getting the job done. I enjoyed doing a job that didn't feel like a job. I liked the responsibility, I liked all the office work, I liked being client facing, I liked the extra pay, and I loved having my own apartment, but trying to be all things to all people is exhausting and eventually my desire to be liked at any cost, cost me.

Resentment is you not giving yourself what you need, expecting someone else to, but not asking them to. It took me years to figure that one out.

I needed to go home. I needed to rest and take better care of myself. But rather than ask, one night I got incredibly drunk for a bet (17 double Jack Daniels with coke and a gross shot) and as she put me to bed in my apartment I told my boss I hated my job and wanted to go home. The next day she lovingly sent me packing. Partied out, and with a chunk of experiences and cash behind me, I moved up to London and got my first TV gig. In a way I think ski seasons prepared me nicely for my TV career. They are far more similar than you might imagine.

Many people believe that working in TV and film is glamorous. Believe me when I tell you it is not. Like working a ski season, it is the people around you that make it worthwhile. They become your family. The hours are long and the demands and expectations are often ridiculous. Being creative and doing something different everyday was what drove me. That, and again feeling like I was part of a family. That I belonged and mattered. Needing people to like you and being a people pleaser are assets in the entertainment business.

Starting out I often felt like I was way out of my depth and most days I had no idea what I was doing. Being in the art department – making stories come alive visually and problem solving creatively – was what I wanted to do, and so I just kept looking for opportunities to prove myself.

The very first paid job I had was in 2004: I got offered a day's work on 'Queer Eye for the Straight Guy' and I jumped in with both feet. I just trusted that I would be OK. Initially a friend gave me her spare room and I stayed there until the end of that job. That one day's work turned into four months. Then I was asked to come back and work on the original American version of the show when the guys from the US came over to London to do a special. From there I moved out of my friend's spare room and in with a friend in Brixton.

I worked on small unheard-of sketch shows and pilots with temping jobs in between. I worked on short films and no-budget music videos for free and for expenses. I always did my very best and eventually found myself working on some very cool stuff. It was not immediate and it was not without hard work and long hours, often for a slice of cold pizza and a travelcard. When I started out in TV land it was still a very old-school world. You apprenticed. You worked for free on jobs in order to get credits and experience. You signed up to 'Shooting People'[40] and you worked on night shoots for that showreel piece until someone you knew got a break and took you with them to a paid gig. I don't think much has changed.

I was lucky and I created my own luck: I'd used my last year at university to make friends with people at London International Film school and Goldsmiths and anywhere else that had film courses and might need an art department assistant. I stayed in touch with those people after I left. A couple of them took me under their wing and taught me everything they knew. Those people know who they are and I will always be incredibly grateful that they saw something in me and invited me in, let me work on their shows and paid me back with paid work later down the line. I worked hard those first few years. I watched and learned from everyone. I didn't like to ask questions or get in the way but I observed and I made notes. I was the first person on set and the last one to leave. I studied my script, I made friends with actors, with all of the crew, with runners; I was helpful to anyone and everyone. I had a standby trolley kitted out for

---

40. *https://shootingpeople.org/home*

every possible eventuality. I took my role terribly seriously even though back then I had no real idea what the job involved or how my work would impact those in the edit suite later.

I was curious and ambitious. I wanted to learn and I wanted to be the best I could be. Throughout my life this has always been true. I have never known where I would end up, or what I was doing. People around me have often commented on my well-conceived plans, but the truth is that although I have always had *a* plan, for the most part they have been naive ones. Trust me when I tell you that that is all you need; a desire to be the best you can be and to get started.

Having someone to learn from helps.

part two:
MASTERY

THE NEXT CHAPTER

MENTOR: AN EXPERIENCED AND TRUSTED ADVISER. FROM THE OXFORD ENGLISH DICTIONARY.

Most of us start out on our own hero's journey looking to our parents, guardians or carers to teach and advise us, but then there comes a time when we must go forth and seek our own wisdom. It is a necessary part of maturity; journeying out into the world to quest alone. It is on this adventure that we find new people and situations to learn from.

There is an expression, 'When the student is ready, the master will appear'. When you are ready to learn something the universe will deliver you a teacher. Sometimes in the form of a person and sometimes in the form of a situation, and often in a package that you do not associate with 'teacher' until way after the lesson is learned.

Learning isn't about schooling or education. Your self-judgment, your socio-economic background, your education and qualifications have nothing to do with how you learn or your capacity to learn. In Step 3: Judgment and Acceptance[41] I talk about this in more depth, but for now when I talk about life as a series of experiments I want you to remember that you are an eternal student and that the definition of insanity is doing the same thing over and over and expecting different results. By this premise the definition of sanity is: trying new things and being open to results without expectation.

---

41. In the work-book section.

'IN THE BEGINNER'S MIND THERE ARE MANY POSSIBILITIES, BUT IN THE EXPERT'S THERE ARE FEW'
– SHUNRYU SUZUKI

Those that know the least may very well learn the most. They have the advantage of the beginner's mind.[42] The problem that most of us face when it comes to learning something new is that we think we already know it all and so we make assumptions. When I was in my teens I knew everything. At least I felt like I did. The older I get the less certain I am about all the things that I know. Each day I remind myself to be open minded, often saying aloud 'I am willing to see this differently.'

If I've gotten stuck in closed thinking, once I realise it I acknowledge it, and ask to be able to see more. It is habitual for me to think I know how a situation will play out, or what will happen as a consequence of an action, based on my experience. But the truth is that assumption is the mother of all fuck-ups. It is our assumptions that keep us stuck, stints communication and stops us from growing. Sometimes we don't even know what it is that we have assumed. During my 20s, I continued to feed my need for certainty by making decisions about how other people would behave and mind-mapping the future like a chess game in my head.

I would try to control all areas of my life: work, relationships and my spiritual or existential spheres. The knowledge I sought was to give me power, the power to control my reality and eliminate fear.

Before I continue to tell you my story I want to explain the stages of learning, so that you can see how and why things change when we decide to learn. Being an autodidact is awesome, sapiosexual might not be a real word, but learning and knowledge sure are sexy!

---

42. Shoshin (初心) is a concept in Zen Buddhism meaning 'beginner's mind'. It refers to having an attitude of openness, eagerness, and lack of preconceptions when studying a subject, even when studying at an advanced level, just as a beginner in that subject would. The term is especially used in the study of Zen Buddhism and Japanese martial arts.

There are four stages of learning, or four stages of competence.[43]

1. *Unconscious Incompetence.*

    In this first stage we do not understand the thing, AND we do not even know what it is that we don't know. We may deny the usefulness of the skill – 'Oh, learning how to drive/speak French/ play guitar/use Twitter isn't relevant to what I do.'

    The truth is that at this point we do not recognise the deficit of skill. In order to move to the next stage we need to become aware of our own incompetence and recognise the value of the new skill. The length of time you or I spend in this stage depends entirely on the strength of the stimulus to learn. There will be something that raises our awareness.[44]

2. *The second stage is Conscious Incompetence.*

    This is when we suddenly get it. We get that there is something that we don't know that would be of great value to us to know. We can quite often be overwhelmed by the realisation that there is SO much that we don't know in this new area and we can feel a lot of fear about being a beginner at something again. The making of mistakes is integral to the learning process at this stage. Remember that, when you are here: it is normal, you are learning, that is HOW we learn. In fact the more mistakes you make the more knowledgeable you are actually becoming.

3. *Step three is Conscious Competence.*

    You know this bit, I know you do, it's where you understand how to do something new, but demonstrating this new skill requires concentration. I remember when I first learned how to drive, or more specifically when I learned how to park – I had to focus with all of my attention: radio off, window open, don't talk to me. I would park well, but I'd get a sweaty lower back and I had to filter out everything else in order to focus solely on the task at hand. I sometimes had to talk myself through the steps out loud. Or

---

43. Attributed to Abraham Maslow but might have been Gordon Training International.
44. See Step 1: From Numbness to Awareness.

when I learned how to build a new page on my website or create a new blog post. I had to run through a mental checklist, again sometimes talking myself through the process. Or when I learned how to navigate my way to a new place in the city – at first I had to focus on where I was going and look out for landmarks to show me I was on track – soon I was going on autopilot.

Which is when you know you are at...

4. **Step four: Unconscious Competence.**

   One day you are just doing it without thinking about it. The same skill that once took all your focus can now be done whilst talking to someone or with the radio on in the background. At this stage you might even be able to teach someone else how to do it... (Maybe not parking, but I bet when you learned to tie your shoe laces it took every ounce of patience and attention you had, but now you could teach someone how to do it with ease and grace.)

There is also a fifth stage that isn't part of the original model: 'Conscious Competence of Unconscious Competence' – this piece is importance for you to take note of as a freelancer, business owner or entrepreneur, this is the bit where you either don't make, or do make your money. This is where the value is. This is where you take the skill(s) that you have and you find a way to pass them on to others. This stage is about reverse engineering what you did and chunking it down into teachable, learnable steps. Which is what I have done with my experiences – The 8 steps from ARGH to AHHH are my version of step five. It is in the teaching of our own unconscious competence that even more learning is made. *Mastery* happens when figuring out how to pass on your wisdom or skills to another.

Maybe now that you have an understanding of how learning works you will cut yourself some slack as you experiment with new ideas and reframing.

In the personal development world there is often talk of an onion. There are always more layers to the onion. Each course you attend, each seminar, webinar, retreat, book and experience will peel back a layer of your onion, and help you to solve the riddle that is you.

If you have ever been to a yoga class you'll know that when you first start out and the teacher explains where to put your limbs, that is often all the information you can handle. As the teacher keeps speaking you zone out as you focus on where your arms and legs should be. After a few classes, the information has been absorbed, you hear more of what the teacher is saying, beyond the anatomical instructions. They are now talking about your breath and perhaps you hear the words 'banda' and 'drishti' but are not quite sure what you do with them. As weeks go by you learn more, you can get deeper into each posture, you hear more of what the teacher is saying, you absorb more and find deeper layers to work on.

Yoga is always a metaphor for your life off the mat, it is never just a physical practice, it is a series of lessons for you to take out into your everyday life.

But, back when I turned 25, I did not know this and what I learned on my mat, stayed on my mat. Like many of my peers and like nearly all twentysomethings nowadays I experienced a quarter-life crisis of sorts. Christine Hassler[45] calls it an expectation hangover. Things in TV land were going well professionally; I had finished working on 'Queer Eye for the Straight Guy', I had identified gaps in my knowledge and had learned the new skills. I had begun to understand what the hell this job actually entailed, I had gotten my head around all the jargon and I knew and respected the hierarchy. I now knew that there were ways of doing things and was doing them as I should to fit in. I was being courteous and diligent in all the right places with all the right people. I could see a line of progression from where I was as art department assistant further up the food chain and had visions of one day being one of the 'grown ups'.

I'd worked on a few shows people had actually heard of like 'Celebrity Big Brother's Little Brother' and had painted The Big Brother house. I was getting to hang out with people like Dermot O'Leary and Davina McCall. I'd been asked to come and work on 'Peepshow' doing Standby Props.[46] I worked on an incredible Film Council project with a local school enabling a group of kids aged 9 and 10 to make a real film – I was one of the industry professionals, teaching these children how to maybe one day have

---

45. American Lifecoach specialising in quarter-life crisis and expectation hangover, *http://christinehassler.com/*. I think we can get an expectation hangover at any age, when we wake up to our own expectations.

46. Which is still to this day one of the best jobs, best crews, best scripts, best experiences of my life. Thank you.

a job as cool as mine. The kids were AWESOME, the ideas they had and the attention and concentration they put in was incredible. I cried tears of joy when we watched the film in the cinema. I think that might have been my first experience of giving back what I had learned. It was taste of where I was headed, I just didn't know it yet. I was working my way slowly on to better-paid jobs with more status and making a name for myself.

I know, you're probably reading this and thinking *And you had a quarter-life crisis because…?*' Things were going well, but not well enough quick enough, and although it looked good on the outside, inside I wasn't happy.

Patience was not my strong suit. Back then the dreaded compare-and-despair mindset had well and truly got me. Rather than being proud of myself I was disappointed that I wasn't further ahead in my career, earning more money, owning a house, getting married, going on foreign holidays, owning expensive and flashy cars, getting famous, being thinner etc, etc. I had very little gratitude for the life that I was living, I wanted MORE. I was incredibly focused on what was next, more, more more… Rather than taking any time to be in the NOW, to stop and take stock, I was always living in the future. I didn't really have a properly thought-out strategy, I wasn't one for goals and milestones back then. I hadn't even contemplated how I would know when I was where I wanted to be. Now it's one of my first questions to clients:

'HOW WILL YOU MEASURE SUCCESS? HOW WILL YOU KNOW WHEN YOU HAVE ACHIEVED WHAT IT IS THAT YOU WANT?'

In July 2005 I just wanted more than what I had. I turned 25 and it was a big deal. I remember thinking, 'FUCK – where has the time gone and what am I doing with my life?' I spent sleepless nights in the run-up to my birthday reflecting on my life. I got really quite depressed. I knew it was time to do something different. For the first time I felt that if I didn't stop partying soon my life would flash before my eyes and I would have nothing to show for it. I began to think about what had to happen in my life in order for me to be happy and proud with what I had lived.

My reality was that I was a work-hard-party-harder girl. Fitting it all in was tough and it was taking its toll. I was just about making the work bit happen, and my social life was a blur of Prosecco, cocaine and sex. I enjoyed the parties and I loved being made to feel special: I loved a guest list and a free drink, but after all the people were gone and the mad adventures were done, what I really wanted was a man to love and a baby. I was incredibly lonely and I didn't know what to do about it. I felt like there was something wrong with me. I had all this love to give and no one to give it to. It didn't occur to me that I wasn't loving me, or that my relationships with others were a reflection of my relationship with myself. I longed for connection, love and intimacy, but looking back now I realise I didn't know what that really meant. Turning 25 made me think about everything. I was reassessing it all, and, as is my predisposition, overthinking it and getting lost in my own thoughts. I tried to focus on what was good in my life. I tried to think about what I actually wanted for myself. Instead I ended up seeing everyone else's outsides and comparing them to my insides.

What do I mean by that?

Everywhere I looked I saw people my age and younger doing better than me. They were getting married, having children, saving money, going on holidays and seemingly doing so much better than I was. They seemed together. They liked and were proud of who they were. I didn't feel good about myself. I was obsessed with my body and my weight and convinced that if I could save up for lipo-sculpture I would finally love and accept myself. Ten years later it's almost funny to me that I remember comparing myself to Britney Spears and thinking she'd got it all figured out. She was at the height of her career and about to have her first child and I was jealous. What this shows me now is that if Britney Spears and I were both creating lives that looked good on the outside but felt BAD on the inside then some of you are too. Not to mention that if Britney can get through 2007 and I can get through 2009 then you can get through whatever is going on for you right now. I promise.

In September 2005, very drunk, in the middle of the night, feeling sorry for myself I wrote a list I called:

10 THINGS I WANT TO DO IN MY LIFE[47]

1. FIND LOVE AND SUSTAIN A RELATIONSHIP.

2. HAVE A CHILD OR TWO AND CREATE A FAMILY.

3. GO TO THE OTHER SIDE OF THE WORLD AND SEE THE SUNSET, LEARN YOGA AND MEDITATION.

4. BE HAPPY WITH MY BODY - THINK IT'S BEAUTIFUL.

5. HAVE A HOME I AM PROUD OF.

6. START MY OWN COMPANY AND HELP OTHER PEOPLE FEEL GOOD ABOUT THEMSELVES DOING SOMETHING I AM GOOD AT AND ENJOY.

7. BE DEBT FREE, HAVE SAVINGS, BE FINANCIALLY FREE.

8. DRIVE FROM ONE END OF ENGLAND TO THE OTHER AND VISIT ALL THE COUNTIES IN BETWEEN.

9. NEVER GO TO SLEEP REGRETFUL OF SOMETHING I HAVE THE POWER TO CHANGE BUT HAVE NOT.

10. JUMP OUT OF A PLANE AND FACE MY MORTALITY.

What strikes me about this list is how much of it is still important to me now. How my values were known to me then, even though I didn't explicitly know them or know the language of them. The thing about values is that they are THE most important things to you. It's why I get my clients to start out with them. It's not about recreating your peak experiences, but about recognising the themes behind them. There is a unique combination of values that is specific to you and which is magically powerful. It is this personalised combination of qualities, feelings, or values that holds your gift to world. In his book *The 7 Habits of Highly Effective People*, Stephen Covey says, 'Be sure that your ladder of success is leaning against the right building...' Which I interpret to mean: make sure you are building a life on the outside that feels good for you on the inside. To work out yours, go to Step 1: Awareness in the Workbook section of this book.

---

47. A list I promptly forgot about and actually only found again for the first time while re-reading all of my diaries and journals as research for writing this book.

The career I was building in the TV industry fitted with some of my values, but not all. If I had worked out what was really important to me then, maybe I wouldn't have crashed so hard. I truly believe that the universe is speaking to us all the time, giving us all little whispers *are you listening?*

I wasn't.

It's OK not to hear the first or second time, but it is my experience that the whisper will become a call, then a nudge and eventually, if you are still not paying attention, it will turn into a smack in the face. When we are children we are able to hear it. The seven-year-old me listened. I see my friends' children listening. The answers you seek are not on your phone or tablet, they are inside you and out in nature. Don't misunderstand what I'm saying, I LOVE technology and what the internet has done for the world BUT (and it's a HUGE BUT) it is SO important to stay attuned to our souls, which are deeply connected to the rhythm of the moon and the waves of the sea, the cycles of the seasons and the whispering of the wind. The universe is whispering to you all the time. This isn't a one-time thing. It doesn't send you a wake-up call and then quit talking to you, it will talk to you the rest of your life whether you are listening or not. Once you are listening it can be a dialogue and the universe celebrates with you as it no longer talks into the wind alone.

I was at an event with Arianna Huffington[48] where she told her story and explained that it took breaking her cheek – waking up on the pavement, mobile phone and blood between her and the floor, to realise that she had to change something, and to start thinking about what she really wanted for herself.

Your wake-up call doesn't need to be that dramatic. It doesn't need to involve homelessness, drugs, or insanity. Losing yourself just enough to find yourself again is fine. Listen to the whispers of the universe and your heart and act on what you hear. Trust yourself. Not just one time, but always.

I first heard a tiny niggly voice telling me to leave the TV industry on my birthday in July 2005 but I didn't actually do it properly until July 2009. Between July and December 2005 my best friend and I toyed with

---

48. Co-founder and editor-in-chief of The Huffington Post. Author and inspirational woman!

the idea of starting a snowboarding-inspired streetwear clothing label for women.

Aside: I realise that I haven't talked much about my bestie. No one tells you how tricky it is to write a book about your life without mentioning or not mentioning the people in it. There are many reasons why I have chosen where possible to leave my family and friends nameless – but let me just tell you the important things about Zoë. She is and will always be my bestie. When I didn't think I deserved friends, when I felt that all women were only ever out to bitch and backstab, when I need someone to listen without judging, when I need someone to make judgments, when I was doing things that were no good for me, when I was doing things that were amazing for me, when I grew and changed, when we stopped seeing so much of each other and when our lives continue to unfold as they will – this woman has always been there for me and I know she always will be. I believe that before we come and live this life we make some choices about what we want to learn and who we'll have as soul mates; souls to guide us home and help us see who we really are, and remind us a little of our purpose – she is one of my soul sisters and my best friend. I am truly grateful for the honesty we have shown each other, for all the tears we have shed in sadness and in joy, in setback and in growth. I believe in sacred contracts and the one we made is lifelong.

So now you know who Zoë is, let's carry on:

Zoë and I have lived together a lot over the years. At that time she and I were living, just the two of us, in a warehouse in Brixton. She had just graduated with first-class honours in Fashion Design Technology from the London College of Fashion. I had done my two ski seasons and the pair of us had been snowboarding together a couple of times. We had friends who were working in that world and we could see that it was a growing industry. There were only a handful of labels specifically catering for women. We recognised a need. Most of the women's clothing out there was awful, designed by men for women that didn't exist. We wanted to create something similar to what Nikita Clothing was doing, but instead of being authentically Icelandic we wanted to do it authentically Brighton/London style. I came up with the brand name, together we came up with the logo, registered the domain, designed our first range and began researching the cost and suppliers. Autonomy Clothing was born, but never made it out of the starting gate.

There is a lot more to starting a company than registering it. But that doesn't mean you need to spend a long time planning, if you don't want to.

It boils down to 6 Ps:

1. FIND SOMETHING YOU LOVE TO DO - PASSION
2. FIND SOMETHING THE WORLD NEEDS - SOLVE A PROBLEM - PROVIDE VALUE
3. BE GREAT AT IT - PROFICIENT
4. GET PAID FOR IT - PROFIT
5. TELL PEOPLE ABOUT IT - PROMOTION
6. KEEP DOING, NEVER QUIT - PATIENCE

I was passionate about the idea as an idea. I was keen on the lifestyle we could have. I really wanted to deliver a product people would love, but I didn't have the first clue about fashion, clothing production or running a company. I didn't have any business background and I wasn't passionate about learning about business. I was just about managing the freelance thing, but being a business owner and running an actual company felt different. I felt like I needed someone to lead the way but I had no idea who to ask or where to begin.

Maybe I could find someone to show me?

The thought flashed through my mind and was gone.

Now of course I'd go out and find someone to show me how, and I wouldn't stop until I found the right person. But then, I didn't know what I didn't know.

I could have gone and got a job that taught me what I needed to learn and learned whilst I earned, but a traditional job where you trade your time for money has just never sat well with me. I have often wanted job security. I often have wanted a regular pay cheque. I have wanted someone to pay me to learn. But I have always felt that jobs come with so much limitation to my freedom. And, whilst inside I have always had the potential to be a Maven (I have not always been one!), I lacked the self-belief – a key ingredient for being an Entrepreneur. Back then, whilst being self-employed was an option, deep down I believed that a person would only ever scrape a living that way. Yet even with that belief living unconsciously in my head I *still* chose the self-employed route, that's how important FREEDOM is to me.

I honestly believed that I would never be rich or 'successful' but I still chose self-employment time and time again. Maybe if I had gotten a job then I would have learned quicker – but there is no right way and no wrong way, just your way and mine. There is no one size fits all. When you are first starting out as an entrepreneur getting a job is a great idea! A job is a great way to get paid to learn. A job can be a great joint venture if it's a values match. A job is a great means to an end and certainly takes the pressure off making your company work straight away.

Autonomy Clothing didn't work out because I wasn't so passionate about it that I would do whatever it took to make it work. The truth is that I liked the idea of it much more than the reality of it. I didn't have the first clue about how to start a clothing label but that isn't what really mattered. What mattered was that starting my own company then was far too far out of my comfort zone for me. It was a goal that paralysed me rather than pushing me. While it was a step toward recognising my values and building a business around them, it wasn't right for me and I'm very glad we only invested a small amount of time and money into that one. I wasn't intrinsically a *businessperson*. I have had to learn about business. As I have grown personally I have grown professionally. My capacity to learn increases every day and is directly correlated to the self-development work I do.

I don't really consider Autonomy Clothing a failure though, not in the way you might. You see, I am thankful for my failures. Here's the thing about failure: it's awesome and to be celebrated. Failure proves that you had a go. Thinking will not get you a business and a life you love. Action will. Start something, have a go – you learn from doing not thinking. Every failure you experience is a lesson you have learned.

> ## 'I HAVE NOT FAILED. I'VE JUST FOUND 10,000 WAYS THAT WON'T WORK.'
> ## – THOMAS A. EDISON

So, I carried on working in TV land, on weird and wonderful shows and events. Whatever came through the door I said YES and figured out how to do it on the hoof. That December, while working on a comedy sketch show called 'Little Miss Jocelyn', I met Alice. Alice became my next mentor. Just as I was getting bored of doing standby and wanted a new challenge, Alice appeared. She was everything I aspired to be. She wasn't so alien and far ahead of me that she was scary and unapproachable, but she was further down the path and she knew so much more than me. I had no idea what a mentor was, nor that I was looking for one, but that didn't matter. She was being, doing and having everything I wanted. She was awesome. She exuded confidence. She was looking for a new petty cash buyer and I really wanted her to pick me. Not like at school, not for validation, but because I wanted to learn from her. I was eager to learn, I was ready for more, there were things I wanted for myself and my future. I trusted life, I trusted that I would get what I needed when I needed it, and so I put myself forward and was open to whatever opportunity presented itself.

She interviewed me and a few other people and on our next job I became her assistant. I learned how to be the very best Production Buyer I could be. I also learned that with the right teacher I could do whatever I put my mind to, with or without sleep.

But before that realisation, before things got better, things got worse – the niggling feeling of dissatisfaction and depression were whispering to me every night. I wasn't sleeping, and the voices in my head telling me how much I sucked as a human being were getting louder.

The girl in the mirror made me cry. I couldn't look at my reflection without feeling overwhelming shame that made me want to vomit. I was binging and starving myself again. New Year came and I wrote a list of things I would do better. I wanted to lose two stone this year. I wanted to find and marry a perfect man and get a cat and live in a one-bed flat by the sea. I wanted to be a housewife, the best darn housewife in the world – if only someone would love me. But no one loved me.

Self-pity, cycles of alcohol, restriction, binge-eating and making myself sick ensued. I needed to change my behaviour. I needed to do something. The urge to leave the TV industry and do something else, anything else, was whispering louder, but it might as well have been speaking in an ancient and foreign tongue. I could hear chatter but I couldn't decipher what it was trying to tell me. I didn't know how to meditate or listen to my heart back then. I didn't know that I had suppressed years of feelings and that they were starting to ferment. The rumblings of dissatisfaction were clear, though. I knew that my life was lacking something, but I didn't know what it was.

Many of you have felt those feelings. Many people I speak to have felt them for years and don't know what to do. I say listen, really listen – you do know exactly what to do. I don't think it matters which retreat or workshop you do or don't do. I think what's most important is gifting yourself time and space to be with who you are. What matters is the container the facilitators provide and that the content resonates with you. I know now that I was looking to connect with or 'find' myself. It's no coincidence that we use that expression. After we progress through childhood and adolescence we must then move on to adulthood. In order to reach adulthood we must go out and slay those that raised us (metaphorically, obviously). We are born idolising them and thinking they are God. It's a survival thing, but then we must knock them off the pedestal we have created for them and go and find our own truths.

In order to progress into true adulthood we must all become our own guru and master, find our own daemons and shadows and confront them. We must check and test that what we have learned from our parents with blind faith is in fact true for us. We must balance the co-dependency and narcissism within our relationships and ourselves in order to become truly autonomous.

It was the start of my journey of reconnection with that six-year-old's intuitive magic that I'd left behind. The first retreat I went to alone was a MythoSelf weekend, organised by Jon Nicoll and Sam Riordan. I have to be honest, I cannot remember all that much of what we did. I remember getting into different 'feeling states' by changing our physiology. I remember doing some NLP-type timeline processes, and imagining myself as a phoenix. I remember that from then on I had tools that enabled me to visualise with sensory detail the future that I wanted for myself. But as with so much in life, whilst I cannot remember what was said, or what we did exactly, I do clearly remember how I felt. I felt scared before I arrived, I made myself show up and then felt good all weekend. And I felt good afterwards. I enjoyed it very much. I loved that someone outside of my 'weird' family was running a *weird* workshop. I enjoyed seeing 'normal' people sign up and pay for the experience. I loved that this kind of thing didn't seem weird to the people here. I liked the people. I tasted a morsel of real belonging that weekend. I got to spend some time connecting with myself. More than that, I spent nearly the whole weekend being myself. My actual self. Not a version of myself that I thought the crowd would respond to. I began my personal journey from Apathy to Aspiration with that workshop. I left happier, and a door had been opened; I wasn't much clearer about what was missing, what I was searching for, or why I wasn't happy, but I was clearer on what I didn't like and what I didn't want more of.

I didn't want to be sleeping with and having a 'good feeling' about a different guy each month. I didn't want to be chasing and fantasising about guys from my teens anymore. I didn't want to be in a relationship that was claustrophobic and suffocating but I didn't want to be friends with benefits either. I wanted love, not just connection, but it terrified me. I didn't cognitively know that it terrified me, but I was sure I was awful at love. I was clear that I didn't want romance or schmaltz or 'lurve'. My belief about love at that time was that it made people stupid.

Another step was made, but I certainly couldn't yet see that I was afraid to be authentically me.

Although I was myself for a lot of that weekend, as soon as I left, I went back to playing the role of Ebonie. I played a role all of the time. I couldn't see that I continually morphed myself into who I thought people wanted to me to be. I believed that men fell in love with low-maintenance, fluffy, sexy, flirty, clever, attentive women and sexy (skinny) women. So I played that. I thought people at work wanted me to be just like them, but not too smart and not better than them. So I did that. I wanted to be loved, but I didn't want to be in love. I was exhausted. It is tiring trying so hard to be all of those things all of the time. And failing. I was tired of fighting for work and still being in debt. I was tired of being angry but refusing to feel it. I was just so tired. But I carried on holding it together, gritting my teeth and being strong, because that's what I thought you did.

I have noticed not just from my own experience but from that of my clients and peers, that when we make the step out of apathy and start feeling and thinking about what we want, what actually comes is a whole load of what we don't want.

The first question I ask new enquirers on their discovery or strategy sessions with me, after the initial getting-to-know-you bit is, 'What do you want?'

Nearly everyone answers this with a whole list of what they *don't* want.

This is because we have been suppressing it until it has gotten so big we can't ignore it anymore and that's where our focus is. It is also because our brains have a negativity bias.[49] Our hunter-gatherer brain seeks out and gives more attention to negative experiences and events because they pose a chance of danger. By default the brain alerts itself to potential threats, so actually drawing your attention to positive aspects takes deliberate effort.

What I didn't want any more was to be fat. I still believed that it was my fat making me unhappy and it was my fat that was leaving me feeling unfulfilled. So I began to look at where I could go, what I could try, who might be able to help me in a way that I hadn't already tried. I felt stuck, I felt like I had tried everything. I had tried diets. Trust me when I tell you

---

49. For more on negativity bias, look at the work of Dr Rick Hanson.

that I have explored every diet going. I had tried not eating, binging and throwing up, eating healthily and exercising, but nothing was working.

I asked around and was told about a friend who had been to stay with a woman in Thailand and done an elimination fast and yoga retreat, which had changed her life. She was now slimmer, happier and more vibrant than she had ever been before. It sounded healthier and better for me than liposuction (which I was still seriously considering) and cheaper too, so I went for it. I think I thought it would be a bit like being on one of those desert island reality shows where the contestants are secretly given rations but all leave the show thin and tanned.

My first elimination fast with Hillary Adrian Han on Koh Samui was in October 2006. Hillary's course is not like the others. The work she does is her Dhama. She teaches all that she knows with love and with spirit.[50] Now I have travelled all over the world and been on all sorts of retreats and courses, workshops and seminars and trainings. But that first overseas retreat trip alone was scary and way out of my comfort zone. I had grown up surrounded by alternative therapies and practitioners, and watched many people doing the 'work', and yet making the step to doing it for myself was scary. I was fearful of the unknown and also of what I had seen others journey through: the anguish and the grief of working through our own personal pain. At the same time I also felt a readiness and a trust that allowed me to take a leap of faith. Many people I have met on my travels have told me about a similar feeling, that feeling of *knowing* that this thing has to be done and that you will survive it. Knowing that some kind of freedom and release will happen, and no longer needing to know *how*. If you are on the edge of that place – and if you are you will know what I mean – follow your fear and you will know when to jump. Trust yourself and remember to breathe.

What I hadn't seen so much of then was what happens after the anguish and the grief; the after effects, the relief and joy that those people felt after they'd done that work.

Not knowing how I would pay off my credit card, I booked a two-week trip to Koh Samui via Bangkok. For the first seven days I knew I would

---

50. *http://www.dharmahealingintl.com/* Hillary's work is incredible, I cannot recommend her highly enough.

be with Hillary.[51] We had exchanged a few emails but I had no idea what to expect and no plans for my second week. I was ready. Armed with this strange feeling that I hadn't felt since childhood: a mixture of fear and excitement. A feeling that I have come to trust to mean: 'you are about to have a life-changing experience'. I arrived at Wasana's Guesthouse and paid the driver by thrusting a handful of Thai baht in his direction and trusting that he would take an appropriate amount and give me the rest back.

Exhausted from a long and chaotic journey, I found my way to my wooden bungalow, dumped my stuff and started to explore. I swam in the sea and lay in a hammock and said hello to the Thai family who owned the bungalow I was staying in. Then at 6pm I went and found the bungalow with a blackboard, sat on a yoga mat and waited for orientation to begin.

Over the next week I learnt so many new tools and experienced so many new experiences. Iridology. EFT.[52] Reiki. Toning. Chanting. Mantras. Colonics. Hillary's mandatory lessons were unlike any nutrition education I had ever had before. Hillary broke it all down into tiny, enzyme-sized pieces. She taught us about fats, proteins, carbohydrates, digestion, elimination, hormones, and the endocrine system. She explained it all down to a molecular level in a super passionate and encouraging way.

Doing yoga outside and working with our bodies to draw all the toxins out was great, different from anything I had done before. Combined with colonics, massage and lots of relaxation time, I experienced yoga as a healing tool for the first time and not just exercise. We were encouraged to journal; I still have all my journals from the four fasts I did with Hillary and nearly every other retreat, workshop and seminar that I have been on since. Detoxing was horrible. The headaches that came with coming off caffeine and sugar, as well as everything else flushing out my system, made me feel like my head was in a vice whilst having a severe case of food poisoning. It was short lived, though. By day three I was experiencing so much joy and feelings of euphoric soberness for the first time in

---

51. *http://www.dharmahealingintl.com/v2aboutus.html*

52. Emotional Freedom Technique, or tapping, is a fantastic tool and a way into experiencing self-acceptance. EFT is a form of counseling that draws on various theories of alternative medicine including acupuncture, neuro-linguistic programming, energy medicine, and Thought Field Therapy (TFT). We tapped whilst using the sentence: 'Even though. [insert ailment accurately] I fully and completely love and accept myself'. You repeat this mantra to a pattern of tapping along the body's meridian lines.

ages: the joys of midnight naked sea swimming, the bliss that comes after detox, the re-found love for food, made every second of detox worth it.

Being in Thailand by myself was also a great experience for me. Before that I would have been reluctant to go travelling or exploring alone. As it turns out, I love the anonymity of not understanding the language of a place. It gives me a chance to go more internal and notice all the beauty in the world. In Thailand in particular, the vibrancy of colour. Wow. The vibrancy of life. The warmth. The massages! There was a lady called Pong who did the best Thai Massage in the whole world. She was incredible. We had many a great conversation without saying a word. That trip to Thailand was another huge levelling up for me. It played a huge part in me discovering who I really am, and no longer playing a role.

I read. A lot. I devoured books like they were food. The three books that stand out from that trip were: *Eat Pray Love*[53], *The Art of Happiness*[54], and *What is Love*[55].

I became aware of how much 'control' had become a feature in my life and decided that I was open to being less in control, less controlling of everything. I chose to try 'going with the flow' more. Instantly an opportunity presented itself. There was a man on the fast that week who had been many times before. He and I got talking one night, and he told me that he had a timeshare in Phuket. He had one week left that year and none of his family would be using it. He asked me if I'd like to take it for my second week.

I embraced uncertainty. 'Yes, please!'

I asked one of the other girls on the retreat if she wanted to come with me and she said yes. We finished our fast, said goodbye to everyone and travelled first by boat and then by bus. The journey was like nothing I had ever done before and yet it felt so natural and easy to me; bumping along the dusty roads, my head rhythmically hitting the ceiling while holding on to someone's chickens.

---

53. *Eat, Pray, Love: One Woman's Search for Everything* by Elizabeth Gilbert
54. *The Art of Happiness: A Handbook for Living* by The Dalai Lama and Howard Cutler
55. *What is Love? - The Spiritual Purpose of Relationships* by Frank Vilaasa

We arrived at the Five Star resort in Phuket. It was AMAZING. I don't know what I was expecting, but it wasn't this. We were so incredibly underdressed in our sarongs and sandals. Upon hearing whose guests we were, the receptionist smiled and had us shown to our room. Our suite, actually. The PENTHOUSE, actually. It was HUGE! It was incredible!

The two of us stayed there together for three days, sharing fruit bowls and one main meal between us in our room because we didn't have the right clothes for the restaurant and our tummies were so tiny after the fast. On the third day Sarah left me there. She made her way back to Kuala Lumpur and then home to the USA. I spent four days alone in paradise. The resort had a seven-mile private white sand beach. I made friends with one of the kitchen staff, who fed me and took me on the back of his motorbike to meet his friends and party with the locals. The whole trip reminded me of how amazing life can be when you say 'yes'. The connection I had to myself through the fasting and the meditation and being so relaxed was so strong and clear that I felt safe to say 'Yes!' and allow the details to work themselves out. I believed that life was my playground and that the more playful and wild and free I was the more I would be supported.

In April 2007 I went back to Koh Samui; my second fast was for ten days. While I was there I also did my Reiki Level One. In between those trips I learned from Alice. She was the exact right mentor for me at the exact right time. She encouraged me to go to yoga; we both snuck in Bikram yoga classes around our gruelling schedule. She was vegetarian and both understanding and encouraging of the food 'rules' I'd bought home with me. I was either food combining or eating mostly raw food. No matter how healthily I ate, no matter how much weight I lost or what size I actually was, I always felt fat and I couldn't see anything but a disappointing fat girl in the mirror. The reality is that I was beautiful. Now I look at this picture and see a beautiful but sad girl. Back then I saw a fat, ugly and frustrated woman. It makes me sad now to think for how many years I hated myself. It makes me sad to think how entwined were my self worth and identity with the number on my scales and the size of my clothes. Whilst I may have felt free and playful in Thailand, back home I landed back into reality with a bump. I struggled with combining the two 'me's: the one I was while out there, and the one I felt I needed to be here.

I moved back to Brighton to be nearer the sea and closer to nature, but I continued working in London. Determined to make the different parts of me work together.

Zoë and I rented a lovely two-bed place together, but almost immediately she landed an incredible 'career job' in Italy so found a friend of a friend to take her room. He was a typical Brighton guy and liked to party! We threw one at the flat before Zoë left; a farewell for her and a moving in for him. It was mixture of all of our friends, no one knew anyone, but somehow it worked. In the midst of all the smoke and laughter and music and noise I looked out into the garden and saw a solitary, hoody-wearing man lying on the floor. He was gazing up at the stars. I went out and joined him. Without saying anything I lay down next to him, my head in the crook of his arm. In silence he passed me the spliff he was smoking and drew me in a little closer to him. We lay unspeaking in a kind of embrace for a long while. Even once the party ended and everyone had left the pair of us just lay in comfortable silence.

We'll call him Tom. Tom was on a break from the love of his life. The fact that we agreed up front that this wasn't going to be a relationship made me feel safe enough to be myself. For about three months he and I hung out. During the week we barely spoke, I was up in London doing my thing, he was in Brighton doing his. On Friday nights I'd race home to be with him, and have sex. It wasn't just sex, it may have started out that way, but it became lovemaking. Tom was the first guy I was more of myself with. Not just the 'cool girl'. Not just role-playing. Consciously straying away from trying to be Little Miss Perfect. I let him see some of my insecurity. I could let him in a little because there were no expectations – he was always going to go back to his girl once she had figured her stuff out. It was safe for me to be me. No one was going to tell me they loved me. No one would get slushy. No one was going to fall in love and be a dick.

Except someone did. I did.

Up until that point I believed that I could be immune to the 'crazy in love' thing. Up until that point there had been many men, but only a handful of *important* ones in my dotted relationship history.

There was the guy when I was 14 who told everyone at school that I'd done all sorts of things I hadn't done. I wasn't sure whether to claim them – be brazen and take the shameful kudos – or deny them and come across as prudish. Consequently I did both and came across as confused and crazy as I felt. *I learned that sex and perception are powerful tools.*

There was the guy not long after that, who was, a friend decided, the male version of me – we were introduced by phone at a house-party back in the days when there were house-phones. We spent ten hours straight talking about everything. We lost our virginity to one another and it was magical. 'Underwear' by Pulp[56] played in the background, it was exciting and new and fun. I trusted him completely, we were friends and we had an agreement. *I learned that keeping relationships short and sweet meant that they never tainted, and could be perfect moments.*

There was the guy whom I seduced and played a game of love with. We wrote each other love letters and acted as if we were in a music video or an American teen TV show. It was incredible – until it got real and he told me he loved me. I freaked out, I wanted love so badly, but I didn't know what to do. I hadn't been an ounce of real with him, so it didn't feel good at all. At

---

56. *https://www.youtube.com/watch?v=VwRfAceTJt4&list=RDVwRfAceTJt4*

a loss as to how to behave, I ran a mile and set him up with someone else. *'You don't want me, I'm rubbish at this; have her – she'll love you right.'*

There was the guy I put on a pedestal, believing he was perfect and so much better and more exciting than I deserved. We went out briefly when we were 17 but again I got scared and pushed him away and then pined after him for years (for ten years…). We slept together quite a few times over those years. It was a deeply unhealthy relationship. I thought I loved him, in reality I had just become obsessed with him. I fantasised about 'us' for such a long time but never once truly believed that I was good enough for him. The last time I saw him properly, everything was finally panning out just how I had imagined it a million times in my head – we were lying in bed and I was telling him about my business idea (he was the first person I told about My Girl Friday) – until he laughed at me and told me it wouldn't work. I realised suddenly that I was in love with a made-up version of him, not the actual him. Lightbulb moment. I learned that for me love is believing in someone and their dreams even if you don't understand them.

There was the guy who was 28 when I was 18. He was everything I dreamt a man could be (even though he was married and had a daughter back at home). We had incredibly honest and intimate sex one time in a caravan at a festival. It was not a relationship, but it allowed me to see that some men didn't take without giving and listening and being your friend. It was two people sharing with honesty their desire to be intimate with one another and even though it wasn't REAL real, it was the most real and intimate I had ever been. *I learned that momentary intimacy was doable and I wouldn't die if I showed someone who I was (fleetingly).*

And then there was Tom. Don't get me wrong, there were other guys – but these were the guys from whom I garnered the evidence that informed the beliefs I had about love and myself.

Our relationships are mirrors, showing us who we are and what we need to see so we can unravel the riddle. Every part of life, including our relationships, is happening for us, not to us. At the time, in those relationships, that's not how I saw it; I only saw my failure to have the story-book, rom-com, fairy-tale love life. Now, however, looking back I can see glimpses of who I needed to become, I can see all of the ways life was happening for me as endless opportunity for growth rather than some kind of penance or endurance test, which is how it felt.

Tom made me feel safe and showed me a part of myself. I fell in love with him for showing me the truth, being real, and caring.

I'll never forget the evening that we broke up, and the kindness he showed me. He told me that I had fallen in love with him and now it had to end because that wasn't part of the deal. I lost control; finally I acted entirely on unfettered emotion – I was furious and grief stricken and desperate. He bore the brunt of all these feelings. I ranted and raved and begged and cried. He left and I chased him as he skated down the road. Wearing just my pyjama shorts, hands over my boobs – yelling in the street for him to come back, tears streaming down my face.

I had become the very thing I would do anything to avoid: I was a crazy in love woman.

He came back. He behaved in such a gentlemanly manner. He took me to bed. He tucked me in and stroked my hair until I fell asleep and then he left.

Before Tom, deep down I believed that men were all out for what they could get away with and women (including myself) were all needy, manipulating victims. After Tom I realised that men were just people. I stopped seeing relationships as a battle, and started seeing them as opportunities for growth and connection.

But whilst I made that hypothesis cognitively, somewhere emotionally I still felt that I was unlovable. That I wasn't good enough, and that if I had been a better woman he would have loved me back and it would have worked out. I was hurt, and rather than simply feel my feelings I collected evidence that feeling feelings sucked BIG TIME.

I'll give you one guess what I blamed.

Yep, you got it: *he didn't love me the way I wanted to be loved because I was fat.*

Did I take some time to explore what I was feeling?

No, of course not.

I threw myself back into work to numb my feelings. At work I could be in control.

Alice and I worked on job after job. BBC dramas and ITV sketch shows. We became good friends and really honed our craft. Then in June 2007 I got a job as assistant buyer on Hotel Babylon without her. It was a step up from petty cash buying, and although I was nervous to do the job alone, I was ready and it was time to make that step. She had taught me everything she could and I was now more than capable of working with new people. I was ready to be one of the grown ups. I was ready to fly solo – to meet and learn from new set decorators and production designers. I was ready to hire, buy and run the budgets all on my own. Scary.

Working on Hotel Babylon was the best and the worst of times for me. I was so proud of the work that I did on that show. But a couple of things happened while I was working on that job that I am not so proud of. Firstly, I started a relationship with a lovely guy not because I thought I could love him, or that we would have fun together, but because he asked and I was lonely. Secondly, I stopped eating almost completely in favour of gin, cocaine and sex.

I was living in Brighton, in my own place now, and commuting to Aylesbury everyday (a 200-mile round trip and a 3-hour commute each way). I drove in and out of London at least once as well on most days, buying props. Most of the time I was able to end my day in South London, making the distance back shorter. Then, the set decorator I was working for got offered a big job on a film. Not a TV show, a film. He asked me if I was ready to take over from him: I was. The production designer was happy to promote me and I was delighted with the extra status and the extra cash. With greater responsibility come longer hours. All of a sudden it wasn't so easy to fit a 5-hour commute and sleep into my already full-on day.

Occasionally I stayed in digs, but they had to be paid for out of my own money whereas petrol costs were a claimable expense. One of the prop guys on our team offered me a room at his place, which was just 40 minutes away.

Yes please and thank you!

I spent one night in that spare room. While I was there I was introduced to one of the other guys who lived in the house. We all stayed up drinking cider and I flirted, because that's what I did with new people – turn up the charm and the sass. He cornered me on the stairs and tried to kiss me. He had a girlfriend and I told him that if he were really interested he'd ask me again when he was single. The next time I stayed over, he was and he did. He asked me out, and it was easier to stay at his than it was to commute back and forth, and he liked me, and I was flattered, and if I said yes I'd have a reason to be in their house – I'd belong.

It wasn't that I didn't fancy him, it's that I had turned off every cell of real. I'd learned a very complex set of behaviours that made it look like I had it all figured out, when in fact I was so incredibly numbed out.

To the untrained eye, everything was going well. I was over my heartbreak. I had the career I wanted. I had the money I wanted. I was living in Brighton renting my own place with a garden in the centre of town. I was beginning to think about getting a mortgage. I was saving. I had a yoga practice and a spiritual practice of sorts. I had a social life: people would come over to my place and party. I would leave them at it in my living room so that I could go to sleep and be up again to drive back to work. Most nights I got home about 9:30pm and would go to bed about midnight. I got up and was in the car again by 5:30am.

I'd just had another birthday and gotten reflective:

23RD JULY 2007

ANOTHER YEAR OLDER, AND THINGS HAVE SHIFTED SUCH A SMALL AMOUNT. SOMEHOW I ALWAYS THINK THAT THERE WILL BE SOME BIG MARKED CHANGE FROM ONE YEAR TO THE NEXT. BUT I'M JUST STILL PLODDING ALONG. SAME SHIT, DIFFERENT DAY.

I KNOW THINGS HAVE MOVED FORWARD, I KNOW I LOOK
SMALLER SLIGHTLY, I KNOW I WEIGH 10 AND A HALF STONE,
I KNOW I'VE FOUND YOGA AND IT MAKES ME FEEL GOOD
WHEN I PRACTICE AND WHEN I EAT RIGHT, BUT I CRY A
LOT AT THE MOMENT, AND I'M REALLY, REALLY LONELY.

I HAVE A CAREER I'VE WORKED HARD FOR, AND THAT I THINK
I AM GOOD AT, BUT I DON'T THINK IT MAKES ME HAPPY ANY
MORE. I THINK IT MAKES ME USEFUL AND INTELLIGENT
AND SUCCESSFUL BUT I DON'T FEEL LOVED OR SOULFUL OR
BEAUTIFUL OR AT PEACE. AND THAT'S WHAT I WANT TO
FEEL. I LOVE MY FLAT, IT'S MY HOME AND I'M PROUD OF IT
AND ALL THE STUFF I HAVE. BUT I WANT TO SPEND MORE
TIME HERE. I WANT TO WALK ON THE SEAFRONT EVERYDAY.
I WANT TO GO TO YOGA. I WANT TO SEE MY FRIENDS. I
WANT TO FIND A MAN WHO LOVES ME AND I WANT TO
HAVE A 'MARRIAGE' AND I WANT TO MAKE IT WORK.

AS I WRITE THIS I GUESS I'M SAYING THAT I DON'T
WANT TO BE THE GIRL WITH THE COOL JOB ANYMORE,
I WANNA MAKE A HOME AND I DON'T KNOW WHAT
ELSE I WANT AFTER THAT BUT I'LL FIGURE IT OUT.

So, when he asked me to be his girlfriend a HUGE box got ticked.

I said yes.

I didn't care about changing anything any more because I had a boyfriend.

It was great; I adjusted my goals so that it looked good! I had a boyfriend who made me feel like I belonged and gave me the space I needed. I had my own home. I had clothes that fitted. I was ticking boxes. If it took a little cocaine, some gin, a tonne of coffee and a carton of cigarettes to make it work, I didn't care. It was working. I was proud of the level of control I was exerting over my life. It was awesome. I was awesome.

At least it looked awesome.

The boyfriend and I hadn't slept together yet; we had been naked and we slept in the same bed each night, but it had only been six weeks and I was playing 'the game'; we were taking it slow. I was in control, I wanted to make sure he was over his ex and I wasn't just a rebound thing. I wanted to do it right this time. I needed to be in control of everything. It wasn't that I didn't love or didn't think I could love him, it was that I was far more concerned with what it *looked* like than what it *felt* like.

The August bank holiday approached. As a family we had a getaway trip to Cornwall planned and I felt sure that when I got back he and I would have had sufficient time to have missed each other and be clear about how we felt. We hadn't been on a proper holiday as a family like this in years and I was excited to spend time all together. My dad, his partner, all five of us kids, my bestie, my brother's girlfriend, and his friend. The whole jumbled lot of us – my proud blended family, hanging out and having fun. I picked up Zoë and drove down on the Friday night after work knowing I didn't need to be back on set until Tuesday morning. Amazing. I remember feeling good about everything – and on a very superficial level everything was amazing. It felt so freeing to drive with the windows down, the breeze blowing through my hair, knowing that we were road tripping to a place with no internet or mobile signal, three complete days without anyone needing anything from me in a hurry.

I wore a bikini on a beach!

(When I look at the photos now, I see a body I'd be proud of! I would love to look like that again, but I don't ever want to feel that disconnected from myself. I don't ever want to do the things I did to achieve it either.)

I still spent so much of the time complaining to Zoë that I was fat, and not enjoying myself for fear that I would be seen enjoying myself whilst being too fat. If people saw me enjoying myself and being fat they would think that I didn't know how disgusting I was. It was boiling hot, but I wouldn't take my top off until I was close to heatstroke. I didn't go in the lagoon we found on our walk even though I really wanted to. I felt a mixture of massive resentment and enormous shame. I didn't want my photo taken and I sulked when people tried. When we sat on the beach I compared myself to everyone else there rather than enjoying the short time we had to really relax together. Aside from my body hang ups, though, it was so good to hang out with my family, to make a fire on the beach, to catch fish, to be real, to laugh. In the pockets of time that I was really present I was so incredibly happy.

It was just a few days, but those few days were wonderful. I enjoyed winding down and slowing down but I couldn't have done any longer: any longer and I may have started to process how I was actually feeling – I needed to keep busy to keep myself from feeling. As soon as we were done it was straight back to London and back to work. I was stressed out of my skull, burning the candle at both ends, but life was GOOD! I was ticking the boxes. I felt proud of what I could say about myself. It wasn't that I felt good in myself, I didn't take the time to check – everything was about how I was perceived. I was pleased with the persona I was creating. I was squeezing in Bikram and green juice, who cares if often they were followed by cocaine and a roll up – they cancelled each other out, right?

Then one afternoon I tripped on nothing, fell and grazed my knee, elbow and chin. In the middle of central London, I flew ass over tit surrounded by suits on phones. I felt weird. It was a weirdly familiar sensation. A lady pulled herself away from her Blackberry momentarily to help me up. I nodded at her reassuringly.

'I'm fine.' I said, not feeling at all fine.

She went back to her conversation and was gone in an instant.

Alone in the throng of Oxford Street I suddenly realised what the feeling I recognised was:

'FUCK, I'm pregnant.'

Again.

Fuck.

How could this happen to me?

I thought I had learned my lesson.

In one fell swoop my charmed little charade fell flat on the floor. In that instant the shine on my practically perfect life fell away and exposed the sham of my relationships – with my boyfriend, with my body, with work, with 'God'.

I didn't finish the shopping and I didn't drive back to set. Head frazzled, with a voice that was screaming at me: 'IDIOT - how, how how!!? How did you let this happen?' I sped down the motorway back to Brighton. I called Zoë as I drove.

'I need you. I need a pregnancy test. I need you.'

By the time Zoë arrived at mine I was a mess of tears and snot.

As I sat on my bathroom floor I was reminded of when Alice had found out that she was pregnant not that long ago. When she told her boyfriend, now husband, he had been thrilled! *Watching as two lines appeared on the stick in front of me, the voices in my head SCREAMED:*

> *'Why doesn't anyone love me like that? What am I doing with my life?'*

My boyfriend already had a son. His son was three and he didn't have a great relationship with his ex. She, like me, had already had one abortion and when they found out that she was expecting again neither of them could not have the baby. I on the other hand couldn't make him *that* guy: the guy with two kids by two different women.

I couldn't be tied to him for the rest of my life.

I couldn't be a mum. I was a mess. I wanted to be a mum so badly!

I rang him.

'I'm pregnant.'

'Is it mine?' – are not the words any girl wants to hear. Ever.

We'd only slept together a handful of times and we'd been careful: it didn't feel possible. Working out the dates, I discovered I'd conceived before the weekend in Cornwall. We hadn't even had penetrative sex. I felt so hard done by. I couldn't believe life could be so cruel.

I shut him out. I didn't let him support me in the way he wanted to. Hotel Babylon ended and I had no reason to see him again. I was strong. I just needed to pull myself together, I'd be fine.

I made Zoë take me for an abortion, warning her I might try and leave, but that she had to make me stay – I wanted nothing more than to be a mum – BUT NOT LIKE THIS.

I acted fast and moved on. I had to.

I didn't move on at all. I shoved everything I felt deep away in a box inside myself.

The air around me every day was thick with it: 'Don't stop moving or you'll fall apart.'

Everything I wanted, the career, the man, the baby – it all felt fake. It was all just there, but none of it was *real*.

I hated that I got a bit fatter. I hated that I got my period again. I hated that I'd almost let my guard down and let someone see me. If I'd allowed myself to feel I would have felt angry, but I squashed it down.

I read a lot. On spirituality. On Buddhism. On happiness. On overcoming and coping with stress.

For six months I was really 'good': no cocaine, no alcohol, no cigarettes, and I ate food. Good, clean unprocessed vegetables – mostly raw with some beans and pulses. I tried to be more present. I tried to meditate. It was hard. I didn't like what was inside of me.

In March 2008 I went back to Thailand again, my third fast, this time for 12 days. I spent a few days in Bangkok first. I wasn't exactly the model spiritual student. I partied hard and didn't sleep for three days straight. In Bangkok I hung out with some friends who lived locally and The Smirnoff crew – beautiful people in their twenties sponsored by Smirnoff to travel the world and party. I arrived on Koh Samui ready to fast full of cocaine and Smirnoff. Consequently, detoxing was painful. Incredibly painful. I thought I was going to die. And then everything was OK again. I was purged.

Because I had done the lessons so many times they were no longer mandatory; instead I spent my time reading and journaling. I went on excursions. To the waterfall, to temples, to local villages. I had massages every day. I did my Reiki Level Two. After my 12 days were done I came home rested and restored. I came back inspired to deepen my yoga practice and prolong this feeling of connection I felt with myself.

Within days the local yoga teacher whose classes I loved (Nigel Gilderson) announced that he was about to open registration for his teacher-training course. It was a 200-hour basic hatha yoga teacher training accredited by the IYN. I signed up straight away. (I later completed and was accredited in December 2009.)

Life is much simpler when you are on retreat. Coming home and back to everyday life is where the real work happens. The effect of the 2007 writers' strike started to hit the UK mid 2008, and work slowed right down. It wasn't sudden, but jobs weren't coming in as easily as they had been. The down time gave me a lot of space to think and to feel. I started to think about what else I could do. I started thinking about my future. I wanted more for myself, and that niggly feeling was back.

And then some work would come in and I would stop thinking and feeling and enjoy having money again.

I flitted between eating everything and eating nothing. Drinking three bottles of wine a night and abstaining completely. I had two personas living inside me: a green-juice-drinking, sprouted-seed-bread-making, bendy, enlightened, good girl and a brooding, adventurous, resentful, sad, tired, lethargic, gloomy shadow self I was desperately trying to ignore. I cried myself to sleep most nights.

In July 2008 I moved back to London, this time to Herne Hill – Zoë was back from Italy and we moved in together again with the addition of another friend. The three of us balanced each other nicely. They were good times! We had great jobs and were all making good money. The house was massive. I named our wifi network 'The Palace'. It was the biggest, most grown-up place we'd lived in yet.

I felt like we had made it.

I was so incredibly happy when we got that house. The whole of the top floor was mine. I had my own bathroom, and a nook I used as an office. It felt like I was living alone, but with my best friends. I had beautiful things and art on the walls. We had a spare bedroom. We had two roof terraces. It was right by Brockwell Park and near to my yoga class. We were surrounded by our friends. We had friends over all the time and hosted the best parties. I'm not sure how or why, but I slipped slowly back into regular drinking, drugs and vacant sex.

I turned 28. To celebrate we went to a music festival and had a 'yes' weekend.[57] The weekend and the hedonistic adventures were a lot of fun, but the come down afterwards was horrid. We had sung and danced on the open top of a double decker bus, nearly tipping the thing over with our passionate vigour. We'd said yes to all sorts of powders and pills and completed missions requiring inebriated intimacy and drug-fuelled, spaced-out trust. I met a guy, the brother of a friend. For a fleeting moment I was hopeful: maybe he was *the one*, we had a connection, something real – it was magical – and then I found out that it was not the magical connection I'd imagined; he had a girlfriend, we'd just been high. I hated myself for being *that* girl.

---

57. A 'yes' weekend is one where you say yes to anything and everything you are offered. You can say no, but it is frowned upon. The idea is to say yes and deal with what and where you end up later. Uncertainty is FUN.

26TH AUGUST 2008

I HAVE NO IDEA WHO OR WHAT I AM. I DON'T LIKE MYSELF
VERY MUCH AND I'M NOT SURE THAT I HAVE LEARNED
ANYTHING IN THE LAST 10 YEARS. THAT'S HUGE. I CAN'T
BELIEVE THAT DAD AND MUM HAD ANYTHING FIGURED OUT,
THAT THEY KNEW WHAT THEY WERE DOING - I FEEL BAD FOR
THINKING THAT THEY SHOULD HAVE. HOW CAN I POSSIBLY
EVER BE A PARENT IF I CAN'T EVEN LOOK AFTER MYSELF?

WHY DON'T I LEARN?
WHY DO I DO THINGS TO MYSELF THAT I KNOW
ARE GOING TO HURT ME LONG TERM?
WHY DO I KEEP ATTRACTING UNAVAILABLE MEN?

I DON'T WANT TO ANY MORE, I WANT MY OWN. I WANT
SOMEONE JUST FOR ME. I WANT TO BE GOOD ENOUGH
TO KEEP. I WANT TO BE GOOD ENOUGH TO HOLD ON TO
AND NOT TO CHEAT ON, NOT TO PLAY, JUST TO HAVE
AND TO HOLD AND CHERISH AND SHARE WITH.

I WANT TO BE SEEN, I REALLY DO. I AM GOING TO BE SEEN AND
I AM GOING TO BE LOVED. IT'S BEEN A YEAR SINCE ****[58]

I NEVER SHOULD HAVE BEEN WITH HIM ANYWAY.

MAYBE THERE JUST ISN'T ANYONE OUT THERE IN THIS
WORLD FOR ME, MAYBE I SHOULD JUST ACCEPT THAT AND
MOVE ON. BUT IT SEEMS SO UNFAIR AND SO SAD THAT I
CAN'T FIND SOMEONE TO LOVE WHO LOVES ME TOO. MY
WHOLE LIFE SEEMS TO BE ABOUT FALLING IN LOVE, BEING
TOO FAT AND NOT BEING ABLE TO MANAGE MY MONEY. I
DON'T KNOW ANY BETTER, BUT I KNOW THAT IT'S TIME TO
CHANGE. WHEN I CONCENTRATE ON MY YOGA PRACTICE, WHEN
I FOCUS ON ENLIGHTENMENT THINGS DEFINITELY SEEM
BETTER. BUT NOT LIKE THEY'LL LAST. I CAN'T KEEP IT UP.

BALANCE.
THAT'S WHAT I REALLY WANT TO WORK ON.
MAYBE I REALLY DO NEED TO SEE A THERAPIST.
MAYBE I JUST NEED TO WORK MORE AND
CONTINUE BEING DISTRACTED???

---

58. The Hotel Babylon boyfriend.

I knuckled down and did the work involved in my yoga TTC: meditating, daily practice, pranayama, regular silent retreats. Slowly I got connected to my body and began feeling my feelings. I could no longer ignore all the residual anger and shame I was feeling. I decided I needed some help.

I started private Independent Cognitive Analytic Therapy (CAT) with Annalee Curran in December 2008. The idea was for us to have 13 sessions together, but my grandma died in between our second and third session and that brought up a lot of extra stuff for us to work with. In total I had 17 sessions, finishing in May 2009.

During our time together we looked predominantly at what I was referring to as my 'sinner versus saint complex'. I felt like inside of me there were an Angel and a Devil. I had these two conflicting personas: big Ebonie and small Ebonie. A 'not good enough' part and a 'really bloody special princess' part.

We unpicked what was going on in my head. We investigated why I had to be perfect. Identified how exhausting perfect and 'should' are and started to look at where all my resentment and anger were coming from. We named ALL the different parts of me that I could identify – there were many, including a gang of four (my negative committee) and two ringleaders who had been running the show; The Driver and The Judge.

We talked about all this for a few sessions; how my behaviour and my story of who I SHOULD be were running my life. Then in a casual comment I talked about my birth, explaining what little I knew.

Annalee made me stop. To her this was a big deal. We dug deeper. I went away and asked my mum and dad for more information. Dad showed me and gave me a copy of the picture of me in an incubator.[59]

I cried, for a whole session.

Underneath the tears and the breathlessness and the panic and the snot, there was a tiny baby who had never grown up. Annalee offered me the opportunity to go on a guided visualisation to symbolically rescue the

---

59. See chapter 1.

baby and bring her home. Back in reality, together we worked out what that baby didn't get that she needed and how I could give it to myself now.

As part of my therapy I wrote a letter to my mum. In it I said everything I was too afraid to tell her. Everything I felt bad for even thinking. I explained my upset, my hurt, my pain, how judged I felt, how small I was making myself to try and make her feel better, how abandoned I felt, how much blame I felt, how unloved and unappreciated I felt, how angry I was, everything I felt and why, and how sorry I was. The point of writing the letter wasn't ever to show anyone, or to hurt anyone, but to get it out. It was never about blame or attribution, it was an exercise in awareness and an opportunity for me to recognise, own and share my feelings. I was amazed how easily it flowed and how much relief I felt afterward.

Trusting the process, I then wrote a letter to myself, from the ideal or mythical mother I wished I'd had – an imaginary mother who told me everything I needed to hear.

<u>MY DEAR GIRL,</u>

YOU ARE PRECIOUS TO ME,

YOU ARE LOVED BY ME,

YOU ARE VALUED BY ME

AS MUCH AS YOU LEARN FROM ME, I LEARN FROM YOU. YOU LEARN FAST, YOU ADAPT TO ALL THE SITUATIONS YOU ARE PUT IN, I'M PROUD OF YOU!

YOU ARE INTELLIGENT, YOU ARE BEAUTIFUL, YOU CAN BE, DO, HAVE, LEARN, ACHIEVE, ANYTHING YOU WANT, AND I WILL BE HERE TO SUPPORT YOU, SHOULD YOU NEED OR WANT ME TO.

THROUGHOUT YOUR JOURNEY, THE TOUGH AND THE EASY, THE GOOD BITS AND THE BAD, I'M HERE. I'M NOT GOING ANYWHERE. WHEN YOU PUSH ME AWAY - I'LL BE HERE. WHEN YOU NEED SOMEONE TO LEAN ON, I'LL BE HERE. WHEN YOU NEED SOMEWHERE TO HIDE, SHELTER, TAKE STOCK - I'LL BE HERE, UNASSUMING, JUST HERE.

WHEN YOU NEED A FRIEND, I'M HERE. WHEN YOU NEED A PARENT - I'M HERE. WHEN YOU NEED A DISCIPLINARIAN - I'M HERE. WHEN YOU NEED A CUDDLE - I'M HERE. WHEN YOU NEED SOMEONE TO RANT AT, OR CELEBRATE WITH - I'M HERE (AND I HOPE YOU'RE GETTING THE IDEA!)
I WOULDN'T HAVE YOU ANY OTHER WAY.
YOU'RE PERFECT JUST AS YOU ARE,

LOVE ALWAYS,
YOUR MOTHER

It felt good to see and hear the words, no matter that I'd written them myself. It was a powerful process. At the end of our time together we ritualised saying goodbye by writing each other letters: summarising the processes we'd been through, highlighting my learning and expressing wishes for the future.

Alongside therapy, wanting to find love and a relationship again, I signed up to ALL the dating sites and I went on about three dates a week for a little over three months. I'd been on them before, and I'd had a run at trying to find 'love' that way before, but this time I treated it differently. I actually really wanted and thought I was ready for a boyfriend and not just a hook up. I wanted to be a keeper and not a sports fish.[60]

I made a vow of celibacy.

After a while in order to maintain it (and also because Hillary had been telling me to for years), I quit drinking.

For the rest of that year I really did take care of myself. Things were different, I felt good about where I was living and I was starting to grow as a person. I hung out with Alice and her son. I took some time out between jobs and I went to yoga and saw friends. I enjoyed being me. I was committed to my therapy; working hard at all the assignments Annalee presented me with. I sat on my meditation cushion every morning and I wrote and reflected.

---

60. *Act Like a Lady, Think Like a Man* is a book by Steve Harvey which describes for women Harvey's concept of what men really think about love, relationships, intimacy and commitment. Women are either 'keepers' or 'Sports Fish' (something you throw back in after you're done having fun.

29TH SEPTEMBER 2008

EVERYONE IS JUST DOING THEIR BEST, FACED WITH THEIR
OWN REALITY, IN THEIR 'NOW' - THEY DO WHAT THEY CAN,
AND IT'S NOT ALWAYS WHAT YOU WOULD HAVE DONE.

LIFE MAY ONLY BE SHORT, BUT IT IS ALSO LONG AND THINGS
HAPPEN REALLY SLOWLY - SO SLOWLY SOMETIMES THAT YOU
CAN'T SEE IT UNTIL OR UNLESS YOU TAKE SOME DISTANCE.
BUT SOMETHING IS ALWAYS HAPPENING. WITH THE RIGHT
INTENTION THINGS WILL CONTINUALLY MOVE FORWARD.

SOME LESSONS ARE REALLY HARD TO LEARN. THERE
IS A DIFFERENCE BETWEEN UNDERSTANDING
SOMETHING, LEARNING IT AND KNOWING IT.

I AM BEAUTIFUL, AND VULNERABLE AND SAD AND
FRAGILE AND SO SO STRONG AT THE SAME TIME!

I AM FUN, AND FULL OF LOVE, WHICH I SHOW EVEN IF
I DON'T SAY IT OR MAKE A BIG DEAL ABOUT IT.

I'VE GOT GOOD FRIENDS. NOT MANY ANY MORE MAYBE,
BUT GOOD, STRONG, LOYAL, LOVING FRIENDS.

But by December I hadn't worked for four months. I was ever so slightly worried but felt sure that financially it was a situation that working on just one commercial would fix.

I read *The Secret* and I became a student of everything Abraham Hicks. I decided to go away for Christmas to get some sunshine and to take the time out while I had no work. Worried that I was becoming co-dependant on Thailand and fasting with Hillary, I looked for somewhere else to go. There was so much more of the world I wanted to see: I picked a yoga holiday with Ali Gilling in Dahab, Egypt. But before I had even gotten on the plane to Sharm el-Sheikh, I knew I *needed* to go back to Koh Samui too. I flew to Egypt for a week over Christmas, flying back to England to spend New Year's Eve in Brighton, and then flew back out to Koh Samui on New Year's Day 2009.

I needed that double dose, my 29th year was being relentless. It was messy for me in so many ways. It was an incredible up-levelling year. At the time it felt relentless, cruel and unforgiving. In hindsight I learned so much. In March 2009 my grandma died. I went to see her just a few days before and she talked to me for hours, sharing many stories I had always wanted to hear but been too afraid to ask for. It was an important day for me. Listening to her shifted many things and enabled me to feel differently about my relationship with my mum. She shared many of her joys and regrets. She talked and talked and I listened, not knowing it would be the last time I saw her. I am hugely grateful that I got the opportunity to spend that time with her.

In May I started the yoga TTC. Everyone involved in that incredibly special and unique IYN accredited Hatha Yoga Teacher Training[61] rocked my world. Nigel's gentle and calm energy was responsible for a huge surge of my ability to really feel adequacy and proficiency. One of the many things I love about yoga is that you get to see your internal progress externally. The patience and practice you put in shows up in physical form for you to see and feel. One of the new goals or desires I set for myself was 'patience' and yoga continues to teach me patience whenever I forget.

Gill Hurst managed to make the learning of anatomy experiential rather than just words and pictures in books. Everything I learnt in those 19 months helped me to go from just 'finding myself', to being able to begin accepting myself. The tools I learned enabled me to get through 2009. I was particularly inspired by yogic philosophy as taught by Christopher Gladwell. His interpretation of The Upanishads and yogic history had me mesmerised. For me, doing the course wasn't about being able to teach yoga afterwards, it was about deepening my practice and my connection to my Self. Immersing myself in yoga and learning all that I did rewarded me with the sense of belonging I had always been searching for.

The physical practice got me into my body and the philosophy captured my intellect and imagination:

---

61. *http://www.awayoga.com/teacher_training.html*

YOGIC PHILOSOPHY IS SOMETHING THAT FOR THE FIRST TIME IN MY LIFE, WITH THE EXCEPTION OF ABRAHAM HICKS'S TEACHINGS, MAKES PERFECT SENSE TO ME AND I FEEL LIKE I HAVE UNCOVERED SOMETHING IN ME THAT HAS BEEN OBSCURED, IT DOESN'T FEEL NEW, JUST TEMPORARILY FORGOTTEN. I FEEL WARMTH IN MY HEART, I THINK THIS IS BELONGING.

- EXTRACT FROM MY YOGA JOURNAL

Be your own Guru – to me this is what yoga allows us to do. No matter which style or flavour calls you, try a variety and step into being your own teacher, be open minded and open hearted and allow yourself to trust and listen to your body's wisdom. So much of who I am now, of how I think, understand and live, is down to that course. Being given the opportunity to explore so many different styles and schools of yoga was eye opening. I explored sivananda, kundalini, Scarevelli, shadow, pregnancy, children's and many other styles and specialisms of yoga. Becoming aware that there was more to yoga than asana was life changing for me. Discovering the four main paths of Yoga – Karma Yoga, Bhakti Yoga, Jnana Yoga and Raja Yoga – was so interesting and inspiring. The fact that each is suited to a different temperament or approach to life, that all the paths lead ultimately to the same destination, and that the lessons of each need to be integrated if true wisdom is to be attained, helped me to see that no one size fits all: each of us journey alone in common pursuit of fulfilment – a sense of connection to self and something larger.

I became more and more disillusioned with the TV industry, the hours and the glorification of busy – the relentless expectation to be constantly on the go and prove that everything possible and more has been done, with no regard for mental or physical wellbeing. And even though I was not in a relationship and didn't yet have children, it became clear to me that I wanted to find a way to make a living that I could go on to fit around a family. Again I started to rethink everything that I wanted to BE, DO and HAVE in my life.

OVER, ROUND, OR THROUGH

A PEARL IS A BEAUTIFUL THING THAT IS PRODUCED BY AN
INJURED LIFE. IT IS THE TEAR [THAT RESULTS] FROM THE
INJURY OF THE OYSTER. THE TREASURE OF OUR BEING
IN THIS WORLD IS ALSO PRODUCED BY AN INJURED LIFE.
IF WE HAD NOT BEEN WOUNDED, IF WE HAD NOT BEEN
INJURED, THEN WE WILL NOT PRODUCE THE PEARL.
— STEPHAN HOELLER

In order to tidy a house or a mind you have to get everything out and look at it. Therapy and my yoga studies did that for me, I was beginning to figure out what I didn't want – it was time to work out what I did want.

I made the decision to start My Girl Friday and I incorporated the company on 23rd July 2009 – my 29th birthday.

No one I knew had done anything like it. I sounded out all the people I admired and trusted. The guy in my bed told me that it would never work. My colleagues in TV land and my close friends wished me well, but it was my perception that they were doubtful. For some reason I was convinced that it would work and more importantly I was willing to do whatever it took to make it work. I knew from my stints PA-ing for high net worth individuals and from all my friends and colleagues in the TV, fashion, photography and creative industries that there were lots of people who didn't have time to renew their car tax or post a letter. There were time-poor, cash-rich people who needed someone they trusted to be their professional 'wife' and that is what My Girl Friday was going to be. I felt sure that an office wasn't important. I felt sure that a good network of the right clients and all my buyer and runner friends who were between jobs would make incredible Girl Fridays. I could see the brand identity in my head.

Fresh from therapy I had the confidence to trust myself and I felt sure that My Girl Friday was a great place to put 'The Driver' persona to work. It would be a healthy way to put 'breathlessly striving' to good use as long as I was also 'kindly responsible' and looked after myself with loving encouragement. My 'Girl Friday' alter ego was the perfect wife, mistress, PA and best friend. She was all things to all people. She was a sort of Mary Poppins. She was practically perfect in every way with a bit of sass thrown in. The idea was to develop the skills I had already and solve a problem for people whilst getting to feel useful and getting paid.

I came up with a tag line. I developed the brand. I made My Girl Friday Ltd more than just a brand; it was something people could buy into and fall in love with.

I identified the problems the people in my target market were facing – *not enough time to fart and no one to trust with their shit* – and I came up with the sales copy (no poop jokes, it was very professional). My Girl Friday was the solution to the blurred lines between work and life for time-poor, cash-rich creative businesses and individuals.

The vision of what I wanted came to me in a dream; I woke up with an idea whizzing around my head and got up and wrote the whole thing out on reams of Zoë's pattern-cutting paper at 3am. I asked a friend to design the logo and invoice header, letterhead, and website. She did an absolutely amazing job. I still love that branding.

My Girl Friday wasn't just a business, though: she was an extension of me, a shiny, perfect, no-shadows-just-gold version of me. I believed this would be a way that I could play that role, the one I had perfected over years, and then go home and be the real me. At that time, it seemed like the perfect solution.

In August 2009 I discovered Twitter. I fell in love with the concept. I started talking to strangers on the internet in 140 characters or less. I had no idea what I was doing, but I spent hours trawling cyber space looking for more information about social media. I followed anyone and everyone; I didn't have a strategy, just curiosity. I spent my evenings online looking for anything I could find out about virtual assistants, my competitors, the trends, what problems freelancers, micro-business owners, and time-poor people were facing. I joined forums, I asked people what their concerns were. I asked them who they felt could fix this problem for them. I asked a lot of questions and I hung out online all night long, joining in and chatting with anyone I could find on My Space, on Bebo, on ASmallWorld, and over the first year or so I joined every single platform without discernment. I wasted HOURS! And I also learned a lot.

I made a business plan. I say *I made a business plan,* in reality I asked a couple of my friends who had businesses that I felt were similarly structured to My Girl Friday to send me theirs and reworked a hashed-together version of what they had said to make mine. When I wrote this book I looked at my archives and found that by page 10 of 21 I had gotten bored and the words were no longer mine at all. The documents have been abandoned, still bearing the original authors' details.

(With The Entrepreneur Enabler, I didn't even attempt a comprehensive business plan. I did a one pager outlining my goals, the assumptions that must prove true, the milestones I wanted to hit and the feelings I wanted to feel.[62]). When I started out there weren't all the systems and courses and training out there that there are now. There were people doing amazing things and creating systems and formulas that we now know to be HUGE and work cross industry for all sorts of businesses, but I didn't know about them or have access to peers who did, yet. We were not yet fully inducted into the information age. My ideas were spot on and I could have been one of the forerunners; I could have been a trailblazer, but I lacked self-belief, confidence and the mindset needed to forge forward. I didn't believe I had what it took to be successful. I didn't really believe that what I envisioned was possible for *me.* I had only just learned that I could be *kindly responsible* or *lovingly encouraging* to myself and I still believed that sharing my vulnerabilities or weaknesses was a sign of failure.

I didn't define what success looked or felt like for me. I did what I thought a grown-up would do, which is crazy really because I had no desire to be that sort of grown-up. For someone who was so full of ideas and intuition I ignored everything my heart and soul and gut were telling me and I followed rules that I didn't even believe in or respect. It's no wonder to me now that at the end of the day, in 2012, it didn't all line up. It didn't feel good on the inside. I was trying to build a saleable asset business when I was running a heart-based, personal brand. I was far too attached to the asset I was building ever to sell.

The insides and the outsides didn't match.

---

62. Head to the Misfit to Maven bonus page for a one-pager template *www.misfit2maven.com/bonuses*

But I had a paper trail and a document for everything:

- The Business Proposal – Executive Summary
- Objectives / Key Personnel
- SWOT Analysis
- Legal Considerations
- Insurance
- Time Plan & Putting Plan into Practice
- Business Premises and Equipment
- Terms of Trade
- Suppliers
- MARKETING PLAN
  - The Target Market
  - The Customers
  - The Competition
  - Competitive Strategy
  - Advertising Plan
- Sales Plan
- Sources of Finance
- Pricing Policy
- Estimated Start-up Costs and Working Capital
- Survival Budget
- Cash Flow Projections
- Profit and Loss
- Break Even
- Letterhead and Business Card
- Customer Profile
- Competitor Profile

These might be useful to you and they might not. You may want to think about all of them, but you may not want to write an actual branded document. Whatever you know to be true for you is right. Trust yourself.

I got myself a business coach because that's what you did. She was from a government-funded organisation. She wasn't the right business coach for me. She was the first person I met with and she didn't cost me anything, but she didn't get me at all. I didn't trust her and I didn't like her *advice*. I felt sure that I could make My Girl Friday work – it would take a little time, it would require me to use that patience I had been developing; I believed whole heartedly that if I just worked hard enough, if I put the hours in, and believed, I would yield results.

She told me to make flyers and post them through doors. She told me to work my way through the phone book and make cold calls. She didn't get my target market, she didn't get that we were niche – but neither did I yet. I didn't have the knowledge or the experience or the jargon. I just knew that what she was suggesting I do was never going to work. My idea was ahead of its time and old-school sales methods didn't feel right to me. So I ignored her and made it up as I went along. But I didn't have a strategy either, I scatter-gunned my marketing; I gave money to whoever asked for it without really considering who my target market were or where they hung out. A guy from Yelp called and flirted with me. I paid for advertising because I was flattered and when I tried to get my money back after realising it wasn't the best use of my cash it was too late and they wouldn't reverse the contract I had signed. I learned my lesson and became more discerning, but I was stuck.

I was struggling to know what to do next. I felt alone, but I didn't want to tell anyone I didn't know what I was doing and so I began to rack up a little debt on my Barclaycard. I ignored all the bits of business creation that I didn't like or understand (numbers, legalities, sales funnels) and I got really into the bits that I loved (branding, marketing, designing, and delivery). Just as I was about to give up on My Girl Friday and go and get a job, a woman on Twitter told me not to. She was the first of the hundreds and hundreds of people that I have now chatted to online and then picked up the phone and became friends with in real life. She became an ally, someone outside of my circle who believed in what I was trying to do. She was the first person to be part of the My Girl Friday team. She freelanced for the company and she helped me to further shape the business. She became My Girl Friday South West (MGFSW).

With renewed inspiration and drive from her belief, we grew. I drew up contracts, for my freelancers, sub-contractors and clients. More business came in. I followed my nose and I started to listen to my intuition a little more, but I didn't ask for help. I stubbornly believed I would be alright as long as I did it all myself.

I started to make a plan for the future. I began making vision boards and working out how I could grow this little venture into a world-changing big venture. My thoughts led me to think about whether I would rather be a little fish in a big pond or a big fish in a little pond. I decided that as a little fish in a big pond there was more room to breathe and swim and fewer people would notice me. I decided that once again – just like in all my relationships – I wanted to be good enough to warrant reward and praise but not big or successful enough to hurt anyone's feelings, rock the boat, or be noticed.

How we do anything is how we do everything.

How do *you* approach something new?

My default setting is to run at a new idea with passion and drive, impulse and attitude, get shit done and deal with the consequences later. My default setting is to start something and then get bored or disillusioned until someone else wants me to continue and then do it for them and not me. Naivety and delusion, sometimes my greatest strengths, are at times also my biggest weaknesses. Knowing this about myself now enables me to identify my challenges; asking for help or collaboration when I myself am not the best solution.

I hadn't thought much past getting enough work to survive without having to get a 'proper' job. I was already in some debt. I needed money, but I also believed that there were some business assets that were vital. I thought that you needed an expensive website and stationery, and I believed that any day now a TV job would come in. I didn't see the recession as a long-term thing. I figured a big cash job was just around the corner and it would provide me with enough to live and build the company.

No work came. I spent more money. It was an investment in my future.

I didn't go and ask for income support or job seekers allowance because I believed that the system wasn't there for people like me. It's not made for self-employed people, and a day of being told 'Computer says no' by an employee who didn't get me at all just wasn't worth my time. Just one day on a commercial would pay me what I'd get from them in a month, and I believed that any day now things would turn around.

They didn't.

I didn't claim housing benefit for six months because I was too proud. I still believe in being self sufficient and I didn't want to be on state handouts, but in hindsight I could have scoped it out before things got as bad as they did. I was stubborn. I spent my 'rainy day' savings. More time passed. My friends still had money, and I hadn't shared with them what was going on. With all the free time I had I went to parties and I kept up the charade of being 'successful' – in my mind I was not just the girl with the cool career any more, now I was the girl who was enlightened, and spiritual, and a yogi, *and* I was starting some other new and exciting thing. I continued to be generous with my cash and resources. I *needed* people to like me, I didn't have a sense of worth or belonging without it coming from external sources.

No work came.

I paid my rent on my credit card. I took cash out on my credit card. I still kept thinking that I'd get a call about a job and then in a few weeks I could pay the whole thing off. Then I got a tax bill. A £16,000 tax bill. I hadn't realised that they would want money on account and that the year before had been such a 'good' year. The jump from petty cash buyer to set decorator meant that a lot more money had come in. I'd spent all that money, though. I buried my head in the sand.

A few clients trickled into My Girl Friday. I kept up the façade of a high net worth (HNW) business. I spent everything that came in. I was 'reinvesting' it. The clients I had coming in were often challenging. I was proud to attract and work for incredibly high-maintenance clients who were renowned for being complicated. Rather than seeing that other people would perhaps set boundaries and say no, I took pride in being able to cope. I got my need for significance met by being needed. I wanted to be liked so badly that I said YES to everything that was asked of me, made myself indispensible, and deep down resented it.

The way we do anything is the way we do everything.

The behavioural patterns of my relationships were now showing up in my business life.

Setting up MGF and running with the idea in the way that I did was a wonderfully brave and stupid thing to do. Circumstance and the universe have a funny way of teaching you what you need to learn. I needed to learn humility. I needed to learn to ask for help. I needed to learn to swallow my pride. I needed to get over myself. I needed to learn to set boundaries. I needed to learn to say NO. I needed to learn to trust.

But before all that I needed money.

I prayed for a miracle.

I went on Twitter. I got in touch with a journalist who was touting for stories, she asked me what I had and I sent her some ideas. She wanted the kind of stories that the *Sun* would pay for. I needed cash, but I wasn't willing to sell out a celebrity – it was more than my career was worth.

Sex sells, and I'd had a lot of it, so I pitched: 'I woke not knowing the bloke I'd slept with. I vowed to spend a year celibate.'

I truly believed that it couldn't hurt anyone, it would be a small story in tiny column in a newspaper that would be here one day, gone the next. A small whisper told me that all publicity is good publicity. I figured I could get a mention for My Girl Friday. I figured 'today's paper is tomorrow's chip wrappings', right?

No. Not anymore. We have the Internet.

They sent a photographer and a make up artist round to 'The Palace'. I got them to straighten my hair and cover me in make-up. I tried to dress as little like myself as possible. *Maybe no one will recognise me.*

Stress does weird things to your brain.

The end of 2009 and the start of 2010 are a blur to me. I do know this though, the story[63] was published in September and it was a double-page spread. My phone rang off the hook. Facebook notifications pinged at me like they never had before. I was pleased, no publicity is bad publicity, right? I had paid my rent AND got a mention in the *Sun*. Maybe it would lead to some new clients and open up opportunities?

Then I read the story. The words I'd used had been tweaked to give them a salacious edge. I hadn't thought about how the piece would affect anyone else – at the time I wasn't thinking about the future. Just like a desperate junkie, I was in survival mode, just looking for the next fix. It did its immediate job; the piece paid for my rent that month. But then I felt ashamed.

The truth is that our society is warped. If the story I sold had been told by a man it would have had an entirely different reaction. In fact I'm not sure it would have even have been newsworthy. I got invitations to speak on high-profile radio shows and more journalists approached me. They wanted to take the theme of the piece and run debate pieces with me as a contributor. I turned them all down because I felt ashamed by how people had reacted.

And, it turns out that 'tomorrow's chip wrappers' are no longer a thing. The Internet keeps things alive for years.[64]

The piece in the *Sun* hurt the feelings of people I care about. In writing this book I spent hours deliberating about whether and what I learned from that article. I have questioned over and over again how personal I need to get, what the implications will be for my family, friends and clients, and

---

63. *http://www.thesun.co.uk/sol/homepage/woman/2617676/I-vowed-to-spend-a-year-celibate.html*

64. The 'right to be forgotten' ruling in the EU goes some way to amending information for some people in some situations, but having stories immortalized whether they are accurate or not is an ongoing privacy and public information issue for many people.

whether I still feel or might end up feeling ashamed. Eventually, I decided that my desire for a more intimate, vulnerable and respectful world requires me to be intimate, truthful and vulnerable with you and that I do not feel ashamed of my story – my hope is that it will inspire.

Photo credit: Jon Bond

The difference between that story and this is in the respect. I have a deeper respect for myself, for the power of sharing stories, for the people in my world, for you.

I am sure that it comes across.

I trust.

Now that I trust myself I am acting from a place that is authentic and real. I believe that people hear us on the level from which we connect with them. When we connect with our hearts and trust what they have to tell us, and then speak and act from our truth, it has a profound effect, a rippling butterfly effect.

The truth is that life is one huge oxymoron. The truth is that it is indeed through your vulnerability that you find your strength.

I am not telling you to go out and make yourself vulnerable. Be mindful. Be discerning.

For me personally, telling that story was cathartic and I enjoyed sharing what had been an important journey for me. I got to pay my rent and at the time of telling it I was not ashamed of what I'd done. I was only ashamed when I needed other people to like me and felt judged.

The truth is that people will judge and they will make comment. Now, first and foremost, I need my own respect. I need for me to like the decisions that I make.

At the time, I wasn't thinking about whether or not I liked my decision and I wasn't thinking long term. I was only concerned with where the next rent cheque would come from. The recession was a real thing. People were losing their jobs and houses. It wasn't just me being 'not good enough.' It was serious and I am proud of my ability to be resourceful.

Then my housemate got made redundant.

He decided to leave London and go home to his parents. Zoë decided she would do the same. I couldn't afford the rent at 'The Palace' alone, or face the idea of finding new people to live with. In fact the reality of the situation was that I couldn't afford to move or find a deposit. I couldn't afford to pay the payments on my credit card. I couldn't afford anything.

They had started putting huge late fees on my overdraft, and on my credit cards. The interest racked up on my debt with the Inland Revenue. Suddenly I owed a lot more than I had borrowed. Every day I received calls demanding money, and not just once – sometimes I got three calls in a day. No one tells you how quickly things can escalate. It's easy to look at people on the street and make judgments. It's easy to look at the sex workers or the drug takers and make judgments. It's easy to think that it will never happen to you. I certainly thought that I was way too educated and self aware to ever end up in over my head.

Before I knew it I was in *way* over my head. I owed in excess of £25k.

DARKEST DAYS

OUR LIVES CHANGE EXTERNALLY AS WE CHANGE INTERNALLY.
— CAROLINE MYSS

In the midst of all good stories the hero confronts death or faces his or her greatest fear. Out of the moment of death comes a new life. We all have trials. Yours will be just as painful to you as mine were to me. The homeless guy you pass on the street. The woman alone and in tears on the train. The friend who hasn't posted an update in a while. They all have a story. Each one is struggling with something. Their struggle may be dramatic, or it may not. Each person's struggle is a very real struggle to them. By the time any external sign is manifest it will have been bubbling away internally for some time.

In December 2009 I finally told someone what was going on. I wasn't in a good way.

I cried and snotted for over an hour.

The relief I felt once I shared my secret was immense.

**I AM SO SCARED AND WEAK, AND FRAGILE RIGHT NOW,
IT'S DIFFICULT TO GET THE MOTIVATION TO GET UP,
KEEP MOVING, SEE THE LIGHT AT THE END OF THE TUNNEL,
LEARN FROM THE JOURNEY ETC..
I FEEL LIKE I'M STILL IN DENIAL MOSTLY...**

I'M NOT SURE I AM STRONG ENOUGH,
AND KNOWING THAT EVERYONE ELSE THINKS
I AM ISN'T MUCH COMFORT REALLY…
I THOUGHT I KNEW FEELING ALONE,
NOW I GET THAT THERE IS ALWAYS FURTHER
INTO SCARED, LONELY, AND LOST TO GO…
I'M SURE THERE WILL BE A TIME WHEN I AM
GRATEFUL FOR THIS EXPERIENCE THOUGH.

The fact that someone else might be able to help hadn't even occurred to me. After keeping the truth of the situation to myself for a further couple of months, I plucked up the courage to share again and I got in touch with a friend who I found out had been in a similar situation. I explained the mess I was in and asked who had helped him. I can't really fully explain how awful I felt, it was a different kind of awful than I'd felt before. I was way out of my depth. I couldn't blag this. I'd lost control.

When my grandmother died she left me a share in her house. If it was sold I would be in a position to pay off my debts, but I was terrified that my family would think I was a failure and a waste of space. I was scared that they wouldn't sell the house in order to give me the money I needed. It was hard for me to explain the facts without bawling my eyes out. I was so caught up in it emotionally. Armed with tissues, a glass of water and deep breaths; it was time to find out where I stood legally and wade through this mess. I got in touch with the financial advisor my friend had used. He told me to come and see him in Newark and bring everything with me. I borrowed £56 and got on a train.

Colin was the most gangster financial advisor I'd ever met. He picked me up from the station in a blacked-out Mercedes. He chain-smoked cigarettes and had the voice to accompany them. He was terrifying on the phone and a sweetie in person. His bark was ferocious; his bite wasn't aimed at me. He saw me for free that first visit. He phoned all my creditors and I gave my permission for him to speak on my behalf. I made him my representative and he told them to stop phoning me every three hours. He was amazing. He explained who I *had* to give money to and who could wait. He explained how the whole system worked. He set me up with a debt management company. I paid them a set fee each month and they distributed it for me. I left feeling able to breathe for the first time in months.

It didn't stop the inevitable, though. A prop truck came and took all my stuff away; I couldn't afford storage and I had left it too late to make a better plan. I'm glad the possessions I had garnered over the years went on to be used on sketch shows and dramas. I got rid of almost everything. A few key pieces of furniture that meant something important to me went to friends. My art and books went into another friend's loft. My dad and step mum had a small storage unit and some things went in there. I kept a suitcase full of clothes, my MacBook and my car. I drove to my friend Ellie's place.

Ellie was amazing.

We set up a mattress on the floor in the living room. She and her boyfriend made me feel welcome in their home. She fed me and kept me in wine and cigarettes (I was back on the wine and cigarettes). I stayed with them for a month or more and I managed to continue with the business. I worked from her place in the daytime while they were out, or from coffee shops and co-working spaces. Slowly I continued to build my burgeoning business, making just enough money to pay my way.

Then one evening while Ellie was away her boyfriend behaved in a way that made me feel uncomfortable. The next day I made an excuse and arrangements to stay with some other friends. (She knows about this now, but at the time I was too afraid to tell the truth.)

Back in Brighton, another kind couple opened up their home to me. A friend I had known since she was five or six years old – when I had been in my teens. I was hugely grateful and yet my pride hated that someone I felt I should be taking care of was instead rescuing me. She and her fiancée were living in a one-bed flat; there wasn't much space but they had a tiny spare room with a boiler in it. The boiler took up most of the space but we found a way to squidge a single bed in underneath it.

I was massively in debt and I knew nothing about running a business. Which meant I had nothing to lose and gave it everything I had.

Bootstrapping a business when you are desperate and resourceful can be a wonderful thing. It isn't how I'd choose to do it, and it isn't something I would recommend, but having a really strong 'why' creates drive, and wanting to stand on my own two feet and be independent once again made me driven.

I worked all night most of the time, learning how to build a website, learning about technology and new systems that meant it was possible to be location independent. It was my dream to earn money in dollars or pounds and be able to live like a king in some far-flung land. I read *The Four Hour Work Week*. I liked some of what Tim Ferris was saying and I implemented the things that made sense to me for my business and my life. I did wonder though why anyone would only want to work 4 hours a week: what would you do with the rest of your time? I think this just goes to show how much of my identity was caught up in work.

Slowly I was given more fantastic opportunities to learn from many wildly inspirational entrepreneurs, business owners and private clients. Something strange happened. As I surrendered to the freedom of the situation I was in rather than seeing myself as a victim of circumstance, small miracles found their way to me. Opportunities came my way and I took them with open arms and a wealth of gratitude!

It may have felt like I was forced to learn to ask for help (and please understand how much I hated it) but swallowing my pride, being vulnerable, allowed me to surrender and receive, and that opened up a whole new world.

Even though it felt like a shitty set of circumstances were being forced upon me, I did have a choice – sink or swim. I learned to make trades. I needed to survive and I needed the business to grow, which meant that I needed to be careful about what went into which bank account. (Anything going into my main accounts was just swallowed up by a huge overdraft or taken instantly by debt collectors.) So I got really creative and I said yes and figured it out as I went, even if it meant staying up all night. It feels strange now to think that I used to do it all alone. Everything. I genuinely didn't really even consider letting others in; it was too uncertain.

> THE QUALITY OF YOUR LIFE IS THE QUALITY OF
> YOUR RELATIONSHIP TO UNCERTAINTY.
> – TONY ROBBINS

> THE QUALITY OF YOUR LIFE IS DIRECTLY RELATED
> TO YOUR RELATIONSHIP WITH UNCERTAINTY.
> – MASTIN KIPP

If there's just one message you hold onto from this book, let it be this: *It is in the places that you feel your vulnerability that you will find your strength.*

Don't do it all alone.

Don't be too proud.

Something magic happens when we co-create.

Today, I actively invite people to be part of my team[65] – I crowdfunded this book for that very reason: collaboration makes my heart sing. In 2010 it felt like weakness. I felt that I should be able to stand on my own two feet and do it all alone.

The phone calls, the letters kept coming. Every day demands and threats of bailiffs continued to be spewed at me. They threatened to cut my phone off. I was scared and I hung on tight. I felt sure that as long as I had my car, my laptop, my phone and the Internet I would keep my business growing and I would sort this mess out. I used my all the strength I could muster. Worried that they'd make me bankrupt and that it would somehow affect me forever, I puffed up my chest and I dug in my heels. Worried that they'd somehow incarcerate me or hurt my family, I kept meditating on a vision of myself safe and surrounded by the people that I loved. Inside I was terrified, but outside I was calm. Each night I dreamt colourful, lucid, big dreams. My dreams were a mixture of visioning my own space – a place I could call home, a place filled with light, where I could shut the door and get some privacy again – and terrifying and incredibly real-feeling

---

65. Connect or contact me on social – I reply to every message about collaboration myself.

anxiety dreams that I'd wake from drenched in a cold sweat. Publicly, I held it together as best I could whilst in secret I wept; quick trips to the bathroom for a pee and a cry.

Those six months when I lived on the kindness of friends and strangers felt LONG and painful and also somehow like a joyful blessing all at the same time. My default when things are tough is to curl up in a ball and hide away. Living in someone else's space, having no privacy and having to share how I felt with people who cared was hard. Having people care made me *feel*. I didn't know how to do this; how to *be* with people supporting and taking care of me. I still feel incredibly lucky to have the friends and people around me that I did. Not everyone does.

It isn't actually about how bad things get, it's not what happened to you or the circumstance that's important, but the attitude with which you frame it and where you go from here.

In your life right now, *is life happening to you or for you?*

Homelessness didn't happen to me, *it happened for me.*

This may sound like a very strange thing to say.

Thousands of pounds worth of debt didn't happen to me, *it happened for me.*

Pregnancy and heartbreak didn't happen to me, *they happened for me.*

The humility that I learned was important. Receiving, asking, allowing others the experience of giving instead of hogging it all for myself, were massive lessons. Before, I thought I was being generous with all the giving that I did, but how stingy is it not to fully receive when someone gives you something? I never used to receive what was given to me. Now I make eye contact and say thank you, and mean it. Thank you.

I began to see that I am accountable for my life. At some point each of us gets the opportunity to understand that we are accountable for our own lives and that it is no one else's fault that we aren't where we want to be.

Shit happens, and when it does all sorts of amazingness does too.

You get to see who your friends are (by which I mean who they are, what they care about, and how they deal with uncomfortable situations). You get to work out what is important. You get to see who YOU really are, what you value, and where the holes in your learning and development are.

Or not. To be fair to myself here (and anyone else that has been through a struggle), I could have stayed the same. I could have fallen through the cracks. I was lucky to be surrounded by awesome people. My friends and family are the best, I feel privileged to be surrounded by such wonderful people – AND – I made the decision to grow bigger than my problems!

When things got really bad for me someone could have found a way to bail me out. They didn't, out of love for me. What would I have learned from being rescued? Rescuing doesn't help anyone. No one learns or grows. Teaching or showing someone how to rescue themselves is way more constructive.

So if you are in the middle of a struggle and you are reading this book – *are you waiting to be rescued?*

Rescue yourself – you can do this! The first step in deciding you are going to. There is no try, you are or you are not. When you decide what book to read or what sandwich you're going to make you don't try, you decide. Decide to become who you need to be to overcome this struggle, and decide it now.

When I was living in the boiler room my friends and I spent a lot of time studying the work of Abraham Hicks in depth. A group of us would gather in the boiler room and discuss what wasn't working in our lives and what we thought Abraham would say.

'MY HAPPINESS DEPENDS ON ME, SO YOU'RE OFF THE
HOOK.' AND THEN DEMONSTRATE IT. BE HAPPY, NO
MATTER WHAT THEY'RE DOING. PRACTICE FEELING GOOD,
NO MATTER WHAT. AND BEFORE YOU KNOW IT, YOU WILL
NOT GIVE ANYONE ELSE RESPONSIBILITY FOR THE WAY YOU
FEEL – AND THEN, YOU'LL LOVE THEM ALL. BECAUSE THE
ONLY REASON YOU DON'T LOVE THEM, IS BECAUSE YOU'RE
USING THEM AS YOUR EXCUSE TO NOT FEEL GOOD.
– ABRAHAM HICKS

And then demonstrate it.

That bit was way harder said than done, but I worked at it.

I thought about all the situations where I maybe expected too much of someone else, or felt disappointed or let down because they hadn't helped me. I read up on blame, and on Transactional Analysis and the Drama Triangle.[66]

I worked hard at letting go of my stuff. I worked my way up the emotional guidance scale.[67] I did exercises like the rampage of appreciation, and the magical creation box.[68] I wanted so badly to be happy and get my old life back.

The amount of debt I was in scared me. (I still sometimes get scared of big money. I still sometimes think that if I keep things small it'll be less of a fall when it all goes wrong. Only now I have the tools to catch those thoughts and manage them appropriately. I know that fear is a universal and impersonal force, like gravity – it will always be there, but unlike gravity I have a choice how I respond to it. I recognise that the negativity bias is there to keep me safe, but that fear of change is often not about my safety but rather a compass pointing me to the most powerful change I could make.)

---

66. The Karpman Drama Triangle was originally conceived by Steven Karpman and was used to plot the interplay and behavioural 'moves' between two or more people. Karpman's original premise was based on the Transactional Analysis (TA) model as proposed by Eric Berne in the 1950s.

67. Go to the Misfit to Maven bonus page: *www.misfit2maven.com/bonuses*

68. Go to the Misfit to Maven bonus page: *www.misfit2maven.com/bonuses*

Sometimes we fall. The bigger the fall the harder it smarts. I went from comfortably earning £60k a year to being £25k in debt in the space of five months. It affected me more deeply and for longer than I first realised.

> **Aside:** In 2014 I discovered that one of my long-standing high-profile My Girl Friday clients committed suicide after a far bigger fall than mine. She didn't have the tools. She didn't ask for help. I don't know the exact figures involved in her situation but I do know that in 2011 I nearly chose that same route. Today and every day I remind myself that the universe has got my back, that I have trust and faith and the tools I need. I choose to let go, to surrender and to allow myself to be supported. I've stopped holding on tight and digging in my heels, because whilst it worked for a short while, it's exhausting. When a baby falls it bounces. When a cat falls it lands well. These days I know that if I treat falling as an adventure in and of itself, if I remain flexible and open, I too can bounce and land well.

We are amazing beings, we learn to stay away from things that hurt us, but our brains were made for a time when those things mostly had big teeth. In recent years I have done a lot of work on my relationship with money and I continue to do so. I am still a work in progress and I vow to always be learning and growing. My container and capacity can and will always be growing larger than the issues and circumstances in my life.

There were moments when I asked, 'Why is this happening to me?'

I felt sorry for myself and I couldn't see the bigger picture. I had no faith. Not in myself, not in anything greater than me. Now I have both. The journey getting to where I am now gifted me with faith in myself and faith in the Divine.

Back then I was asking rubbish questions. The quality of the answers you get is determined by quality of the questions you ask. The answers to 'Why is this happening to me?' Or 'What did I do to deserve this?' will never be useful or constructive, and will never be empowering.

I have now learned to ask better questions – instead of 'Why is this happening to me?' I ask, 'What am I learning?' or 'Who do I want to be?'

For me, being an entrepreneur isn't about the cash or the cars or the freedom, it's about who I am becoming on the way to those things.

You can grow your container bigger than any problem you have. That's the best piece of advice I can give. Become self aware, learn how you learn, discover what inspires you and grow along the way. Find people who teach in a way that turns you on and ignites your inner light. There are 50 billion people in the world and the Internet – your people are out there, go find them!

For six months I lived on sofas and I had hard conversations. I put my name of the list for housing co-ops and signed up for every bursary or grant I could find. I stood in queues at the housing office and asked for help. I was told I was too old, too white, too middle class, too childless and too sober to be considered vulnerable. It would take six years for me to be housed by them. I went and spoke to my mum about selling her mum's house so that I could use my inheritance to pay off my debts. It is not how I had envisaged using my inheritance. I had mentally made a promise to use the money as a deposit on a house. I did not want to let my grandma down. I didn't want to have screwed up my chances of ever owning a house. I didn't want to be behind everyone else. I was still comparing myself to my siblings, my friends, peers, strangers.

The gang of four – the negative committee, led by The Judge and The Driver in my head – were back on at full volume:

'How did you end up here? You stupid idiot.'

'Why did this happen to me? Life's so unfair.'

'You are such a fuck up!'

'Suck it up Nancy! You loser.'

'How will I ever have the life that I want?'

'You've got exactly the life you deserve.'

When you have fallen out of the system it is really hard to get back in. When you have no address you can't get a job, without a job getting anyone to rent you a place to live is really tricky. Having no deposit is one thing, but having no references, being self-employed and having a business that is less than a year old and is making a loss whilst you are living in your car and on people's sofas is not ideal. Knowing that I had some money coming and that I would be able to get out of this mess eventually kept me going, but barely. I was so frustrated and disappointed in myself that I would have to spend my grandmother's hard-earned money on getting myself out of my self-made hole. It felt so tricky to me, if I told anyone in the system that I had money coming they would consider it an asset and not help me with housing benefit and demand I pay back the money I owed in full. I didn't have the money yet as it was a house, my grandmother's house; my mum's mother's house. I had to ask my mum for help. I had to ask her to sell the house in order to help me out of the mess I had gotten myself in. I'll let you imagine how fun that conversation was for me.

All the time that I wasn't paying off the debt I owed the Inland Revenue it was collecting interest. My debts were getting larger. How I managed to build a business and keep a happy smiley face on is beyond me. Thankfully, I was and can still be as stubborn as an ox. When a job did come in I gave it everything. I was good at what I did and made sure I over-delivered. Living in this way was taking its toll. I was surviving on adrenalin and my cortisol levels must have been sky high. One day I was in a meeting with my caseworker at the housing office and I lost it. I burst into uncontrollable angry, desperate tears. I couldn't hold it together anymore. The waiting room was full of homeless people who had given up and decided that this was their life. I didn't belong there. I was scared. My future had to be brighter and bigger than this. I was destined for great things. She listened while I ranted at her and wept. At some point during my impassioned speech she softened in front of me and went from being a form-filling robot to someone who wanted to help me. Together we came up with a plan.

I got in touch with the estate agents I had rented from the last time I lived in Brighton. I asked if they had any one-bed properties for rent; my plan was to ask if they could use my previous reference checks. It was a long shot, but given my circumstances I was willing to try anything. My biggest problem was that if anyone credit-checked me now they wouldn't trust me to be the stand-up citizen that I knew I was and could be. I was way outside my comfort zone, but I had limited options so I just did it.

'Ebonie, hello, yes I remember you. I'm sorry but we only deal in commercial properties now.'

FUCK.

I could feel the warm wetness of fresh tears forming in my eyes, whilst still on the phone.

My only hope of getting out of my friends' cupboard was gone. I was devastated and not hiding it well.

She asked me what was wrong. She asked if I was OK. I cracked open. Why is it that someone being kind stops us from being tough? I told her the whole story, I told her that I could get housing benefit if someone would just give me a break and rent to me. She went away and came back and told me that one of the company directors had a studio flat that was about to become available. (Hello, miracle.) I arranged a time to view it.

She met me at the property with the company director. The three of us went in together to see it. I couldn't believe it, I'd seen this place before: it was the place I had been dreaming about each night. The whole of the back wall was glass looking out over a small garden. The light, which in my dream might have been heaven, was in fact daylight streaming into a large L-shaped studio room. I just knew I was home, and everything was going to be OK.

They agreed to let me move in if I could show proof that I would be in receipt of housing benefit. Filling out the forms, speaking to people who didn't care and were just doing their job, for days on end, queuing and being moved from pillar to post, from one department to the next, explaining that I didn't have the paperwork they needed because I was currently of no fixed abode: it all became easier when I could see a goal.

I got what they needed and I moved into the flat and everything got better and better each day. I started to rebuild my life. I refused to let the situation I was in rule my life. I refused to let the depression win.

Somehow I went on a yoga holiday, I have no idea where the money came from, or how I paid for it, but I went back to Dahab in Egypt with Ali Gilling. The whole place had changed, or maybe I had. Now I enjoyed the culture and being treated like a royal princess. It didn't feel sleazy like it had the first time. My perspective had changed, everything seemed different, I viewed the world through appreciative eyes.

I hung out with a local guy about my age who told me about his life. He took me out to the desert on his motorbike. He took me to meet his mum. He told me about his religion and shared with me his dreams of traveling the world and coming to live in Europe.[69]

Back home I continued my personal development journey; dancing The 5 Rhythms© and practising many different styles of yoga. I organised and attended many seminars and conferences. Through My Girl Friday I got to work for many incredible people whose work I admired and from whom I was able to learn and get access to powerful information and resources.

Having my own space after six months was AMAZING! Suddenly I was able to digest so much of what I had been through. I spent a lot of time alone. I love to be sociable and I love to fill myself up on people, but once I am full I am FULL and there is only really one person in the world I can be around when I am that sort of full: Zoë.

I didn't have a best friend I felt equal to, without feeling as though I were their sidekick, until I was in my mid twenties. I didn't think I'd ever have a woman as a best friend if I'm honest. I'd had lots of men friends, but there was always a slight agenda, and let's remember, I didn't really trust anyone. Then I met Zoë. Zoë is someone I can be 100% myself around. Zoë has seen me at my best and at my worst and every step in between and our relationship has taught me about unconditional love. To me she is family.

She was having a really hard time at work. I was too caught up in my world to ask more and she is a very private person, so she mentioned it once but then not again.

---

69. He did, we stayed in touch for a while, he came and lived in Germany for a year.

Eventually my grandma's house was sold. Feeling stronger I took back control from the debt management company and used some of the money to pay off my creditors. I played the long game. I got organised and every month I rang to see who my debt had been sold to and I offered them a settlement figure. Every month they said no. I paid them their monthly payment and got on with my life. I had learned to separate the emotion from the facts. I learned to be patient. I invested the rest of my money; put it away for five years where I wouldn't be able to touch it and it could make me some money. I figured in five years I'd be solvent again and be in a position to buy the house I had always dreamt of.

In August 2010 Zoë came and worked for My Girl Friday. Disillusioned with the fashion industry she needed something to tide her over and I needed some support. I was ready to grow My Girl Friday, and I needed help. I wanted to prove that I wasn't a failure and that I could be a proper grown-up, sane human being. Business was going well, gaining momentum and including Zoë I now had six freelancers working for the company.

I was still feeling wobbly and whenever I was alone, whenever I stopped, I couldn't stop crying. I went to see an Ayurvedic practitioner. I thought maybe he could help. As a result of our consultation he told me about Woman Within™ and also offered to front the money for the residential weekend if I wanted. There was one to be held in a few weeks' time, I could pay him back when I was able.

I didn't take him up on his offer. I paid for the retreat myself. I was stubborn, starting to feel more like my old self – I wanted to be in control of my life again and that meant paying my own way. However, the fact that a man that I had only just met had offered to help me out financially spurred me into wanting to do the course and do the work. I wanted to be as open-hearted and authentic as he was. I wanted to be as comfortable and confident in my own skin as he was.

Woman Within™[70] is set up so that you have no idea what to expect from the weekend. You are asked to arrive with no makeup or jewellery and with an open mind. The rituals and experiences that you go through

---

70. *http://www.womanwithin.org.uk/ http://womanwithin.org*

during the weekend allow each woman to connect with the woman within herself, rather than her little girl.

I don't often talk about the how the work I did on the Woman Within™ weekend changed me. It wasn't just the weekend, but afterwards too – something changed on a core level and I continue to see the impact it has had on my life every day. Before that weekend I felt deep down that women were my competition; I had never experienced or felt that I needed to experience intimacy with another woman and quite simply I didn't trust women. My experience of them was that for the most part, en masse, they were bitchy, manipulative and/or needy. Zoë was the exception that proved the rule.

After that weekend, I now have deep, connected, authentic and intimate relationships with other women. I experience other women as my sisters, I have found companions and friends, I have made joint ventures and partnerships, I have found trust and empowerment and I cannot articulate what this has done for my relationships with men also. I have so much gratitude for the community that I continue to be a part of. If you are a woman who is fearful of other women in some way, as I was, I really empathise and I invite you to have a look at the organisation and the weekends they hold. If you are a man reading this, I invite you to look at The Mankind Project.[71]

Within weeks of that weekend, on a personal development mission, I attended a Shadow Work® Weekend.[72] Shadow Work is similar to the work on a Woman Within™ weekend and a lot of the other closed-group retreats and workshops I have attended and been a part of organising; it includes a set of facilitated processes that allow individuals to identify, explore and change behaviour patterns. The idea of the weekend is to reframe and transform parts of your character that you'd like to change with compassion and understanding.

The Shadow Work weekend I did was with a small group of both men and women. Having a mixed group brought up new and different things for me and I was able to see the work I needed to do next around intimacy.

---

71. *http://mankindproject.org/*

72. Based on Cliff Barry's unique synthesis of ancient and modern tools, Shadow Work® uses a four-directional 'map of the mind' to identify and process your 'shadows.' *http://www.shadowwork.com/*

I got to see how overwhelming just the tiniest bit of physical touch, eye contact or receiving love was for me when I stayed present without numbing or zoning out. I got to see some of the patterns I had of numbing out rather than communicating, or slowing down. I got to confront my need for and my complete terror of touch and intimacy.

Over the course of the rest of that year I went on many retreats, I did a lot of yoga, I did the work and got more and more able to be in the present moment. I became aware of just how much of my life I spent in the future or in the past. I made an effort to catch myself and make changes.

My Girl Friday grew. We had eight Girl Fridays in different parts of the country all working and things were going well. I was proud of us. We were running a real-life grown-ass company!

Then one day just as I was beginning to feel comfortable, I got to see just how much I still had to learn. We had a HNW client with two daughters, both of whom were getting married. My Girl Friday SW worked her ass off, over-delivering at every opportunity. The first wedding was a roaring success! Not sitting on her laurels she cracked on with the next one, making sure to treat each equally and manage the emotions and family dramas that go with working so intensely with a family on something so emotive. The client was hugely grateful and often called me to tell me how amazing we were. I loved how relaxed and friendly we were able to be with our clients. The second wedding was delivered and MGFSW prepared to take some time off, but the invoice didn't get paid. Upon investigation it seemed that the client had decided that she didn't want to pay us. She decided that MGFSW hadn't done her job properly and that she had ruined her daughter's wedding by letting a photographer leave before the end, thus denying them of precious memories they would never get back. She went on to completely contradict everything she had previously told us about the work and how happy she had been.

She threatened to sue us. My girl rang me in tears and I was out of my depth. I got scared. I didn't know what to do and although I wasn't doing a great job of communicating such, I had too much on my plate as it was. Legal issues on top of everything else were just too much for me to cope with. Although I felt as though I ought to know how to deal with this situation, I didn't have a clue. I felt like a failure. Instead of holding my hands up and asking for help, seeing it as an opportunity for growth and greater connection, I let my freelancer (and friend) down and we walked away from a large amount of money because it was easier than standing up for ourselves.

Aside: a few years later, in 2013, a different client tried to do a similar thing to me. By then I was wiser, I had more self-confidence, I knew my own worth and I decided that I was worth fighting for. I did my research and I took her to the small claims court. I wish I had done that the first time, but I didn't have it in me, I wasn't ready – but I did grow and learn. I have learned to contract work properly. It has taken me years but I now know that people who are worth working with will never mind a contract.

I am now able to see so many of the lessons that My Girl Friday taught me, and I am sure I'll continue to find more along the way. It really all is feedback, not failure. That's not just a nice sound bite. Whatever you are doing now is a training ground for what will come next: In business, in your relationships, and in your connection and knowing of yourself and the Divine.

My Girl Friday had the potential to be an incredible business, but it was more than my business, it was my *everything*. I stopped being or doing anything outside of work and I began to believe that I actually was the Mary Poppins-type character I had created. What was supposed to be a brand identity became *my* identity. I couldn't see the wood for the trees, I became completely immersed in my business and not in an objective or business-like manner.

It is important to have an identity outside of work.

Who do you want to be?

How do you want to be remembered?

The first time I crashed I learnt some stuff. The second time I learned more. There is still more for me to learn, of that I am sure. These days I listen out for the whispers telling me to slow down, or ask for help. I make time to check in with how I am feeling every day and I do the internal work to keep my mind and my body healthy.

I wanted an office. I decided that we needed one. To make it work financially I needed to move out of the place I was renting alone and I decided that sharing with other people might also give me a life outside of work. I moved out of my studio flat and into Kings Mews, a Brighton version of 'The Palace' in some ways. In our new house were Ben (and his band), a tattoo artist, and us: Zoë and I.

Zoë and I lived together, worked together and hung out together. It wasn't the most sensible idea in hindsight. I lost sight of what I was trying to create and why. In fact I don't think I was ever that clear on my *why*.

Your *why* is what gets you out of bed. It's what motivates and inspires you. It's the legacy you want to leave behind. Growing a business takes work and real focus. I can't stress enough how important it is to know why. Your *why* is what gets you out of your comfort zone and pushing yourself. It's what helps you make good choices and keep you on track.

I was working and working and working – why?

Because I had to keep a roof over my head and pay off debts.

Beyond that – now what? Why was I doing this and not something else?

So I didn't have to be a normal, cookie-cutter grown-up.

Hmmmm.

It is not lost on me now that I worked really hard trying to be a normal person, so that I didn't have to be a normal person! I wish I'd gone and found a coach or a mentor; maybe then I wouldn't have crashed the second time. In truth though, I wouldn't change any of it: it needed to happen just the way it did.

Kings Mews was a party house. I fell into old habits. We partied a lot. I fell back into numbing my feelings with alcohol and food, eating things that were quick and cheap and easy.

The way you do anything is the way you do everything.

In my relationships I was quick and cheap and easy.

Why have I told you so much about my relationships, about food, about drugs?

Why has this book, which is all dressed up as a business book, got so little reference to business in it?

Three reasons.

Firstly, a book just about business is boring and you won't remember or learn from it. We learn better from stories, from shared experience.

Secondly, business is all about relationships. People buy people. People buy because of how they FEEL not because of how they THINK. In most developed countries we do not need very much, but we buy a lot. We buy because we feel we will be healthier, have more sex, live longer, be more youthful, be smarter, richer, thinner, or more likable if we do.

Thirdly, love is the great leveller. In love everyone is equal, there is no relationship trust fund. There is no amount of money that buys you intimacy. Nepotism won't hook you up where real authentic feelings are involved. How we are in our relationships, how we treat other people and how we let others treat us, tells us a lot about our self-esteem and self-worth.

And, *how you do anything is how you do everything.*

At the beginning of this book I explained that I break life into three sections for the purposes of my coaching and for the purposes of being able to compartmentalise that which is un-compartmentalisable. The first section is work – or the gift that you have been given with which to make your living and serve the world. The second is relationships – that thing that happens in your belly when another person enters into your space. And the third is your relationship to the paradox that is ego/enlightenment, self/God, Individuation/Universal energy.

There is a reason to break it out into sections like this. It becomes easier to see where we are getting our needs met. Where and how we choose to get our needs met isn't always healthy. Often we have found ways of getting our needs met in childhood that no longer serve us now that we are adults. Often we haven't recognised our behaviour patterns and so we keep on behaving in ways that are detrimental to our own fulfilment.

Let's take the need for *significance* as an example. Where are you getting your need for significance met? At work? In relationships? In your spirituality?

If you trip over others for significance then you may well get that box ticked, but how is your need for connection and love? Are you demonstrating narcissistic behaviour? Have you become co-dependent?

> IF THERE IS AN OUTCOME YOU ARE AFRAID OF AND YOU
> DO NOT TAKE ACTION BECAUSE YOU ARE AFRAID – YOU
> PRODUCE THE ACTION YOU ARE AFRAID OF.
> – MASTIN KIPP

I was terrified of becoming a victim, so I became one.

I was terrified of loosing my sanity and not learning from my mistakes – so I completely lost it and didn't learn from my previous mistakes.

CHOOSE LOVE, CHOSE LIFE, CHOOSE JOY

I have '*choose love, choose life, choose joy*' tattooed on my wrist, and yes, it is a reminder.

People have asked: 'So, it's like a post it note that won't fall off?'

Yes.

My Girl Friday continued to grow. I got ambitious. I wanted more and more. Somewhere I knew that I couldn't do it all alone. I needed support. I was saying yes when I meant no. Things were starting to spiral, but I didn't do anything about it. I hadn't actually learnt that lesson from the first fall at all. I still felt that sharing my feelings was a sign of weakness and instead I just became silently resentful of everyone around me.

Resentment is a sign that you are not listening to yourself, not giving yourself what you need.

Instead of slowing down and internally taking stock I looked externally for answers. I compared myself to everyone else but me.

Eyes on your own mat.....

Be yourself, every one else is taken...

Whilst my identity had changed massively I was still playing by old rules and looking for old validation points. If you're to fully step into a new life the old life has to die. The butterfly doesn't bring its cocoon with it.

From the outside my business looked great. We had survived the toughest part of the recession. I had made my best friend my business partner, the company was growing larger, our reputation and reach were extending. We were being invited to attend amazing events. We were being nominated for awards. We were 17 freelancers strong. We had clients in five countries. I had navigated all sorts of obstacles. I should have been happy.

I was FUCKING miserable.

Inside the business I was stuck and lost, and definitely not having fun. I wasn't delegating, I was pushing people away again. My clients wanted me and no one else and I had to 'sell' them the other girls, whilst getting very little reward for doing so. I began to resent them for all their wealth, their fulfilment, their creativity, and their freedom. I was working round the clock, but not making enough profit. I was not running my business, my business was running me!

The patterns of my past were repeating themselves. I felt trapped and overwhelmed. I doubted everything. I felt like a massive fraud. I felt discomfort and I numbed it with food and alcohol, I felt no real pleasure and no real pain, I felt disconnected from my clients, from my business partners and from my purpose. All I could hear were demands, dissatisfaction, the voice of my own disappointment, and silence...

I stopped listening and found myself alone and disconnected.

I was in a pattern of feeling separate, of not belonging, of feeling like a failure, and again I saw my vulnerability as weakness. I was in a cycle of picking myself up and just getting through it. Day by day I survived on will-power and determination, followed by burn-out... Physically my body got fat and ill. I would get tonsillitis at least once a month. My mind became un-stimulated and full of cotton wool. I became apathetic and cared about very little, I could not see the point in anything and was too ashamed to share my shame.

I was awful at setting or keeping boundaries.

I was constantly people-pleasing – I couldn't stand the idea of someone not liking me.

I didn't know what my priorities were or should be.

I was using food and cocaine to numb my pain. I craved connection, but I couldn't let anyone in – I'd fall apart if I allowed anyone to be kind to me or see my truth.

Our house was a party house. There were people over every night. I tried to stay in my room and out of the temptation, but I couldn't sleep through the noise and, as the saying goes, 'if you can't beat them, join them'. I got wasted and found myself hooking up with other people's boyfriends. It was just a kiss here and there, I told myself it was OK, *I wasn't the one cheating, and it wasn't ever the same person.* I just needed quick, simple connection. Acting like this made me feel awful about myself, adding to the evidence I was accruing to support how much of a failure and a fuck up I was. Yet again, getting involved with unavailable men was a safe way to connect without being seen.

But it all added to my self-loathing.

I hated the girl in the mirror.

Any time I was alone I spent crying and feeling ashamed.

Most days I felt like something out of Alice in Wonderland; self-medicating to keep myself awake and smiling when all I wanted to do was curl up in a dark hole and sleep. I became concerned about my mental health. One of my clients was a therapist who specialised in the treatment of depression, anxiety, eating disorders, stress, relationship problems, obsessions and low confidence. He and I had talked here and there about the work that he did using a combination of cognitive therapy, hypnotherapy, positive therapy, NLP, schema therapy & psychotherapy. I went to him in confidence and I had six sessions with him. They didn't teach me anything I didn't already know. If I am honest I copped out and just told him what I thought he wanted to hear: I'd done it all before and he wasn't showing me anything new. I did my homework; I kept a food diary.

We analysed my behaviour, but the truth of the matter is I was tumbling down a rabbit hole and no amount of talking was going to dig me out.

One day in September 2011 I woke up and found some cocaine that someone had left behind after another party. It was 7:30am and I got high in order to leave my bedroom and face the day. I needed it to get out the door without crying.

As I sat on the edge of my bed and looked at myself in the mirror I realised I was contemplating suicide. Not for the drama, but as a choice, an option.

My brother phoned. My brother makes me feel safe. When I feel safe enough around someone I cry, I am such a crier, and how I feel tumbles out of my mouth unedited.

I told him I was contemplating suicide; I was tired of my own shit. I was aware enough to know that it was me that was the issue. I recognised that I was creating the same patterns over and over and I felt as though I had tried everything within my power to change but I wasn't changing, nothing was changing! I told him that I felt trapped in a samsara cycle that I didn't know how to break out of. I told him that I felt that there is always an option and a choice and that I thought my choice was to end it all. 'It's too hard, I'm too tired and I want out.'

When it feels personal, pervasive and permanent, suicide starts to seem a really good and viable option.

My brother told my mum. My mum called me and asked me if I'd like to go for a walk.

Going for a walk, being in nature, is one of the ways that my mum and I are able to connect with one another. We share a love of being outside and noticing all the seasonal changes. I didn't know how to say no, so we went for a walk.

Out in the countryside, in the middle of nowhere with no place to hide, she asked me to explain what was going on in my head.

Why did I want to kill myself?

For a moment I felt tricked, I was angry that my brother had told my mum, but then another feeling overtook that: *She wants to understand me!*

I tried to explain as best I could. She didn't get it, I don't think she ever will, but I'm hugely grateful for that intervention; that conversation got me to seek a different sort of help. I knew in that moment that she loved me. I went to the doctor and asked for antidepressants. I never thought I would take antidepressants. I grew up using and believing entirely in holistic modalities. For some reason I didn't believe the science. By that point if they had taken me to a loony bin and locked me up, I would have been relieved. That day was my was my rock bottom – no yoga, diet, CBT, retreat, or advice was going to pull me up from the floor. I felt flat, my life was completely grey, there was no colour. I would have taken any help I could get and, frankly, a padded white room and no responsibilities sounded like heaven.

The antidepressants were amazing. In the first week the buzz they gave me was very similar to the cocaine I had been doing, but once that wore off something incredible happened. It was although someone had opened a window and let in some light and some air. The suffocating dark black box I was in expanded, and for the first time in a long time I could breathe and see. I felt like me again. The cotton wool in my mind disintegrated and I could think again.

I made some decisions. I decided that if My Girl Friday was a business and not just an extension of me, I should be able to go away for a little while and get well. It should be able to survive. In fact it might thrive without me. I sublet my room and I sold my car.

> 'THE SOUL ALWAYS KNOWS WHAT TO DO TO HEAL
> ITSELF. THE CHALLENGE IS TO SILENCE THE MIND.'
> – CAROLINE MYSS

I bought a flight to Bali

I wanted time out to silence my mind and figure out who I was.

I needed a focus, though, so I decided I would use the time to start writing the novel I'd always dreamt of writing.

A friend I'd met in Thailand all those years before was now living in Bali and said I could stay with her until I found my feet and worked out what I was doing.

I stopped taking the antidepressants the day I got on the plane to Denpasar and I haven't taken them since. (I haven't used any other substances to self-medicate, either.)

That trip to Bali changed my life, changed me forever. The people I met, the love that I felt, the energy of the place, the femininity, the time out to just be me… Bali is magic and I was ready to receive magic.

I met so many incredible people and learned so much so fast in my time there.

I was lucky enough to work with Jeremiah Abrams,[73] both assisting him and as a participant in his incredible immersive *Removing the Barriers to Love* retreat, where I began to unpeel yet another layer, this time around my relationships with men. I became an assistant to Margot Anand[74] and many other wonderful trailblazing, heart-centred entrepreneurs. However, within six weeks of being in Bali I had somehow pretty much recreated my whole life over the other side of the world: instead of spending my time 'being' and figuring out who I was, I had six clients, all healers or coaches or therapists, and I was doing their admin and marketing and organising their travel. It finally dawned on me that it doesn't matter where you go, you take your stuff with you.

I did an OK job of the work I was doing, but I wasn't Mary Poppins anymore, I had a resentful edge. One of my wise and intuitive clients said to me:

'Ebonie, you are great at what you do, but you don't want to be a Girl Friday anymore, you want to be the one with a Girl Friday.'

---

73. Jeremiah Abrams is a Jungian therapist and author who is considered a leading expert on the human shadow. He is a pioneer in the field of breath work innovation and consciousness research, going back over 35 years. His books include the best-selling *Meeting the Shadow: The Hidden Power of the Dark Side of Human Nature, The Shadow in America*, and *Reclaiming the Inner Child*. http://www.jeremiahabrams.com/

74. Margot Anand is an internationally acclaimed authority on Tantra, best-selling author, and teacher and founder of *SkyDancing Tantra*. http://margotanand.com/

I told her she was wrong, but she wasn't.

I wanted to help people. I wanted to enable them to be, do, and have everything that they desired. I wanted to help them get out of their own way, but I was not sure what I had to offer anyone as a coach or therapist or counsellor or consultant. I didn't know if I wanted to go back to school and study and I didn't see any other way. I was still very fragile and I wanted to rebuild myself cautiously.

My time in Bali was coming to an end; I needed to decide what I was going to do next. I looked at extending my visa and found a gorgeous local family to sponsor me. Then I received an email from a friend who presented me with an opportunity and a reason to come home. He offered me somewhere to live and a way to make some money. I wasn't sure what to do. I was at a crossroads: stay in Bali or come home?

That evening I went out with friends, mulling my future over in my mind. At the end of the night I found my wallet had been stolen and with it all the money I had left. I saw it as a sign to come home.

Back in the UK, My Girl Friday was not doing great. The girls had all gone and gotten jobs. Unsure about what I wanted to do next with my life and scared what ploughing back into running my own business would do to my fragile mental health, I focused on getting a personal life. I wanted a man and a home and a body I was proud of.

And a job. I wanted a clock-in, clock-out, get-paid job!

For over a year I tried to get a job.

At one end of the scale I was told that I was far too experienced. At the other end I was told that I didn't have quite enough experience in an agency environment and that I was too entrepreneurial. I applied for more than 300 jobs. Each one had over 200 applicants. I went to interview for more than 50 of those jobs and I got down to the last 2 applicants for approximately 30 of them. I got offered none of the jobs.

Each time the reasons were the same – *You have an incredible skill set and we'd love to have you work for us, but the other candidate has got actual experience of this exact job and whilst we think you could bring something fresh to the table we are worried that you'll get bored.*

It was so frustrating. At the time I just wanted money. I would have kept my head down and worked. I really wanted a *job*. I was fragile and I didn't want to do my own thing any more, I felt weak and uninspired; I just wanted someone to tell me what to do. I felt sure that I wanted to clock in and clock out for a while. But my soul had other ideas.

I kept myself busy doing up the house I was living in and looking after the tenants I had living there with me. I wrote every day, working on the book I had started in Bali. I made a vision board, with a lover, getting paid to travel and a relaxed English countryside lifestyle squarely in the centre of it. I started to look after myself and care about how I was treating my body. I ate well and I went to the gym every day. It became a priority to be mindful of how I was looking after myself. I wanted balance. I felt sure that abstaining from everything completely wasn't the way, I wanted to be allowed to eat or drink whatever I wanted. I wanted to be someone who ate intuitively but deep down was resentful and mistrustful of my body and believed that it would never be how I wanted it to be. I read *The 4 Hour Body* by Tim Ferris and followed his guidelines for a while, never noticing the results for myself but being told that I was losing weight. Rather than encouraging me, each comment made me more and more angry. Not the kind of anger that is visible – the kind that festers unacknowledged. I was resentful that I had to try so hard.

That summer at a festival I met a guy. He was physically fit, outdoorsy, strong, mature and intelligent. He told me he didn't drink alcohol, which was hugely appealing to me. He was laid back. He was a gentleman. He courted me. I was flattered.

He took me on dates. I'd never been treated so well before. He ticked a lot of boxes. I took him home to meet my family – he didn't have a family of his own and it was Christmas so I invited to come to ours. He was and still is actually the only man I have ever taken home. It was a big deal for me.

Life was going well. An ex My Girl Friday client got in touch and talked about a big job, coordinating the VIP element for Sarah Brightman's world tour. He asked if I wanted to set up the event at each stop along the route as well as host them? It would mean going on tour, getting paid to travel across Asia and North and South America, leaving April 2013. Was I interested?

Hell yes!

Things with the guy were going OK, but he was starting to make me feel uncomfortable. I decided that it was me; I told myself that I was rubbish at relationships. Even so, I was feeling more and more claustrophobic and controlled but the voices in my head told me that I ought to stay with him and make it work just until I went away on tour.

There were some issues with the tour dates and my start on the job was pushed forward to June. I should have been excited; it meant that this guy and I would have more time to be together. All I'd ever wanted was to be in a mature relationship like this. *Why was I so unhappy?* I began to notice not only that he was drinking alcohol, but how much alcohol he was drinking and how much weed he was smoking. I began to notice that he kept filling my glass up when I had said no, I didn't want to drink. I began to notice that I was scared. I finally realised that it wasn't the intimacy that scared me, it was his behaviour.

I felt more and more on edge, manipulated and controlled. I am grateful for those feelings now, they enabled me to recognise that I was in a pattern of picking men I knew could hurt me, putting myself in situations that made me feel unsafe. I decided it was time to break the pattern. Just because I wanted to be in a relationship and prove that I could 'do a relationship' was not reason enough to be with him.

We stopped seeing each other.

I stopped drinking completely. I decided that I wanted to be completely sober in all areas of my life all the time. In my soberness I realised that the house I was living in wasn't working. I moved again. I picked somewhere in the countryside, near enough to all the places I needed to get to but far enough away from people. I needed to spend time alone, quietly and in my own space. For work I was freelancing as a private personal assistant, doing the same as with My Girl Friday, but this time it was just me. Word spread that I was back in business and work started to roll in. I wasn't excited by the projects I was working on, but I was making ends meet.

I found a personal trainer I liked and worked out regularly with him. I really enjoyed lifting weights and getting strong. As I got physically stronger I also became emotionally stronger. I was finally ready to look at what I wanted for my future. I made it my mission not just to figure out who I was and like it – I decided that it was now time to create the life I wanted for myself without 'should's or 'ought to's.

I decided that it was time to learn from all the crazy adventures I had been on, all the books I had read, all the people I'd met, all the businesses and trailblazing entrepreneurs I had worked with. I was tired of trying to be someone else, and never living up to my self-set standards. I raked through all the retreats and workshops, therapy and courses; all the journals I'd kept, all the money I'd lost, all the diets and the drugs – everything! I got really honest with myself and worked out what my strengths and shadows were. I looked at the clients and the work I had enjoyed and why it had worked. I realised that the commonality was 'enabling' and 'entrepreneurs' – and The Entrepreneur Enabler was born. I realised that I wanted to build a personal brand, built on my values and on my truth. I wanted to find a way to build a business that could help other wild and true misfits to grow and evolve, whilst leaving space for me to grow and evolve too.

The tour was pushed for a second time; my start date was postponed until October.

By chance as I was surfing the Internet I clicked on a banner ad for The Coaching Academy and ended up booked onto a free two-day course they were running that weekend. I'm not sure how I stumbled upon it, but I travelled up to London alone and spent the weekend immersed in coaching. I loved it: I applied to be on their courses and started work on my Personal Performance Diploma immediately.

Life was good. I loved everything about the course and finally all my experiences up until this point made sense. I could see with some sort of clarity a future for myself again and I was excited. On top of all of that new excitement, the new tour date was approaching; I was finally going to start on this dream job of mine. I was going to be getting paid to travel across America whilst still having time to do my course work and work remotely with a couple of the private clients I had on retainer.

Everything was coming together. I was the happiest in my body and in my self I had ever been. I was inspired and content and feeling fulfilled. I guess with everything going so well I should have expected it; I met a man and I fell in love. I wasn't expecting it, it came out of nowhere - I fell in love instantly.

We hung out for two weeks before I went on tour. He made me laugh. He made me feel safe. He was sexy and fun. We could talk about anything. It was a whirlwind. Then I was off, on a plane and onto a tour bus. I joined a crew who had already been together for three months. They had already been in Asia using a different VIP team. I was thrown in at the deep end, co-ordinating the VIP experience across America for Sarah Brightman's biggest fans. Getting paid to travel across the US had been a long-standing dream of mine and finally, after a year of planning, negotiating, and contracting, I was doing it. I should have been over the moon. What I had not prepared myself for, however, was not enjoying the experience that I had worked so hard to manifest.

I hated it. I didn't love Sarah's music. I didn't have the passion that her fans had. It was a hard tour, and I wasn't the only one who left. I got ill but had to work through it and I was homesick; something I had never experienced before. I missed him. We spoke all day by Messenger, unsure what time it was where the other one was, but a continued conversation back and forth only made me miss him more. The tour was far more gruelling than I had anticipated and I didn't get a day off for two weeks. Emotional, unwell and in love, I ached to come home. I could have given it longer, but I didn't care about the job, I cared about *him*. I had no idea if it would work out, but it was a risk I was willing to take.

I'd never put my career second before. I'd spent years with my career being my *everything*. **Full of fear, I had no idea how to go about saying to my employer:**

'Hey, this isn't fun for me, I need to go home.'

My head was full of questions and uncertainty:

Am I making the right decision?

Will I regret this?

Does this compromise my integrity?

What will people think?

Will I ever work again?

Am I crazy?

I meditated on it, neck-deep in a bubble bath at the Doubletree Hilton in Detroit.

'Wild and True' sang softly in my heart.

So I told the truth. And, I came home.

We found someone to replace me on the road and I was able to continue doing some of the work; advancing the shows and running some of the logistical bits from back at home in England.

The experience taught me about living in the moment, communicating from the heart, staying true to myself and really enjoying the journey – massive cliché though it is, I finally figured out that if you can determine your happiness by the very adventure of *being*, rather than the outcome, then whatever happens is A-OK.

You know what? It didn't work out with the guy. He didn't feel the same as I did, but I'm still glad and grateful for every moment we had together. I was heart-broken for a really long time and I cursed this new place of FEELING everything. I lay on the floor for two weeks sobbing; the feeling in my chest so deep and dark and dense. And then gradually, with time, I was OK again.

Part Three:

MYSTERY

MYSTERY MASTERY MYSTERY

'WISDOM COMES ONLY WHEN YOU STOP LOOKING FOR IT AND
START LIVING THE LIFE THE CREATOR INTENDED FOR YOU.'
— HOPI PROVERB

Since then two years have passed, and in a way my journey has only just begun.

It's all very simple.

Which doesn't mean it's easy.

I was born curious…

…and I have discovered that I have access to all the answers to all my questions.

I have learned how to love me. I have relearned how to feel. I have discovered that I can control how I think.

Every day I am mastering how to process, to connect, to engage or to numb and to run away.

I get now that everything I seek is seeking me, it is all here for me. Everything I have ever had the notion to desire or want or not want for myself, others and the world is all here for me. I have come to see the misunderstanding, that common and widespread misunderstanding, which led me to believe that what I seek is out there in the world. I now see that the truth is not out there, it is inside of each of us.

When we are just starting out life is a mystery. Our monomyth begins with a departure, followed by some kind of initiation and a return. Each one of us is the hero in our own story. We are a riddle to figure out and the journey of discovery is laid out in front of us. We do not know how much we have to learn and eagerly we go out and consume experience and knowledge.

In the beginning everything is a mystery and with beginners' eyes we revel in it. Then we start to learn, we collect evidence. We think that we have it all figured out. We have experience under our belts, we have read the books, been to the seminars and bought the merchandise. We believe we are Masters; we have made it to enlightenment.

But, this is only the beginning.

'IT'S NOT WHAT YOU LOOK AT THAT MATTERS, IT'S WHAT YOU SEE.'
– HENRY DAVID THOREAUX

On the other side of mastery, with eyes anew, it all once again becomes a mystery to revel in. For me now, every day is a chance to step into my vulnerability further. I have found that by accepting the misfit, I have been able to let the angst go. I have found that it's only by embracing my fear, the uncertainty, my crazy-insanity, my fat, my un-lovableness, that I have become able to see my beauty and how loveable I truly am.

With every step into my own vulnerability I find more strength, more connection, freedom, adventure and love. I decided to share my story because it is my hope that you will identify with some of it and see the universality of the growth that we share. My story isn't one so far from yours, it isn't one that happened to someone in a far off land – I'm no wealthier, or skinnier, or cleverer, or less crazy and fucked up than you. If it is possible for me to find my way, then it is possible for you too. Every single one of us can experience connection, belonging and fulfilment. (I know this because if I can stop smoking once and for all, using my values and principles, it is ALL possible!)

For years now I have been fascinated by the psychospiritual journey I have witnessed so many people undertake and I invite you to look closer at where you are on yours. I found that mine has closely followed that of The Heroine's journey[75] but yours might be more like that of The Hero's journey[76] and it might be as unique as you are. You will probably have many of these journeys in your lifetime. Wherever you are right now, whether your landscape is littered with trials or ogres or dragons, whether you are on your descent or return. Whatever is next for you, I know that freedom, adventure, duty and love or whatever you value and hold dear is out there seeking you too.

The word Entrepreneur comes from the French word *entreprendre*, which means to undertake – and so my dear Maven in the making – undertake to live your life moment by moment, wild and true and full of heart!

ON PURPOSE, WITH PURPOSE, XOXO EBONIE

---

75. *The Heroine's Journey* – Maureen Murdock, a Jungian-oriented American psychotherapist, found that her female clients went on a slightly different variation of the traditional Hero's journey:

76. *The Hero's Journey* – originally introduced by Joseph Campbell in *The Hero with a Thousand Faces* (1949), Adapted by many over time, with the most recently used and acclaimed being by Christopher Vogler

FROM ARGH TO AHHH

The next step in the journey for me was to relax into being me. To surrender into life and let go of the tension of who I thought I should be.[77]

> TENSION IS WHO YOU THINK YOU SHOULD
> BE, RELAXATION IS WHO YOU ARE.
> — CHINESE PROVERB

I refined and distilled everything I had learned and I came up with eight essential steps. This is a cycle, a progression; it provides a way of thinking and tools for life that you can carry with you and utilise wherever you are and wherever you go.

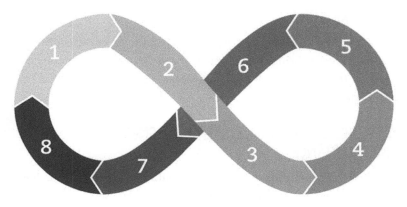

---

77. Which is still an ongoing practice, much like going to the gym – it is not a one-time thing to build a muscle, but something I practise with regularity.

I now refer to them as principles rather than steps, but the first time round it's more useful to use them consecutively in a more masculine, linear fashion. As you become more familiar with them you can pick and choose which principle you want to work on in a more feminine, fluid way:

PRINCIPLE I: AWARENESS. STEP I: FROM NUMBNESS TO AWARENESS.

The first step is moving from a place of numbness to a place of awareness. Awareness means doing a reality check, looking at and facing the facts. The facts, not the emotion or the story or the desire. The truth is that I was not seeing the truth, but rather a skewed version of reality. It was time to get clear on the rules. You have probably figured out by now that I am not one for 'the' rules. I like to question them, and I encourage you to do the same, but the rules I am talking about here are *your* rules, and these aren't really rules, they are values. They are the filters through which you view the world and they will be the filters through which you make decisions and prioritise.

PRINCIPLE 2: ASPIRATION. STEP 2: FROM APATHY TO ASPIRATION.

The second step is moving from a place of Apathy to a place of Aspiration. Aspiration means being clear about what you desire, how ambitious you are, what the objective is. It is about goal setting but more than that, it is about fulfilment.

PRINCIPLE 3: ACCEPTANCE. STEP 3: JUDGMENT AND ACCEPTANCE.

The third step is finding a way to accept all of who we are - the light and the shadow, the bits we are proud of and the bits we're ashamed of. I had to make friends with ALL of who I am. I had to fall in love with my judgmental, crazy, bossy victim before I could truly accept and let go of my wounds. It is also about accepting that which you cannot change, identifying what you can and discerning appropriately.

PRINCIPLE 4: ACTION. STEP 4: FROM INERTIA TO ACTION.

The fourth step is about actually taking action, getting things done. Once you have made it this far you are ready to make inspired choices and take action. Sometimes this will be about *being* over *doing*. Sometimes less is more, sometimes thinking or resting is an action.

PRINCIPLE 5: ACCOUNTABILITY. STEP 5: FROM BLAME TO ACCOUNTABILTY.

The fifth step is all about opting out of the drama and understanding that you are accountable for yourself. It's no one else's fault. When all those excuses and limiting beliefs about why you can't be, do, or have the life you want for yourself come up – and they will – it's time to become self-responsible and ask for help and support when you need it. This step is about reframing failure as feedback and taking stock of the information coming back at you.

You are a grown-ass adult – and that means being self-responsible.

I had to learn how to be *Kindly responsible* and *Lovingly encouraging*. You can too. This is about learning how to and actually mothering or father-ing yourself. Setting your own boundaries and loving yourself with good, kind, loving discipline.

PRINCIPLE 6: ACKNOWLEDGEMENT. STEP 6: FROM IGNOR-ANCE TO AKNOWLEDGEMENT.

The sixth step is first and foremost about Self Love.

Looking externally for love and acknowledgement doesn't work. You won't hear it or believe it until you believe it for yourself about yourself. The more you look externally for love, recognition, kudos and reward, the less you will FEEL them. You must delve inside as deep as you are extending outside. The more you want by way of love, recognition and reward, the more you must be able to do this for yourself and for others.

The truth is that the more you love your decisions, the less you need others to love them. The more you are able to define your self-worth by the measure you have of yourself, the more confident and complete you will feel. When you know your own worth, no one can make you feel worthless. When you know your own worth you will expect others to treat you a certain way and there will be no exceptions.

It only works when you are first able to treat yourself this way!

PRINCIPLE 7: APPRECIATION. STEP 7: FROM CRITICISM TO APPRECIATION.

The seventh step is about cultivating an attitude of gratitude. Whilst you believe that you will be happy when XXX, you are constantly striving and living in the future and missing out on today. The truth is that when you are able to appreciate what you have now, you become happy. Happiness is a feeling of progression and a series of recognised moments. There isn't really a trick to happiness; it can be found in any moment that we APPRECIATE. Learning to take stock and appreciate what we have is a skill, and it *can* be learned.

Once your basic needs are met, once you can take care of the first four stages of Maslow's famous hierarchy of needs,[78] then the motivation for self-actualisation begins. Tony Robbins calls those first four needs 'basic human needs' and he claims that the other two (Growth and Contribution) are 'needs of the spirit'. Answering the needs of the spirit, to me, means living on purpose with purpose.

> 'PURPOSE IS AN EMOTION WITHIN YOURSELF
> THAT YOU GENERATE AND GIVE AWAY.'
> – MASTIN KIPP

---

78. Maslow stated that people are motivated to achieve certain needs. When one need is fulfilled a person seeks to fulfil the next one, and so on. The earliest and most widespread version of Maslow's *hierarchy of needs* includes five motivational needs, often depicted as hierarchical levels within a pyramid.

I love the way Mastin is able to articulate and define so many of the words that can be difficult to have a shared understanding of. For me, purpose is also the attitude that you bring to life, it is about leaning into life's adventurous twists and turns and encouraging everyone you meet to reconnect with the wisdom we all carry within.

I believe that it is our responsibility to shine, to bring our gifts to the world, and to encourage others to do the same.

Which is where the eighth principle comes in…

PRINCIPLE 8: AD INFINITUM. STEP 8: FROM APPRECIATION BACK ROUND TO AWARENESS.

This eighth step is about making a commitment to continue to remain aware. It leads back into the first principle of Awareness. As you evolve, you can pick and chose for yourself which principle, and which set of tools, is most appropriate.

In the workbook that follows you have an opportunity to work through these eight steps for yourself. I have given you taster exercises and tools for you to try on your own, with a friend or partner – or indeed with me.[79]

---

79. *'Misfit to Maven in 80 Days'*, my signature programme, goes into more depth and offers the opportunity to work with me on this material.

MORE

My first word was 'more'.

MORE. I do still, and will probably always, want more. There have been many times in my life though when I have been ashamed of my desire for more. There have also been times when *more* was just too overwhelming for words.

Today, I'm ready for more, the idea of more excites me – I have finally built my container, my vessel, my capacity large enough for the *more* that I have and I continue to grow it so that I might always be able to be in receipt of more.

My dream is for more for you too. My desire for you is that you grow your infinite insides so large that you have the capacity to receive and keep and grow everything that you yearn for.

What is next? What more is there?

Well, my journey is ongoing too. My goals continue to change. My capacity for intimacy and real relationships grows daily. The quality of my life is directly related to my relationship with uncertainty and so is yours.

I have a vision of a community. Of a group of people who interact and support each other in being unique and trusting themselves. Please come and connect with me. Head over to *www.facebook.com/groups/misfitentrepreneurs* to join in.

Share your actions, stay accountable.

The Workbook

FROM ARGH TO AHHH!

1. AWARENESS
2. ASPIRATION
3. ACCEPTANCE
4. ACTION
5. ACCOUNTABILITY
6. ACKNOWLEDGEMENT
7. APPRECIATION
8. AD INFINITUM

STEP 1: FROM NUMBNESS TO AWARENESS

NUMBNESS: DEPRIVED OF THE POWER TO FEEL OR MOVE NORMALLY, EMOTIONALLY UNRESPONSIVE; INDIFFERENT.

In this day and age, when everything is on show, where we all want to be the best versions of ourselves, it can feel like no one wants to hear anything other than good news and positivity. There is a lot to be said for optimism, don't get me wrong, but we live in a culture that promotes numbing. Everyone has a drug of choice. Alcohol. Food. Work. Exercise. Sex. Each, used to produce feelings of euphoria or to stop feeling something, has the same effect.

Numbing how we are really feeling. Initially to remove stress, or to stop the pain, or anger or sadness or grief, but eventually numbing the good feelings too.

You can't have it both ways, if you are going to numb your feelings, over time you will numb them all.

- *How many times have you sat in front of the TV eating a meal you are not really tasting?*

- *How many times have you been asked by your partner or friend 'How are you?' and said 'Fine' or 'Good'. But not really thought about it, checked in, or meant it?*

- *How many times have you taken money out of an ATM without looking at your balance, because if you don't look you won't know?*

- *How many times have you gone to the gym or yoga and refused to feel your feelings, preferring instead to sweat them out and induce an endorphin high?*

- *How many times have you eaten bread or potato chips without tasting them until that carb coma kicks in and nothing matters anymore?*

AWARENESS: NOTICING OR REALISING SOMETHING. HAVING COGNIZANCE.

When you read this are you thinking, 'shit, that's me'? Is this a completely new thought? Or one you have been aware of for a while?

- *How aware are you?*

- *How much cognizance are you exercising in your life?*

- *Are you sleepwalking through your life, coasting from Friday to Friday?*

- *Are you living a life on purpose? So very on purpose that you haven't yet hit all the targets you set for yourself and deep down know that you are heading for burnout and breakdown?*

In order to know who you are, where you are, what is or isn't working, what you do or do not want, and how you are going to get what you want, you have to do a reality check.

You have to know the facts. Not the story or the assumptions, but the facts. Then separately, afterwards, you can work out how you feel about it; the emotions that you have attached to the facts. After that you can then look at the evidence that you have to support the stories that you have been, or are still telling yourself. And then, only then, can you work out where to go from where you are. BUT, first up, you need to know the facts.

REALITY CHECK. HERE AND NOW.

You have to know where you are now before you decide where you are going.

Research[80] shows that the most successful people share a common trait of heightened self-awareness. They recognise the situations that will make them successful, and this makes it easy for them to find ways of achieving objectives that fit their behavioural style.

They also understand their limitations and where they are not effective, and this helps them understand where not to go or how not to be as well. Those who understand their natural behavioural preferences are far more likely to pursue the right opportunities, in the right way, at the right time, and get the results they desire. The problem is that we are comparing our worst selves to everybody else's best selves. Or we have not really looked at who we are now, but have an out-dated assumed identity from our childhood or teens, with matching behavioural patterns that no longer serve us.

Nearly everyone I have ever met believes the lie I am about to share with you. Every adult and a fair amount of teens and children believe this:

LIE: NO ONE WANTS TO HEAR THE BAD STUFF

How sad is that? We are all walking around with shadows and truths, feelings and insecurities buried deep, hoping that they'll go away on their own. No one wants to hear the 'bad' stuff.

Is that true?

NO!

---

80. There have been many scholarly articles written on the subject as a result of Daniel Goleman's book *Emotional Intelligence* (1975)

TRUTH: YOUR VULNERABILITY IS WHAT MAKES YOU ATTRACTIVE

I want you to think about the last time some brave or desperate soul shared something that made them feel vulnerable with you. Afterwards, did you feel more or less connected to them? Did you respect them more or less?

Here is the thing. I haven't shared my story – all of my deepest, darkest secrets – with you for shits and giggles. I have done so to illustrate what happens when we believe that no one wants to hear the bad stuff. Including ourselves. It slows us down. It stops us feeling joy. It stops us from living with vitality.

The receptors we have for feeling happiness and love and belonging are the exact same ones we have for feeling shame, sadness, anger and guilt. If we numb one set of feelings, we numb them all. Finding ways to block out feelings or to control ourselves is all the same, it's numbing vulnerability.

'VULNERABILITY IS NOT WEAKNESS. I DEFINE VULNERABILITY AS EMOTIONAL RISK, EXPOSURE, UNCERTAINTY – NUMBING VULNERABILITY IS ESPECIALLY DEBILITATING BECAUSE IT DOESN'T JUST DEADEN THE PAIN OF OUR DIFFICULT EXPERIENCES; NUMBING VULNERABILITY ALSO DULLS OUR EXPERIENCES OF LOVE, JOY, BELONGING, CREATIVITY, AND EMPATHY. WE CAN'T SELECTIVELY NUMB EMOTION. NUMB THE DARK AND YOU NUMB THE LIGHT.'
– BRENE BROWN.[81]

The process of 'numbness to awareness' happens when you really feel a feeling and choose to stay with it. Most often it happens when we have pushed or numbed so much that the feelings explode all over the place. Often described as 'rock bottom', 'dark night of the soul' or, more positively, an 'awakening', it can be BIG and involve being checked into a clinic. It can also be a quiet and tearful MOMENT. It can be the moment you catch

---

81. *Daring Greatly*, p137.

yourself losing it at a child, or it can be when you simply want something else more than what you have right now.

It's when you finally realise that what you resist, persists. You catch yourself shouting out loud or in your head: 'OH!' or 'ENOUGH!!'

The point is: it's also a decision. There is a moment when you decide that you want to be different more than you want to stay the same. Once you have gotten there, you are ready. You can do this. I promise.

EXERCISES: FROM NUMBNESS TO AWARENESS

So, are you ready to do some work?

EXERCISE I: DEFINING YOUR VALUES

Your values are the things that you believe are important in the way that you live and work. They (should) determine your priorities, and, deep down, they're probably the measures you use to tell if your life is turning out the way you want it to.

When the things that you do and the way you behave match your values, life is usually good – you're satisfied and content. But when these don't align with your values, that's when things feel... *wrong*.

Incongruence of belief and behaviour can be a real source of unhappiness or confusion.

Values exist, whether you recognise them or not. Sometimes we have outdated values or beliefs that conflict with our new-found values. Life can be much easier when we acknowledge our values – and when we make plans and decisions that honour them.

Identifying and understanding our values is a challenging and important exercise.

Your values are a central part of who you are – and of who you want to be. By becoming more aware of these important factors in your life, you can then use them as a guide to make the best choice in any situation. Some of life's decisions are really about determining what you value most. When many options seem reasonable, it's helpful and comforting to rely on your values – and use them as a strong guiding force to point you in the right direction.

If you value family, but you have to work 70-hour weeks in your job, you feel internal stress and conflict. If you value freedom, but you are told what to wear and your every move is micromanaged, you will feel internal rage and resentment.

In these types of situations – and many, many more – understanding your values can really help.

When you know your own values, you can use them to make decisions about how to live your life, and you can answer questions like these:

- *Should I start my own business?*
- *Should I compromise, or be firm with my position?*
- *Should I follow tradition, or travel down a new path?*
- *Do I want to say 'yes' or 'no' to this?*

Values are usually fairly consistent and yet they don't have strict limits or boundaries. As you move through life, your values may change. For example, when you start your career, success – measured by money and status – might be a top priority. But after you have a family, work-life balance may be what you value more. As your definition of success changes, so do your values.

Many of the people I work with have had a life-altering event happen and are feeling confusion because there has been a value shift. Maybe they recently became a parent, or turned 30 or 40 or 50. Maybe they sold a company, or got a pet. Maybe they sold their home and decided to be a full-time digital nomad. When life stuff changes, so too do your values. This is why keeping in touch with your values is a life-long exercise;

although your core values are set very young and will essentially stay the same, the order in which you prioritise them and the way in which you choose to meet them will change. By continuously revisiting this exercise you can stay on track and make sure you are living in line with your own values. As you go through the exercise below, bear in mind that values that were important in the past may not be relevant now.

Taking the time to understand the real priorities in your life will mean that you are able to determine the best direction for you and your life goals!

So, finding somewhere comfy and quiet, perhaps with a cuppa and a notepad, make this time your time, sacred time. This is you honouring and being kind to you. Throughout this workbook, gift yourself the time and space to work on these exercises without distraction.

Look back on your life – identify when you felt really good, and really confident that you were making good choices. Identify your peak experiences. We want to determine what made them memorable and how you were feeling in each one. *Find examples from both your career and personal life to ensure your values are all-encompassing and come up with three or four stories for each:*

1. *Identify the times when you were happiest:*

   What were you doing?

   _____

   Were you with other people? Who?

   _____

   What other factors contributed to your happiness?

   _____

   _____

_____

_____

_____

2. **Identify the times when you were most proud:**

   Why were you proud?

   _____

   Did other people share your pride? Who?

   _____

   What other factors contributed to your feelings of pride?

   _____

   _____

   _____

   _____

3. **Identify the times when you were most fulfilled and satisfied:**

   What need or desire was fulfilled?

   _____

   How and why did the experience give your life meaning?

   _____

   What other factors contributed to your feelings of fulfilment?

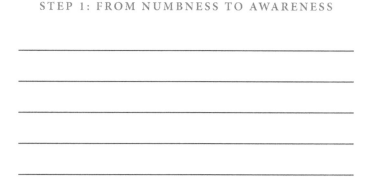

It is likely that The Six Human Needs[82] will come up for you whilst you are remembering. Most people have an issue or a limiting belief about one or more of these, you are not weird, and we will come back to this. For now, just know that you need to be honouring all of them in your life. *The memories you identify should and will cover all six:*

1. *Certainty*

2. *Uncertainty / Variety*

3. *Significance*

4. *Love / Connection*

5. *Growth*

6. *Contribution*

4. ***Collate a list of your top values, based on your experiences of happiness, pride, and fulfillment:***

Why is each experience truly important and memorable? As you remember write down the describing words you use, or if you are doing this with someone else, have the other person write down the key words while you tell the story. Make a note of any 'feeling' words that come into your mind as you remember or share.

---

82. I refer to the six human needs throughout the book and in my work A LOT! They determine what and why we do what we do. Find out more here: *http://training.tonyrobbins.com/the-6-human-needs-why-we-do-what-we-do/*. Mastin Kipp also covers them in detail and uses them in his work.

_____

_____

_____

_____

_____

As you speak or think you will find that you repeat the same words often. These are your values. Find at least 10, ideally 15.

The next step is to work through them and see if any naturally combine. For instance, if you value new experience, fun, and adventure you might roll those all into 'adventure.' These words don't have to make sense to anyone else and they don't have to be 'real' words. One of my client's words is 'bestness' and another has a gesture for which the most accurate word-form description we have come up with is 'essenceful'. I cannot stress how important it is for you to find *your* words, it's about a feeling that you get or a state the word induces in you. One client uses 'treacle-tart' as one of her words and another shines when I remind her of her 'glitter'. These are for you, and what is important is reminding you and linking to the feeling that you felt in these peak experience moments.

5. **Prioritise your top values**

This step is probably the most difficult, because you'll have to look deep inside yourself. It's also the most important step, because, when making a decision, you'll have to choose between solutions that may satisfy different values.

You have got time.

You don't need to rush.

Listen to your gut.

There is no wrong answer.

Work your way through the list and compare one with the next asking:

- 'If I could satisfy only one of these, which would I choose?'
- Work through the list comparing each value with each other value, rolling words into one another where appropriate, until your list is much shorter and in the correct order.

Some coaches will get you to keep them all.

I get you to distil it down to your core three.

1. _____

2. _____

3. _____

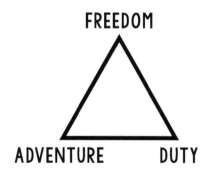

FREEDOM

ADVENTURE   **DUTY**

Mine are FREEDOM, ADVENTURE and DUTY – that means that I have created a filter through which to view the world. My very own filter. Yours will be unique to you. When we look through our one personal peak-experience filter at our day, or at an opportunity or threat, when we ask 'how can I use my values to support me?' or, 'what would I do if I was honouring my values?', it becomes much easier to say yes or no.

Mark in yours here.

Take your words and make your own little triad filter.

When you are clear on your values, 'should's disappear and in their place is a clear strategy for making an empowered choice. Raising awareness of your self, what governs and motivates you, is an empowering understanding.

6. *Reaffirm your values:*

   Looking at your triad of values:

   - Do these values make you feel good about yourself?
   - Does this look like your list or triangle?
   - Are you proud of your top three values?
   - Would you be comfortable and proud to tell your values to people you respect and admire?

7. *Measure the extent to which your values are currently being met:*

   Give each of your values a score from 1–10 indicating the extent to which you are honouring these values in your life right now.

   If you are scoring less than 7, you might want to make some goals or get some coaching.

'BE SURE THAT YOUR LADDER OF SUCCESS IS
LEANING AGAINST THE RIGHT BUILDING.'
— STEVEN COVEY

A WORD ON OPERATIONAL VERSUS ASPIRATIONAL VALUES

A lot of us build and build and plod on through life, adding to what we have and creating a future, without necessarily understanding what we are building that future on, or for.

Steven Covey's words are a great way of thinking about your values and your goals. If you can work out your values, your rules, then building on that foundation is always going to create something meaningful for you.

It is also really important to acknowledge the difference between operational, or practised, values and aspirational values. Aspirational values are the ones you aspire to, that you want to do, be, think and feel, the ones you believe are right, but which you may not necessarily on a day-to-day basis practise or embody. If you scored below a 7 then it's likely that the values you have recognised are currently aspirational rather than operational values.

Brene Brown explains that between our aspirational values and our practised values is what she calls 'the disengagement divide,'[83] she talks about the power of aligned values, in the family, in the workplace, and everywhere that has a culture. I say, starting with yourself is a bloody good place to start.

Becoming aware, noticing what was important to you once, is important to you now and checking in every now and then to see if you are compromising your values, is so incredibly important. If you do nothing else in this book, do this. Become aware of what is really important to you underneath everything.[84]

When you check in with yourself, you might find that you have compromised on your values. That's OK. You are not alone. There is a logical

---

83. Brene Brown, *Daring Greatly,* pg 177 (Mind the Gap).
84. If this isn't clear to you or you need help with this exercise, check out my video on *www.misfit2maven.com/bonuses*

explanation for it. You, like everyone else, probably have conflicting values or beliefs about those values. For example maybe you found that FREEDOM was one of your values, in your triad even. You might then be wondering why you are staying in a job that makes you feel trapped or un-free. You feel the ARGH of the incongruence but you're not sure why. Well, it might be that your operational value of SAFETY is trumping your aspirational value FREEDOM in real, everyday life.

Please do not judge yourself for these decisions, just becoming aware and being clearer on why you have made or are making the choices that you are making will empower you. As your emotional intelligence and awareness grows so too will your ability to step out of your comfort zone and make some changes. Be gentle and forgiving of what you are uncovering about yourself.

Our beliefs about ourselves and how the world works heavily govern the decisions we make, and our happiness or perceived lack of happiness. Years of numbing may mean that who you really are and what you are discovering about yourself is all very surprising.

Values can and probably will change after life-altering events. Having a child, getting married, buying a house, starting a company[85] – all these changes shift the goal posts and re-order the priorities we have in our lives.

Plus, we all have some conflicting values and beliefs.

Growing up with all sorts of important 'truths' being flung at us, by our parents, our role models, our peers, the media, religion, experience, means we end up with a bag of mixed messages. It is totally understandable that we are pretty good at forming an opinion and then sticking to it forever without questioning if it still holds true for us. Most of us never take the time to explore whether this new 'rule' contradicts any earlier ones. Most of us decide 'the rules' about life very early on and then never re-evaluate the status quo.

Like a lot of people, I held conflicting beliefs about work and money for a long time. I was brought up to value hard work, I believed that in order

---

85. This list is not limited to the things I have mentioned…

for my work to be valued I had to work hard for my money. I also believe that we all have some unique gift to offer the world and if you make that your job, you'll never work a day in your life.... Can you see the issue?

Here is the thing, without realising that both of these messages were running in my mind, I 'gave away' my gift to the world and struggled hard to earn money doing something else. It was only when I made the connection, and then made a choice to change the belief, that I was able to change my behaviour.

Working with a coach, a buddy or alone can help you to identify, challenge, change, transform, adjust and develop your beliefs.

A belief is what you perceive to be your reality. A conviction, right or wrong, of which you feel certain. A fundamental view of life. A guiding principle. Our beliefs are stories that we tell ourselves and stories that others have told us about what we can and can't do in life. They come from our peers, tradition, family, friends, culture, experience and religion.

These stories can take us closer to or further away from our goals and that all-important sense of fulfilment or AHHH.

The beliefs that you hold are either empowering or limiting. It isn't a question of one belief being right or wrong. Your mindset and your ways of thinking either help you, or hold you back. Your beliefs become your reality. Whether your belief is a way of thinking that will help you achieve your goals or not, you will always find evidence to support your belief, and to have it become your reality.

We humans have an average of 50,000–80,000 thoughts per day[86] and according to some research, as many as 98% of them are exactly the same as we had the day before. Talk about creatures of habit! Even more significant, 75–80% of our thoughts are negative. This is because of the human brain's negativity bias.[87] It is important because of the mind/

---

86. According to the National Science Foundation of America, *http://www.mind-sets.com/html/mindset/thoughts.htm.*

87. Negativity bias is a psychological phenomenon by which humans have a greater recall of unpleasant memories compared with positive memories. Useful in our caveman days when threats were greater than they are now but arguably less so today. According to Charlie Munger there are 25 cognitive biases that affect our judgments. *http://25cognitivebiases.com/*

body connection (psychoneuroimmunology).[88] You know when you have spent the day doing something physically demanding, and at the end of the day you're tired physically AND it's hard to think clearly? That. Similarly, if you've been using your mind doing mentally strenuous work all day, you're likely to also feel the effects physically, too. Negative thoughts are particularly draining. Thoughts containing words like 'never', 'should', and 'can't', complaints, whining or thoughts that diminish our own or another's sense of self-worth, deplete the body by producing corresponding chemicals that weaken the physiology. So, it is no wonder that if you spend the day mentally berating yourself you feel exhausted and weak at the end of the day.

The good news is, that we can change our thoughts. By changing your thoughts you will have more energy, more vibrancy and more life force! We'll come back to how you can change them later. I want to share with you as many tools as I can to help you become more mindful, and empower yourself through your thoughts and actions.

Let's first continue with building awareness.

---

88. Psychoneuroimmunology (PNI) is the study of the interaction between psychological processes and the nervous and immune systems of the human body. PNI takes an interdisciplinary approach, incorporating psychology, neuroscience, immunology, physiology, genetics, pharmacology, molecular biology, psychiatry, behavioural medicine, infectious diseases, endocrinology, and rheumatology. The main interests of PNI are the interactions between the nervous and immune systems and the relationships between mental processes and health.

EXERCISE 2: I AM

The words I AM are very important and very powerful. They can be used to empower and affirm a more conscious and expanded notion of ourselves or they can limit our beliefs and consequently our behaviour and actions. The words we put after them have tremendous power over us. When we use the words, 'I am...', we are telling ourselves who we believe ourselves to be. With these two words we deliver a pronouncement to ourselves and the world about what to expect from us, what we are capable of, how much success, money, love and happiness we will allow ourselves to have.

I invite you to look at how you are currently 'I am-ing'.

If you say, 'I am stupid', 'I am bad', 'I am no good at _____ (fill in the blank)', or 'I am inept/powerless/undeserving/a failure', you are affirming and investing belief in a limiting and stressful idea about yourself. Doing so leads to behaving in ways that will lead to the very outcome you are 'owning' with the pronouncement, 'I am.'

With the words 'I am' you formulate and take possession of a definition of yourself.

It starts in childhood when we introduce ourselves, 'I am Ebonie', and continues from there: Every day we make assertions about who we are. Giving life to our identity through thought, word, and then behaviour.

We use these two words to announce our status in life with such phrases as, 'I am poor (or rich), 'unloved (or loved),' 'unlovable (or lovable)'. Whether the mantra, 'I am' manifests for or against us depends on what follows those first two all-important words. This exercise will allow you to see how you are shaping your own identity.[89]

---

89. A really important one for me has been to rephrase 'I have fat', rather than 'I am fat'. In the same way that I have fingernails, not I am fingernails.

Don't think about it too hard, complete the sentences below with the first thing that comes to mind.

I am _____

I am _____

I am _____

I am _____

I am _____

I am _____

What did you learn?

EXERCISE 3: PIES AND GOING A LITTLE DEEPER

What is actually going on here?

Let's look at the PIES (Physical, Intellectual, Emotional, Spiritual).[90]

By breaking it down in this way we can process each piece individually. It can be really easy for us to blend all this information together and make something personal when it isn't or misunderstand the information we are processing by telling ourselves a story about it. I have a predisposition for being emotionally sensitive, and I can intellectualise and overthink things, so having this tool in my metaphorical tool kit enables me to process information with more accuracy. This is a resource you can use over and over and in all sorts of circumstances.

Don't spend hours agonising over this, just note down the answers that come to mind and if more questions come up, ask yourself those too.

---

90. This is a common way of categorising Maslow's hierarchy of needs to take a holistic approach to wellness, but is a useful model for analyzing complex issues too.

(P) Physical: **What are the data, the facts?**

_____

_____

_____

_____

_____

_____

(I) Intellectual: **What story are you telling yourself about these facts?**

_____

_____

_____

_____

_____

(E) Emotional: **How do you feel?**

_____

_____

_____

_____

_____

_____

(S) *Spiritual:* What do you want instead?

_____

_____

_____

_____

_____

_____

You can use PIES in all sorts of situations to help you divide up the situation into the facts and the story, the emotion and your desire.

Let's take it a step further now. Make a list of everything that is working and that you are pleased with or proud of.

- What are you proud of?

- What do you value?

- What goal or dream or target have you set yourself and achieved?

- When was the last time you felt excited?

- What are your natural gifts / abilities / passions?

- When do you feel at peace?

_____

_____

_____

_____

_____

_____

And let's not leave out the other stuff. Make a list of everything that is not working, about which you feel sad, angry, ashamed or resentful.

- What conversations are you not having?

- What situations are you avoiding?

- What is currently impossible | difficult | limiting you?

- What are you putting up with in your life?

- What or who threatens your peace?

- What is missing?

_____

_____

_____

_____

_____

_____

Don't worry, I'm not going to keep you focused on your negative feelings, but pushing what you don't want down or away does not make it actually dissipate, it just relegates it all to the shadows.

Where it will fester and grow.

Out there in the Universe there is a place of '*success*' and a place of '*not success*', a place of light, and of shadow, a place of what you are wanting and a place of not what you are wanting. Both exist. Fact. In order to *do*, *be* and *have* all of what makes us happy, we have to accept all of what *is*.

When you first start this journey from Numbness to Awareness there will be a lot of feelings. Feelings that you are not used to and that you have been supressing and ignoring. I want to make sure that I've said this, because you may feel a lot of 'bad' feelings surfacing and it may feel like it'll be this way forever. It may feel like this awareness lark is just not worth it. Listen to me and believe me when I say it is not going to be like that forever. I promise.

I speak to people all the time who say:

'Ebonie I am just so ***angry/sad/ashamed/fearful****ALL the time. This fucking sucks, it's not worth it, I'm going to just go and ***get drunk/watch tv/eat cake/have sex****.'

*delete as appropriate.

Here's the thing, you have been numbing these feelings, pushing them down or spacing out, for years and now there is a backlog to process. It will not be this way forever I promise!

BONUS EXERCISE: DEALING WITH FEELINGS

When you aren't used to feeling feelings they can be overwhelming! And let's face it, our society is not yet set up for you to call in to work, or say to most of your friends:

'I'm not coming because I am feeling sad and I really just need to sit with this feeling until it subsides.'

So, here is a technique for allowing you to feel those feelings and function without reaching for your numbing drug of choice. If you can take some time just to be with your feeling – whatever it is that has come up – and allow yourself to explore it with curiosity then do. Don't wallow in it, but with the eyes or receptors of an adventurer explore this new terrain. If it isn't appropriate then try the technique I am about to share with you. I have used many versions of The Sedona[91] method over the years, before I knew it by this name. You can use this process and series of questions in every area of your life where you would like to feel better.

---

91. *http://www.sedona.com/about-us.asp*

1. **Focus on the issue that you would like to feel better about, and then allow yourself to feel whatever you are feeling in this moment**

   This doesn't have to be a strong feeling. In fact, you can even check on how you feel about this exercise and what you want to get from it. Just welcome the feeling and allow it to *be* as fully or as best you can. This instruction may seem simplistic, but it needs to be. Most of us live in our thoughts, pictures, and stories about the past and the future, rather than being aware of how we actually feel in this moment. The only time that we can actually do anything about the way we feel (and, for that matter, about our businesses or our lives) is NOW. You don't need to wait for a feeling to be strong before you let it go.

   In fact, if you are feeling numb, flat, blank, cut off, or empty inside, those are feelings that can be let go of just as easily as the more recognisable ones. Simply do the best you can. The more you work with this process, the easier it will be for you to identify what you are feeling.

2. **Ask yourself one of the following three questions:**

   - *Could I let this feeling go?*
   - *Could I allow this feeling to be here?*
   - *Could I welcome this feeling?*

   'Yes' and 'no' are both acceptable answers. You will often let go even if you say 'no'. As best you can, answer the question that you choose with a minimum of thought, staying away from second-guessing yourself or getting into an internal debate about the merits of that action or its consequences.

   All the questions used in this process are deliberately simple. They are not important in and of themselves but are designed to point you to the experience of letting go. Go on to the next step no matter how you answered the first question.

3. **No matter which question you started with, ask yourself this simple question: Would I? In other words: Am I willing to let go?**

Again, stay away from debate as best you can. Also remember that you are always doing this process for yourself—for the purpose of gaining your own freedom and clarity. It doesn't matter whether the feeling is justified, long-standing, or right.

If the answer is 'no,' or if you are not sure, ask yourself: 'Would I rather have this feeling, or would I rather be free?'

Even if the answer is still 'no,' go on to Step 4.

4. **Ask yourself this simpler question: When?**

This is an invitation to just let it go NOW. You may find yourself easily letting go. Remember that letting go is a decision you can make any time you choose.

5. **Repeat the preceding four steps as often as needed until you feel free of that particular feeling.**

You will probably find yourself letting go a little more on each step of the process. The results at first may be quite subtle. Very quickly though, if you are persistent, the results will get more and more noticeable. You may find that you have layers of feelings about a particular topic. However, what you let go of is gone for good.

STEP 2: FROM APATHY TO ASPIRATION

APATHY: LACK OF INTEREST OR CONCERN, INDIFFERENCE, LACK OF EMOTION OR FEELING, PASSIVITY, DETACHMENT.

I believe that when feeling our feelings becomes too daunting we look to numb them, and whilst one way we can do that is with actions another way is to tune out. If life is operating on different frequencies and this universe is channel 1, then occasionally we all just tune out into the white noise between channels. Some of us do it by spacing out, and others by spacing in.

Many of us have become masters of disguise – we can continue to talk and function whilst actually being some place else entirely – and others personify apathy.

Sometimes this is as a result of trauma and sometimes it's just a learned comforting behaviour.

I have done both. I am capable of being a highly functioning person and looking like I am engaged while actually being absent. I learned how to engage with men and have sex or feign intimacy whilst not being present at all, I learned how to speak to a counsellor or therapist intelligently, looking like I was doing the work, whilst actually faking it. At other times in my life I have disappeared into a black hole of inertia and apathy where interaction with anyone was impossible. If you haven't experienced this for yourself you may well have seen a glazed look in someone's eye and intuitively known they weren't really here.

Step two is moving from that place to being 100% present. When we are 100% present, we have desire. It is a human law. We aspire.

ASPIRATION: STRONG DESIRE, LONGING, AIM, AMBITION, A GOAL OR DESIRED OBJECTIVE.

In this step, denial or indifference are overtaken by a desire to change what is.

Aspiration or determining a goal, an ambition or merely a desire is the second stage. Making the connection that there is some place you want to be that is not where you are right now means that you can move. Change can now occur because quite simply there is somewhere to go, and some energy to do so.

Each step has a lie and a truth.

LIE: PEOPLE WILL REJECT ME IF I HAVE EVERYTHING I WANT

Somehow we believe that we don't deserve what we want. We think that other people will judge us for achieving or having those things that we want. Even if those things are simply feelings.

TRUTH: THE MORE YOU HAVE, THE MORE YOU HAVE TO OFFER

In step one we looked at values. Couples often think they have the same values. Workplaces think that because they have a manifesto stating their values hanging on the wall, their employees all share the same values. *Friends often think their friendship is based on shared values.*

- *Are they, though?*
- *Were the meanings you gave to the words really quite personal to you?*
- *What if the interpretation of the language is different?*

- *What if the words themselves have shared meaning, but the level of importance differs?*

- *What if the beliefs that uphold the values are different?*

What if you and I both share the value of freedom, but to me freedom equals being a digital nomad and having no fixed abode whereas to you freedom means owning our house outright and not owing the bank money?

Can you see how important is it not just to recognise your own values and beliefs but also to be able to communicate them?

Here's the thing: I had so many beliefs that were holding me back from what I wanted and I was focusing on these beliefs and not what I wanted instead. What you think about, you bring about, so while I was focusing on being fat, on having to work hard for little return, on men who didn't value me and treated me like a sleeper and not a keeper, that was what I was getting. I believed that in order for my work to be valued I had to work hard for my money. I also believed that if I got the body I wanted I would turn into a *'mean girl'*. I also believed that rich people were stingy and cold-hearted. I also believed that people would reject me if I wasn't doing something for them and making them feel good about themselves – I believed that I needed to at all times be smart, kind and funny, but less so than the people I was trying to impress. I believed that if I was 100% myself I would be rejected. I believed that anyone who fell for my 'cool girl' act was stupid and I didn't want to be with anyone stupid – in relationships or business – so I rejected everyone who liked the false me I was projecting.

Exhausting just reading it, right?!

Does it sound like these beliefs were empowering or limiting me?

Beliefs are a feeling of certainty about what something means. Most of our beliefs are generalizations about our past, based on our interpretations of painful and pleasurable experiences. Most of us, at first at least, do not consciously decide what we're going to believe. Instead, our beliefs are often misinterpretations of past events.

Tony Robbins says:

> 'Think of an idea like a tabletop with no legs. Without any legs, the tabletop won't even stand up by itself. Belief, on the other hand, has legs. To believe something, you have references to support the idea—specific experiences that back up the belief. These are the legs that make your tabletop solid and that make you certain about your beliefs.'[92]

There are only two types of belief, ones that empowers and one that limits. Right at the beginning of this book I mentioned the RAS at the base of the brain. Its job is to collect evidence to support whatever belief you give it. If you believe you're extremely intelligent, you likely have a lot of references to back it up. Maybe you did well in school, people always tell you how smart you are, you catch onto things quickly, etc. You can find experiences to back up almost any belief. If you believe you are stupid instead, you will also find evidence to support that belief.

In 2007 I lost a substantial amount of weight. I dropped two dress sizes but I maintained the belief that I was fat and I truly believed that the shops were cutting their clothes bigger – that was my evidence. That is the power of belief. The evidence isn't always logical. The key is to make sure that you're consciously aware of the beliefs you're creating and the evidence you are basing them on. If they don't empower you, if they are in fact limiting you, and if you *want* to, you can change the belief. The process involves choosing a new belief and finding new evidence.

It's simple, but it's not easy. It requires some dedication.

You are worth it.

When you know your own worth, no one can make you feel worthless – your value is not determined by how many people like you, your value is determined by whether you like you. It sounds like a cliché, but doing the work on liking yourself first and foremost regardless of others is the key. When you have found and accepted all of who you are, then your tribe will find and accept you too. Like unto itself is drawn. Whilst you are

---

92.   *https://training.tonyrobbins.com/stop-your-limiting-beliefs-10-empowering-beliefs-that-will-change-your-life/.*

masquerading as someone else you are disguised from the very people you are seeking out.

STOP!

This is important. Now is the time to move from apathy to aspiration. It is the time to look at what you are building your life on instead of blindly plodding on through – creating a future without necessarily understanding what you are building that future on.

'Be sure that your ladder of success is leaning against the right building.'

Steven Covey's words are a great way of thinking about your values and your goals. You now have awareness of the foundations of your life (your values). Building on these foundations will always create something meaningful for you, as long as you watch your beliefs and are mindful of which values you are building on. Remember that there is a difference between your operational or practised values, and your aspirational values. Aspirational values are the ones you aspire to, that you want to do, be, think and feel, the ones you believe are right, but may not necessarily on a day-to-day basis practise or embody. Every day you have the chance to practise your aspirational values.

You now have a triad of three words. These words are the most important words you have. They remind you of what is important to you. Checking in with these every time you make a decision will let you know if you have compromised your values.

If you have compromised that's really OK. At the beginning it's hard. You are building a new neural pathway. There may be a conflict of values. There may be out-dated beliefs getting in the way.

It was only when I made the connection and then made a choice to change the belief that I was able to change my behaviour. Most of us have grown up living from the outside in, rather than the inside out. As a society we have a massive OUTSIDE-IN v INSIDE-OUT issue....

What do I mean by that?

I mean that we think, 'When I fix this thing OUT in the world (body, money, relationship) I will FEEL good.' But the truth is that unless you work on the inside you will not be able to really receive the things you want, and receiving them will not make the slightest difference to how you feel.

When you work on what is going on inside of you, and when you feel GOOD on the INSIDE, when everything on the outside shows up you will really be able to see, hear and feel it!!!

The model that most of us grew up with is an outside-in one:

HAVE	→	DO	→	BE
Perfect body	→	What impresses others	→	Happy
Possessions	→	One better than our peers	→	Successful
Power	→	What feeds the ego	→	Satisfied
Status	→	What makes us 'important'	→	Safe

On some level we all know that this model doesn't work. Focusing on having and doing as the way to being happy, successful and satisfied with life comes up short every time. When the model is turned around and becomes **BE → DO → HAVE** – when we let our life choices be an extension of our being – our true self comes out; this is living from the inside out.

Inside → Out:

BE	→	DO	→	HAVE
Authentic	→	Work that feeds mind & spirit	→	Life that satisfies us
Fearless	→	What you are passionate about	→	Heartfelt desires
Healthy	→	What takes care of your body	→	Mental & physical energy
Happy	→	What makes you feel proud	→	A sense of achievement

EXERCISES: FROM APATHY TO ASPIRATION

So, are you ready to do some work?

EXERCISE I: IDENTIFYING LIMITING BELIEFS

There are just two types of belief. You can have a belief that empowers you, or a belief that limits you. Think about it. Do your beliefs inspire and encourage you or do you also have beliefs that are holding you back?

Do you know which beliefs are limiting you from achieving your goals?

This exercise will help you appreciate to what extent your beliefs impact your goals.

All you need to do is complete the sentences. For the best results, take a moment to centre yourself. Take a few deep breaths in, and out. Make your breath fluid and audible to yourself, like a seashell.

Take your focus to your heart centre and visualise your heart glowing with a green light. If you want to you can chant internally or out loud YAM (pronounced 'yum'). Spend a minute or two and then when you are fully focused and present, begin. Using the other hand than the one you usually write with (so if you are right-handed, use your left) finish the sentences below. ***Don't think about it too much, just fill in the gaps with whatever comes to you.***

I should _____

I should _____

I should _____

I should _____

I should _____

I should _____

I must _____

I must _____

I must _____

I must _____

I must _____

I must _____

Now for each sentence, ask yourself: what would happen if I didn't?

_____

_____

_____

_____

_____

_____

Interesting, huh?

The next sentence completion will help you look at how your belief has a bearing on what you think you cannot do.

Again, just write the first thing that comes into your head.

I can't _____

I can't _____

I can't _____

I can't _____

I can't _____

I can't _____

Then ask yourself the question, what stops me?

_____

_____

_____

_____

_____

_____

What will you do with what you have learned?

_____

_____

_____

_____

_____

_____

What's the belief that you tell yourself over and over, which if it weren't there would free you to DO, BE or HAVE what you want?

_____

_____

_____

_____

_____

_____

What belief would you like instead?*

_____

_____

_____

_____

_____

_____

***NB:** If this doesn't just come from somewhere and you are making this up, don't make this new belief too far from where you are now, just rephrase it in the positive. I invite you to practice this new belief every day when you brush your teeth at night. Just try it on for size for 3 minutes a day.

Now that you have identified what limiting beliefs you have and for now have 'parked them' on a page – let's look at your aspirations.

EXERCISE 2: THE 'EXIT INTERVIEW'

Take yourself somewhere comfortable and when you are ready close your eyes. I want you to imagine yourself into the future.

I want you to imagine that you have reached the end of your life here on earth and are having an exit interview with your maker.

This interview is your opportunity to reflect upon the experience this incarnation has gifted you, what lessons have been learned?.

What has happened in your lifetime that you are proud of? What legacy are you leaving behind? What could have gone better? What would you do differently given your time again? What has happened because of your unique blend of you-ness?

Write down the story of your incredible life, the amazing things you've done, the fantastic things you've seen, the people you have touched and the changes you have made in your own and other people's lives.

_____

_____

_____

_____

_____

_____

_____

_____

_____

_____

Now that you have an idea of all the things that have to happen in your life in order for you to enter your exit interview with God feeling good about your life, let's talk about goal setting and what makes a good goal.

I often get asked about goal setting. For a lot of people the hardest part of living a life on purpose is actually working out what they want. Often people find it much easier to reel off all the things that they *don't* want, and while that is a great place to start, being clear on what you *do* want is even better. We have parked all your limiting beliefs, all the reasons why this couldn't possibly be your life – let's continue as if you knew you could have everything you want for yourself and for the world.

It's really important that your goals are set in positive language. This is because our subconscious brain cannot process negatives. If we say 'don't eat that' or 'don't smoke', our brain only hears 'eat that' or 'smoke'. The word 'don't' isn't processed. When we are focused on not being poor we are in fact focusing on the lack in our lives, so by changing it round you will find that more of what you actually want appears.

Here's the science bit… There is a small bunch of cells at the base of our brains (I know I have now mentioned it a few times – the RAS, or reticular activating system) which acts as a filter for everything our brains need to process. It gives more importance to the stuff that we're actively focusing on in each moment and basically goes about collecting evidence to support our beliefs — so if you say to yourself 'I can't do X, I can't do X', sure enough your incredibly clever brain will find evidence to support your belief. Where attention goes, energy flows and what we think about, is what we bring about – these aren't just woo-woo clichés, they are based on evidence.

If that isn't enough, when we frame things in the negative we actually stress ourselves out, producing debilitating neurochemicals. The power of negativity is astonishing. If you have never tried the rice experiment[93] then please do, or look into the work of Masaru Emoto and the power of

---

93. In this experiment, Dr Emoto placed portions of cooked rice into two containers. On one container he wrote 'thank you' and on the other 'you fool'. He then instructed school children to say the labels on the jars out loud everyday when they passed them by. After 30 days, the rice in the container with positive thoughts had barely changed, while the other was mouldy and rotten. You can try this at home and let me know what you find.

negativity.[94] Humans are about 60% water: how we speak to ourselves and carry ourselves affect the vibration of our water.

So when setting yourself goals remember the 4 Ps:

- *Positive*

- *Present*

- *Personal*

- *Possible*

Really good goals are phrased in POSITIVE language.

Great goals are also set in the PRESENT tense.

By saying 'I will...' you are subconsciously pushing and keeping the goal in the future.

'I am...' or 'I have...' are the best way to state your goals.

Get practice at saying them out loud. If you can't even **say** 'I am 'X'' then how will you ever **be** 'X'?[95]

Really good goals are also PERSONAL, by which I mean that they are **yours**, not your mum's, your partner's or society's. If your goal starts with 'I should...' then I'm guessing it's not really yours.

Anything starting with 'should' doesn't inspire action.

The best goals, the goals you will be motivated to achieve, are the goals that are in line with your values, and which make you smile when you think about them. They are INSPIRING....

Good goals are also POSSIBLE

By which I mean that they are something you have control over, and do not involve changing other people. By all means **dream big,** breaking down big dreams into smaller manageable steps is completely possible. No matter how big or small your goals are, though, they also need to be

---

94. *http://www.masaru-emoto.net/english/water-crystal.html*

95. By the same token, there is evidence to suggest that saying things you don't believe is more stressful on the brain, so making the statements incremental is useful. I have written about self talk and differing ways of reframing your beliefs here: *http://www.womenunlimitedworldwide.com/self-talk-yourself-to-success/*

MEASURABLE – if you don't know what it will look like when it's done, if you can't tell how you will measure success, then how will you know when you've got what you wanted?

I go on about this a lot, but painting a picture in your mind, or on paper with words, is a really important step. The more clearly you can describe what it is that you want, the easier it will be to move toward it.

Perhaps you are called to write what you want in words, or maybe recording yourself speak or making a vision board feels more inspiring to you. Whether you collect things that make you feel how it will feel, or make a playlist – you need to know what it will be like when you have gotten there.

Getting clear on your time frame is also really important. If you are anything like me, you want to achieve your goals yesterday, but here's the thing: the journey, the getting to the thing, is just as important, and can be just as rewarding, as the end result. Learning to set realistic time frames is all part of the learning curve. It will come with practice, and you might not be great at knowing how much you can achieve or by when at the beginning. You will learn, though. Actively rewarding yourself along the way will keep you motivated, and remembering that it's all just feedback (not intrinsically good or bad) will allow you to focus on where you are going positively rather than ending up back in a negative spiral. We'll cover more on this later in principle six, 'Acknowledgment'.

Being really clear on what it is that you want will make saying 'No' to things and people much easier. You will have to learn to say no to some stuff, because you only have 24 hours in a day and 7 days in a week just like everyone else, and I know you want to be a kind and helpful person, but you also need to look after your own needs and find a way to prioritise. You are your first priority. You cannot be kind or helpful if you are not taken care of.

Being really helpful but poor, unhealthy, unhappy and resentful is not what you are striving for, is it? Saying 'NO' is much easier when it's saying 'YES' to something else. You *can* have it all, but not at the same time.

Learning to be realistic, set boundaries and honour your own needs is a really important part of the journey to AHHH!

Here are some great questions to get you thinking about your goals:

- *How will achieving this goal benefit you, and/or those around you?*

- *What will happen if you don't achieve this goal?*

- *What impact does having or not having this goal have on you and on others?*

- *What is motivating you to achieve this goal?*

- *How challenging is this goal for you?*

- *What support or resources do you need to put in place for you to achieve this goal?*

EXERCISE 3: DEFINE THE GOAL

Write down or record your goals. Remember that if the word 'goal' turns you off, that's OK – what are your aspirations or desires and how will you measure them?

Current situation:

_____

_____

_____

_____

_____

_____

The impact the situation is having on your life:

_____

_____

_____

_____

_____

_____

_____

Desired state you would like to achieve:

_____

_____

_____

_____

_____

_____

_____

Earlier I encouraged you to dream HUGE, saying that we'd chunk it down into manageable pieces if necessary – let's do that.

By the same token, if you are looking at your goal and know that you are going to be able to achieve what you have written down in a month or two, this is your chance to go back and ask yourself 'What would be even better than that?!'

This is the bit where you get to check if these are the right goals for you.

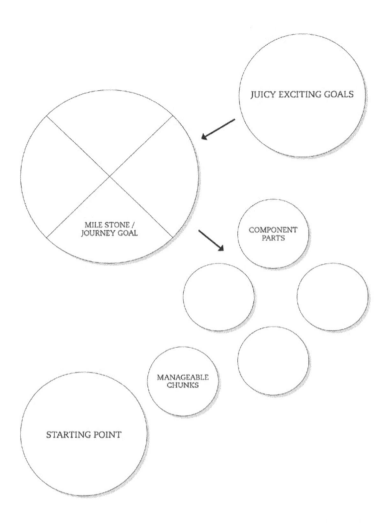

Setting the right-sized goals is important. The goals you have written down are your End Goals or JUICY EXCITING GOALS.

This goal or picture of 'success' is your INSPIRATION.

Along the way you will have Journey Goals or Milestones. These are where you will see growth and personal successes – these are what will keep you motivated.

Rather than looking at the enormity of that end goal, and being so panicked by it that you are frozen, the aim is always to get to the next journey goal.

The journey goal gets broken down into component parts, then manageable actions, and that is where you start.

When the goal is too big, we try and take action but don't because we are in our 'panic zone'. This is a place where we are terrified and the fear paralyses us. Conversely when we set targets that are too easy for us, we are in our 'comfort zone' – this is also problematic because we know we can do it, and because there is no challenge we don't bother. It's just not juicy enough.

Knowing this, look at your goals again. For each one, ask:

- *Is it believable?*

- *Is it the right size?*

- *Is it inspiring?*

- *What are the journey goals or milestones?*

- *What are the component parts?*

- *Do you need to adjust anything?*

Apathy is the result of confusion or being in your panic or comfort zone. If the goal is exciting and a stretch for you then you will stay motivated. Keeping your actions at the size that leaves you saying 'yes – I will do that' is what will keep you moving forward.

If you are still not able to move from apathy to aspiration then it may be that there are issues of self-esteem and debilitating limiting beliefs that need to be addressed. Coaching may be able to help, or NLP or CBT or another modality.

BONUS EXERCISE: THE NOW/FUTURE GAME

Once you know where you are going and you know where you are, you are ready to analyze the gap in between. Using my Now / Future model you can look at what milestones you want to pass along the way and also what assumptions have to prove true in order for you to get where you are headed. To get your free NOW / FUTURE game PDF, head to my website: *www.misfit2maven.com/bonuses*.

STEP 3: JUDGMENT AND ACCEPTANCE (DISCERNMENT)

JUDGMENT: THE EVALUATION OF EVIDENCE TO MAKE A DECISION. TO DISCERN. TO CRITICISE OR CONDEMN FROM A PLACE OF MORAL SUPERIORITY.

This is not about moving *from* Judgment *to* Acceptance. This step is slightly different. This step is about looking at both, becoming discerning. It's about exploring what judgments you are making, without judgment, and practising acceptance.

ACCEPTANCE: TO ASSENT TO THE REALITY OF A SITUATION, RECOGNISING A PROCESS OR CONDITION WITHOUT ATTEMPTING TO CHANGE IT, PROTEST, OR EXIT.

In human psychology, acceptance is a person's assent to the reality of a situation, recognising a process or condition without attempting to change it, protest, or exit. The concept of acceptance is close in meaning to 'acquiescence', derived from the Latin 'acquiēscere' (to find rest in). Acceptance is being really clear about what you do and do not have the power to change.

You have control over your thoughts, your attitude, your behaviour and your reactions.

That is it.

The situation may not be how you want it to be, but that does not leave you powerless. You have the power to choose your response to it. Understanding that whilst your goal and your ideas of success exist, so too does the lack of it. Placing judgment and ultimate importance and worth on 'getting what you want' over and above the alternative of 'not getting what you want' does not work. Accepting, and surrendering to the reality that both outcomes are possible, and becoming less attached to one certain outcome, embracing surrender instead, is scarier initially but much more powerful and a lot less ARGH-inducing in the long run.

Understanding, not just cognitively but *really* understanding in your body, soul and spirit, that which you have control over and that which is not yours to control is a huge part of life and the focus of this step. Acceptance, giving in to, letting go of, surrendering to uncertainty are also part of it.

Acceptance is not the same as resignation.

Understanding and accepting uncertainty, relinquishing the attempt to have control over those things that you have no control over, is a practice. It's something I have not fully mastered yet. Some days I get it, some days my need to control is HUGE! Even though I know that I have no control, I'm still there – metaphorically banging my fists against an immovable wall. So, although this is the third step in my eight steps to a life of AHHH it is also the one that is and will probably always be for me a daily practice. It is not a case of read the information, get the concept and you are done.

I wish it was sometimes, I really do!

All religions and spiritual paths talk of Acceptance in some form or another. Most talk of Mindfulness as a practice that can help. Mindfulness is now recognised as an inherent quality of human consciousness, a capacity that can be learned, empirically measured, and is free of religious, spiritual, or cultural beliefs.

But here's the underlying belief that trips us up:

LIE: THERE IS A RIGHT WAY AND A WRONG WAY...

Let's be clear, this is a LIE and it gets us all. Remember The Riddle, right back at the beginning of this book? Every single one of us has our very own rulebook but we've forgotten that the answers are inside us. We forget to remember that we have the answers to our own questions.

So many of us, especially creative self-employed people, feel like we are frauds; blagging our way through this life as a human being, terrified that we'll get caught out. Well I'm here to tell you that you are not alone. Imposter syndrome is a thing.[96]

TRUTH: THERE IS NO ONE SIZE FITS ALL!

The truth is that you do deserve all that you have achieved. The truth is that the less focused you are on the outcome, the more focused you are on the journey, the experiment, the experience – the more present you can be, the more real your experience will be.

This step in some ways is the trickiest one of all because I am not asking you to stop making judgments, rather to watch and be mindful of the judgments you are making. I am not asking you to resign yourself to believing that you have to accept that your life is the way it is right now. *Right now you might think that there is a certain way of doing things, which will equal certain results:*

- *If I eat fat, I will get fat.*

- *If I follow that formula for marketing my business I will make a six-figure salary.*

- *If I am agreeable and attractive (s)he will love me.*

- *If I do exactly what (s)he did I'll get the same results.*

- *If I drink green juice, go to yoga and only think good thoughts I'll be happy and enlightened...*

---

96. The term 'impostor syndrome' first appeared in an article written by Pauline R. Clance and Suzanne A. Imes in 1978 *http://www.paulineroseclance.com/pdf/ip_high_achieving_women.pdf*. More information can be found here: *http://paulineroseclance.com/impostor_phenomenon.html*

But the truth is that there is no one-size-fits-all approach to anything. This step is about learning to use your judgment to make decisions that are right for *you*. You must learn to listen to your 'gut' feeling. You may be thinking, 'but I am not an empath, I am not magic, I am not special in that way,' and whilst it may be true that *feeling* may not be your dominant sensory receiver, you HAVE been gifted with a gut feeling or an intuition. I have not met anyone yet who hasn't. You have been given a personal guidance system that knows what is right for you; the hard part is learning to listen and trusting yourself. Once you have spent time tuning into the whisper without judging harshly or unfairly, that whisper will grow. It may appear differently to you than it does it to me. For me it is always a feeling. For you it may be a voice or visualization.

As you practise this step you will begin to see that life is not so much black and white, just endless shades of grey.

Be kind to yourself.

> Eat like you love yourself.
> Move like you love yourself.
> Speak like
> you love yourself.
> Act like you love yourself.
>
> ———×———

Be kind to others.

Try not to judge others by your view of the world. Remember we all process the world differently. How each of us interprets a situation will be dependent on so many factors. Being mindful of this can make all the difference.

It's the main reason why I coach rather than mentor or advise. No matter how empathetic anyone is, they will never fully be able to view the world in the same way as someone else. Each of us has our very own blend of insecurities, vulnerabilities and neuroses. When someone assumes they understand it can make us defensive, which for the most part isn't conducive to great relationships, creativity or good thinking.

Listening, asking questions and trying to understand is GREAT! Telling someone what to do, making and sharing snap judgments, not so much. Sharing what worked for you, without expecting the other person to act on what you have shared, is beautiful.

Personally, I am incredibly stubborn and while that can be a great thing because I stick to my guns and I keep going when things tough it can also mean that I think I know the best way to do something, and I can forget that each of us are on our own journey, with our own lessons to learn. I can also look at how other people building their businesses or living their lives and judge and compare myself. (You too, huh?)

There are so many people out there telling us how to grow our businesses, how to market, find clients, fall in love, make a relationship work, take the next step. The truth is that what works for them may not work for you. Advice is dangerous. Don't get me wrong: learning new skills, asking people who have trodden the path you want to tread is a great thing to do. There is no need to reinvent the wheel, I advocate standing on the shoulders of giants – but no one knows what is best for you better than you. No one has the same world view, the same lens as you. So please don't take this as me saying that you shouldn't ask for help or learn from other people – PLEASE DO. But also remember to trust yourself and be as open minded as you can be.

This step is all about becoming mindful of the judgments you make, but not judging yourself for them. It's about becoming accepting of yourself and of others, accepting what is and is not controllable and embracing certain uncertainty.

If you are anything like me then you also judge yourself more harshly than you would another person. It is a practice of daily discipline to be kind to myself and to accept that which you are capable of. I am super, but not superhuman. I only have control over my thoughts, beliefs, behaviour and actions and not anything else, and so do you.

We all have the same 24 hours in a day and as I have said before, we can have it all – just not at the same time! *(Let's be clear about this, you can't enjoy it all at the same time anyway, and if you don't even have gratitude for what you do have, why do you think you'd be grateful for more?)*

Often when I am frustrated and believe that the world is against me, there is something else at play that I am not privy to. Some days the world and its mysterious ways are bigger than my to-do list and personal objectives. I have to remind myself that right now I may not be able to see the bigger picture and that the journey and its lessons and experiences are the reward – not the destination. It's all about awareness and mindfulness. It's about balancing the big and the small, the detail and the bigger picture, being patiently impatient.

Once I had accepted the idiosyncrasies of life I became able to celebrate what had previously baffled me. Once you are able to reframe life as being X AND Y, not X OR Y, then everything gets simpler. The world is an inclusive and abundant place by default rather that an exclusive place driven by lack. Really understanding this requires a paradigm shift, achieved by a change in many little beliefs.

So, we have looked a little at beliefs – the thoughts that you perceive to be your reality. Our beliefs are stories that we tell ourselves and stories that others have told us about what we can and can't do in life. These stories can take us closer to or further away from our goals.

The beliefs that you hold are either empowering or disempowering. It isn't a question of one belief being right or wrong. Your mindset and your ways of thinking either help you, or hold you back. Your beliefs become your reality. Whether your belief is a way of thinking that will help you achieve your goals or not, you will always find evidence to support your belief, and to have it become your reality.

In Step 1 we looked at how many thoughts you have a day and I told you that you can change the way that you think. Your brain searches for and finds the easiest and quickest thought pathway. Tony Buzan,[97] a leading expert in the field of discovering human potential, offers an excellent analogy. He describes the brain as a jungle – a huge neural jungle with billions and billions of potential connections and neural networks. The first time someone tries to make a new pathway in that jungle it is thick and dense

---

97. Tony Buzan is an English author and educational consultant. Buzan popularized the idea of mental literacy and a thinking technique called Mind Mapping, earlier used by the likes of Leonardo da Vinci.

and he or she has to battle their way through. The next time the path is slightly trodden and easier to find. After a dozen or so times, the path is flattened, clear, and anyone coming through the jungle will automatically use that path rather than go into the undergrowth. The new pathway eventually becomes automatic. At the same time, the old one which is now not being used becomes forgotten as the jungle grows up around it.

When I work with clients we find new beliefs that feel possible and then they work with them every day until the new path is trodden and the old one a weed-filled territory. I wish it were as simple as deciding to delete a mind file, as you would a file in your computer, but in my experience it requires a more mindful approach.

Mindfulness is no longer just a buzzword reserved for spiritualists. Over the last 40 years there has been scientific interest and investigation into the effects of mindfulness practice. Whilst it is great that mindfulness is now recognised, it can still be confusing.

'MINDFULNESS MEANS TO REMEMBER TO PAY ATTENTION TO WHAT IS OCCURRING IN ONE'S IMMEDIATE EXPERIENCE WITH CARE AND DISCERNMENT.'[98]

'A CAPACITY OF ATTENTION AND AWARENESS ORIENTED TO THE PRESENT MOMENT THAT VARIES IN DEGREE WITHIN AND BETWEEN INDIVIDUALS.'[99]

'PAYING ATTENTION IN A PARTICULAR WAY: ON PURPOSE, IN THE PRESENT MOMENT, AND NONJUDGMENTALLY.'[100]

'WAKING UP FROM A LIFE LIVED ON AUTOMATIC PILOT AND BASED IN HABITUAL RESPONDING.'[101]

---

98. Shauna Shapiro, PhD, a professor at Santa Clara University, a clinical psychologist, and internationally recognized expert in mindfulness. *http://www.scu.edu/ecp/faculty/counselingpsychology/sshapiro.cfm*

99. David S. Black, PhD, MPH, Founding Director of the Association for Mindfulness Research, offers a very thorough definition: *http://www.mindfulexperience.org/resources/brief_definition.pdf.*

100. Dr Jon Kabat J. Zinn, *Wherever You Go, There You Are: Mindfulness meditation in everyday life* New York: Hyperion Books (1994).

101. Dr D Siegel, *http://www.drdansiegel.com/about/biography/*

Even more than just paying attention and waking up from a life lived on autopilot, what I am talking about also includes coming to terms with the fact that you cannot change anyone else. Being realistic about what you have control over is a really big piece of Awareness. I know I'm repeating myself, but let's just get this really clear – *you have control over your thoughts, your attitude, your behaviour and your reactions.* That is it.

How many people or situations have you spent time and energy trying to change? It is like trying to make something fall upwards. Gravity is a law. So is this. You cannot change anything or anyone other than YOU.

You are not powerless though; you always have the power to choose your response.

For a long time I believed that this practice of acceptance and surrender meant letting go of my idealistic goals, or hours of meditating and becoming able to detach while still being present and not spacing out. It felt impossible. In fact it's less about letting go of the desire and more about letting go of the judgment placed on the achieving or not achieving of the desire. The cliché is that it is the journey and not the destination that is important, and like all good clichés it exists for a reason. When the lessons, the joys, the disappointments, the stories, ALL of the journey truly become as important as the outcome or reaching the destination, then we are living Acceptance. Then it doesn't matter if you reach the goal really – and let's be honest, the likelihood is that what you want will change as you progress anyway.

I get that it is easier said than done.

In relationships especially.

How often would you like someone else to change? Be honest…

Like I said, it is a practice. Something we can draw our awareness, our attention and our focus to everyday.

Formal meditation may be a way to do this, as might yoga, or dancing, or boxing, or walking in nature, painting, singing, dancing, tarot, gardening or even washing the dishes…

If you have not paid attention like this before, when you start becoming aware of the judgments you are making you might decide that you are a bad person. You are not. Judgments are not bad, Often they have kept us safe. I am not asking you to remove your judgments, just watch them.

If you decide that you want to create new beliefs, then new thoughts can be constructed, and you have the power to change your mind. The research that has been done into the effectiveness of building new neural pathways – neuroplasticity – evidences just how much power you actually do have over your thoughts.

Jeffrey M. Schwartz[102] has spent his career studying the structure and neuronal firing patterns of the human brain. He pioneered the first mindfulness-based treatment programme for people suffering from OCD, teaching patients how to achieve long-term relief from their compulsions. In conjunction with psychiatrist Rebecca Gladding, Dr Schwartz has refined a system[103] that explains how the brain works and why we often feel besieged by bad brain wiring. He found that, just as with the compulsions of OCD patients, bad habits, social anxieties, self-deprecating thoughts, and compulsive overindulgence are all rooted in overactive brain circuits. They discovered that the key to making the life changes that you want is to make your brain work for you by consciously choosing to 'starve' these circuits of focused attention, thereby decreasing their influence and strength. The first step is just being aware of your thoughts.

'A MAN SHOULD NOT STRIVE TO ELIMINATE HIS COMPLEXES
BUT TO GET IN ACCORD WITH THEM, FOR THEY ARE
LEGITIMATELY WHAT DIRECTS HIS CONDUCT IN THE WORLD.'
– SIGMUND FREUD

When I think over my time attempting to work the 12-step programme, the one thing that really sticks in my mind is all the time I spent saying the 'Serenity Prayer' out loud with others. Out loud on my own. In my head in moments of fear and confusion. That prayer is about acceptance.

---

102. *http://jeffreymschwartz.com/about.html*
103. In their book *You Are Not Your Brain*.

The rest of the steps and the programme I personally can take or leave, but that prayer was a lifesaver:

GOD, GRANT ME THE SERENITY TO ACCEPT
THE THINGS I CANNOT CHANGE,
THE COURAGE TO CHANGE THE THINGS I CAN,
AND THE WISDOM TO KNOW THE DIFFERENCE.

In my teens I had a friend who became a Buddhist and every morning she would get up and chant. I didn't understand it at all until I was at university and there were times where I would look myself in the mirror and say the Serenity Prayer over and over until calm washed through me and I felt connected to something larger than me.

Chanting is something I have never found easy. The sound of my voice out loud felt embarrassing. I'm not sure why, I am not shy of an opinion, but to chant anything at volume was tricky and hugely uncomfortable. During my yoga teacher training course I pushed through that discomfort and at times found something wonderful in the rhythmic waves of a group chanting sound. Later in my Kundalini yoga practice I found chants soothing and powerfully transformational.

I still don't chant out loud alone. I repeat mantras in my head, though.

'DEAR GOD, I AM WILLING TO SEE THINGS DIFFERENTLY.'[104]

If it's good enough for Marianne Williamson... I heard Marianne tell a story about how she uses it and I now use it similarly; when I catch myself being closed minded I ask for a miracle and remind myself that I have a sense of humour:

---

104. Marianne Williamson is an internationally acclaimed spiritual author and lecturer, whose bases a lot of her work on *A Course in Miracles*. http://www.marianne.com/ http://www.acim.org/AboutACIM/

> Don't be afraid
> to be open minded,
> your brain
> isn't going to fall out.
>
> ——×——

When I turned thirty I began doing mirror work.

What's mirror work?

Talking to yourself in the mirror, a little more each day.

Finding things to say that are kind. I started working with affirmations. I still find affirmations a really helpful way to reframe my thoughts. The way we talk to ourselves is incredibly powerful.

Self-talk has a really significant impact on our confidence and self esteem. It also has a huge impact on our happiness and success. When I first heard of self-talk the stories of Beyoncé and Victoria Beckham talking to themselves out loud, came to mind and for a long time it seemed a little too far-fetched thing to do for me.

Each moment of each day, whether consciously or not, we all have an inner dialogue running. The thoughts that run through our minds and the things that we say are what form our beliefs, which we know impact our behaviour and in turn our results.

So I began to think about what I was thinking:

- *What are you telling yourself over and over?*
- *Do you talk to yourself like you would someone you love?*

I certainly didn't.

Mirror talk is a way of consciously and on purpose talking to your self.

I invite you to have a go: tell yourself something you would tell someone you love, and use your name.

I really mean it, have a go, find a mirror, say something kind and use your name.

The evidence shows that actually using your name and addressing yourself like you would another person makes a significant difference to your choices and actions.

Talking to yourself in the third person, whilst it may feel ridiculous at first, may not be stupid at all, quite the contrary in fact. Ethan Kross of the University of Michigan conducted research published in 2014,[105] which suggests that talking to yourself using 'I' can stress you out, whilst referring to yourself by name or as 'you' enhances self-distancing, which allows you to review and assess the situation and choose to exert self-control when faced with tempting options in the short term, from skipping a meal or a yoga class to not taking a business opportunity which would be great for you but is outside your comfort zone.

Over the years I have had many moments of self-doubt and self-judgment. We all have days when our own personal negative committee comes out and says 'You can't do this.' or 'You are worthless.' or 'You're not good enough.'

Natalie Nahai[106] explains that by addressing ourselves by name and self-talking in the third person, we give ourselves a level of authority, which makes us more likely to listen to ourselves.

I am a big fan of affirmations. I use my wisdom cards[107] daily to give myself something to ponder on and I believe that the key is saying something positive to yourself and being enquiring.

I invite you to play with a mixture of questioning, affirmations with and without a mirror. It's about finding what works best for you. Just saying an affirmation that you don't believe is not helpful. For example, repeating to

105. *http://selfcontrol.psych.lsa.umich.edu/wp-content/uploads/2014/01/KrossJ_Pers_Soc_Psychol2014Self-talk_as_a_regulatory_mechanism_How_you_do_it_matters.pdf*

106. *http://www.thewebpsychologist.com/*

107. *http://entrepreneurenabler.com/goodies/*

yourself 'I am awesome' when you are feeling depressed or unworthy will probably leave you more frustrated than before.

Be mindful of the emotional guidance scale;[108] jumping from feelings of insecurity to optimism is just not going to work. There are layers of feeling. Moving through them incrementally is not only more logical but takes the pressure off. Aim to move one or two steps up the scale at a time rather than expecting more.

Try it all out. Don't be afraid to experiment. Be playful with it.

The thing with some affirmations or mantras is that your clever brain simply won't accept statements that you don't believe. Humans are wired to seek for answers. If I ask you *'Why is the grass green?'* your mind immediately starts searching for the answer. 'Afformations' use this to your advantage, according to Noah St John:[109] his process is a way of asking a question that changes your mindset and gets you thinking differently.

Trying:

'How do you run your businesses and life with such ease and grace?'

Certainly gets me thinking differently to:

'I run my businesses with ease and grace.'

Which is different again from:

'Ebonie, you can do it, you have all the tools and resources you need to run your businesses and life with ease and grace.'

I invite you to have a go at trying out these differing forms of self-talk and let me know how you get on. I'm fascinated to find out which way works best for you.

So, now you have gotten a grasp on what you have power to change and have begun looking at the judgments you are making, let's try some

---

108. This scale was first introduced to me by Abraham Hicks: 1) Joy/Knowledge/Empowerment/Freedom/Love/Appreciation; 2) Passion; 3) Enthusiasm/Eagerness/Happiness; 4) Positive Expectation/Belief; 5) Optimism; 6) Hopefulness; 7) Contentment; 8) Boredom; 9) Pessimism; 10) Frustration/Irritation/Impatience; 11) Overwhelment; 12) Disappointment; 13) Doubt; 14) Worry; 15) Blame; 16) Discouragement; 17) Anger; 18) Revenge; 19) Hatred/Rage; 20) Jealousy; 21) Insecurity/Guilt/Unworthiness; 22) Fear/Grief/Depression/Despair/Powerlessness

109. *http://afformationsbook.com/more/*

exercises to get you even more aware and to help you overcome the obstacles and resistance that you find in both business and relationship and with your relationship to your God and your self.

EXERCISES: JUDGMENT AND ACCEPTANCE

So, are you ready to do some work?

EXERCISE I: NOTICING YOUR THOUGHTS

1. **Carry your notebook with your for the next three days and make a note of:**

   - *Your recurring thoughts*

   - *Whether you think thoughts that empower or limit you*

   - *Whose opinion matters to you*

   - *Who are you accountable to*

   - *How often you say 'I should' or 'shouldn't'*

   - *How often you want to or try to manipulate others*

   Practise being mindful; paying attention in a particular way: *on purpose, in the present moment, and non-judgmentally.*

   _____

   _____

   _____

   _____

   _____

So what do we do with all the 'obstacles' that come up?

EXERCISE 2: OVERCOMING 'ROADBLOCKS' AND FINDING A WAY OVER, ROUND OR THROUGH

'ROADBLOCKS' FALL INTO 3 CATEGORIES:

1. *(lack of) Resources (including the big two – TIME and MONEY)*

2. *Doubters: headed up by the negative committee in your head, but maybe including your friends, family, peers, the bank etc.*

   NB You have begun to pay attention to these, and now that you have Awareness, you can work out what you want instead (Aspiration) and then Accept what you can and cannot change. From here you are able to take some ACTION (Step 4) ☺

3. *Assumption(s) – The mother of all F-ups.*

Let's unpack these a little more:

I. RESOURCES:

These are the things that make it possible to do what it is that you do: everything from your laptop and your phone to your mum. Being an entrepreneur in my mind is about developing your resourcefulness to overcome the lack of resources. This is something that you CAN do, often with the support of a coach, mentor, peer or mastermind group[110] you can find ways of looking at things differently and come up with creative and innovative solutions to a resource issue.

The main gripes that come up for everyone are:

---

110. Join mine here: *www.facebook.com/groups/misfitentrepreneurs.*

Time: not having enough time is something that is common to all of us and my personal opinion is that it all depends on how you look at those hours, minutes and seconds. We all have the same amount in one day. *It's all about what you value and how you prioritise.*

- *What is important to you?*

- *Do you still say yes to everything? How is that working out for you?*

This is the time to go back to your values, your ▲ which is your WHY and use that triad of words and their meaning as a filter in your life. When a request for your time, energy, focus or attention comes in, ask yourself if it is contributing to your overall goal(s). If not, say NO.

Money: Please don't fall into the trap of thinking that money will solve your problems. Please don't use it as an excuse. *Sure, money is helpful but get really clear and honest with yourself:*

- *What is it that money would give you?*

- *How else could that be achieved?*

- *How much do you need?*

- *Specifically?*

_____

_____

_____

_____

Not enough of ME to go around: Please remember that you are a resource. Look after yourself. Remember that your health is VITAL. You want to avoid burnout. Also remember that you can't do everything well. Learn to delegate.

Being resourceful is the key to success. It's something we are all capable of developing. Lack of resources is sometimes a blessing in disguise. You can come up with all sorts of unique and game-changing ideas when the resources are limited.

What is the main obstacle in your way right now?

_____

_____

_____

_____

_____

_____

2. DOUBTERS:

The doubt might come from the outside, but if you didn't share it in some small way it would be water off a duck's back and roll away. Things stick when we ourselves are unsure. This all comes down to our beliefs.

As I've said before there are only two kinds of belief: ones that empower and ones that limit. Most of what comes up for us when we listen to or give thought to a doubt, as raised by a friend, or a family member or the bank, is fear.

Fear of not being enough.

I know that you are enough.

I know that I am enough... but I still have wobbles. I still have days when PERFECT is the enemy of DONE. When you are having a wobble ask yourself:

- *Who am I listening to?*

- *Why does their opinion matter?*

Surround yourself with people who are on your team. Who believe in you and want you to succeed.

Go and investigate. Go and find the evidence to support your beliefs.

- *What area is concerning you right now?*

- *Is your concern based on fact?*

Go and ask. Do some RESEARCH.

What is your biggest doubt right now?

_____

_____

_____

_____

_____

_____

When you hear 'I can't...' try reframing it by asking 'How can I...?'

Defining your goals so that you can measure them is SO important. I know I keep banging on about it, but it a BIG deal. How you achieve it doesn't matter nearly as much as working out and defining how you will know when you have achieved what you have set out to achieve.

Being mindful of *Deliberate* and *Emergent* strategy[111] is also something to bear in mind when you hit a wall. The most successful entrepreneurs have got this balance right: they know where they are headed, have clear defined goals AND are open to going with the flow. They have their eyes open for opportunity and are flexible and adaptable when it comes to making a detour.

3. ASSUMPTIONS:

Not being able to see the wood for the trees is an inevitability of running your own business. From time to time we all make assumptions. ***Taking time to look at things from a range of angles can really help:***

- *Who can help?*

- *Who is doing what you want to do?*

- *Who is doing it well?*

- *Who is doing it badly?*

- *What makes you believe that? What evidence is there?*

- *What can you learn from them?*

- *How can you use this information to aid you?*

- *What if this roadblock set me on a different path?*

---

111. See Step four: *From Inertia to Action.*

- *What else could I do?*

_____

_____

_____

_____

_____

_____

EXERCISE 3: MIRROR WORK OR SELF-TALK

Using the principles of Affirmations, Afformations and self-talk, what new thoughts can you create and work with until they become the quickest and easiest thoughts for you?

Take the limiting beliefs that you uncovered in the last chapter and rework them in your own way into a question, an affirmation or a mantra that you can repeat to yourself.

Here is an example of one I made for myself when I did my yoga teacher training:

- **Limiting belief:**

  It will be really hard for me to earn good money as a yoga teacher.

- **Mantra that I used to change my belief:**

  I will find work in a wonderful way. I'll give a wonderful service for a wonderful pay.

_____

_____

_____

_____

_____

_____

NB: I am not saying that mindfulness practice is a cure for OCD or mental health issues for everyone. Sometimes medication is advisable. I am not a doctor, brain or mental health specialist. Please make sure you speak to one of these if you are concerned. The brain is complex. There is a unique blend of thoughts and chemicals in everyone, and whilst I am an advocate for holistic approaches, I also found medication very useful at the right time, and in the right way. You must do what is right for you.

STEP 4: FROM INERTIA TO ACTION

INERTIA: A TENDENCY TO DO NOTHING OR TO REMAIN UNCHANGED RETAINING A STATE OF REST OR CURRENT VELOCITY ALONG A STRAIGHT LINE SO LONG AS NOT ACTED UPON BY AN EXTERNAL FORCE.

So finally it's time to move and take some purposeful, inspired action.

Action – as far as I am concerned – is not doing just for the sake of it. This is your chance to take what you have cultivated internally out into the physical realm. Action is the bridge from your inner to your outer world.

ACTION: THE PROCESS OF DOING SOMETHING, TYPICALLY TO ACHIEVE AN AIM.

There is a reason that ACTION is Step 4. Working through all the other steps first means that you will not be taking action for the sake of it, but working smart. Doing things that are in line with your values and that you know (believe) will take you incrementally to where you want to be. Things that have integrity and make you feel good about yourself.

I am so over working hard for the sake of working hard. *Yes. You too?*

LIE: HARD WORK IS ALL IT TAKES

The truth is that if you are reading this book then you are probably one of life's do-ers rather than one of life's be-ers. This means that your default is *look busy*.

TRUTH: INSPIRED ACTION IS THE ONLY ACTION WORTH TAKING

What I'm about to say next may feel like a contradiction, but life is full of these wonderful idiosyncrasies. Sometimes ACTION isn't what needs to happen. Sometimes 'being' and surrender are action in and of themselves. This step is about trusting yourself again. It's about listening and being mindful. Being busy for the sake of busy isn't going to build you a business or a life you love. Choose to step away from the glorification of busy. Choose to take only inspired action.

SOMETIMES IT'S OK IF THE ONLY THING YOU DID TODAY WAS BREATHE!

Print by Will Blood (contact Will or myself for copies) – all profits go to the Cystic Fibrosis trust in honour of our Moonbeam, Freya, for whom this was a daily reality.

DOING AND BEING

We are human BEINGS not human DOINGS.

As a society we glorify busy.

Have you played 'Busy Top Trumps'? You know, when your friend or partner asks:

'How was your day?'

And you reply:

'Oh, I was soooo busy – I didn't even stop for lunch.'

And then they say:

'Well, I can't even remember the last time I had a lunch break,'

And you say:

'I haven't had an evening off in weeks, I mean, I just seem to be doing stuff all day long and even then my to-do list isn't any shorter.'

'Well my to-do list is twice as long and most of the things on it are impossible!'

Sound familiar?

STOP!!

Everything integrates when you stop… take time out and remember what's important here. Some of your best 'work' happens when you stop.

You go to the gym to build muscle, but it's actually on the rest days that the muscles rebuild and you get stronger.

Make sure you are taking time to integrate, digest, ponder and think. The learning happens when we stop reading and stop pushing and stop trying so hard. When you stop and just *be* you. It is in the moments in between that we are able to realise that we know a lot more than we think. When you feel as though your have tried it all, stop.

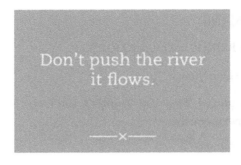

Don't push the river
it flows.

——×——

Some of us are born do-ers, and it is our lesson to learn how to *be*.

On the flip side, some of us are be-ers and could *be*, all day every day, waiting for the action to take itself. I'm going to mention The Secret[112] and the Law of Attraction just once in this book, now: **It (whatever it is) will not magically attract itself to you while you sit on your parents' sofa smoking weed. The red Ferrari will not magically appear in your drive whilst you sit on your arse!**

Of course mindset and belief are important! Of course visualising, being on the same frequency, having the ENERGY it takes are integral, but this is still the human realm where you need to take action too.

Apathy, inertia and laziness won't get you anywhere.

Perfectionism is a form of procrastination.

Perfect is the enemy of done.

Fear of failure is a mindset issue. Failure isn't bad – it means you are experimenting!

You can have it all. Everything that you want. But there are two caveats:

1. *You can't have it all at the same time – you wouldn't enjoy it all at once anyway!*

2. *You need to know what that is that you want so that you can measure it.*

And then there is balance. Balance is not easy. It is hard work.

112. *http://thesecret.tv/*

Have you tried standing on one leg in various yoga asana?

It takes strength, discipline and involves focus and also more than anything else BREATH – if you just breathe and relax into your own infrastructure, trusting your bones and breath, you will balance.

How does this relate to this step of the process?

Sometimes you need to engage your muscles and take action, and other times you must breathe. Yoga is not just for your mat. Take its lessons into your life.

Are you faffing or being busy because you have things to do or because you don't know what else to do, or because you are not comfortable in those pauses?

It's in the pauses in life, in my experience, that the magic exists. Yoga changed everything for me. Actually, learning to breathe changed everything for me.

DELIBERATE VERSUS EMERGENT STRATEGY

'GIVE ME SIX HOURS TO CHOP DOWN A TREE AND I
WILL SPEND THE FIRST FOUR SHARPENING THE AXE.'
– ABRAHAM LINCOLN

Preparation is so very important, but sometimes just say YES and figure it out on the way.

Maybe you think that you have to work hard, all the time, to the edge of your capacity, in order to get the life that you want.

OR maybe you think that if you visualise it, believe it will happen enough, then somehow magically it will just appear – attracted by your vibration – et voilà.

The truth is somewhere in between. Action for action's sake is not helpful or fulfilling. The trick is to look at your motivation. You attract what you are.

Inspired action is action that will give you the biggest win.

The biggest win isn't just about results, but about the journey too. The best strategy is a balance between deliberate versus emergent strategy. Making a deliberate plan, and yet being flexible, open to opportunity. Whilst you need to have a deliberate plan, you also need enough resources and flexibility to change course, and make way for an even better, emergent plan.

This step is all about recognising that:

1. *We determine our fate by where we pour our energy and resources.*

2. *Where you are putting your resources, your time, energy, talent and wealth, is where you will see results.*

3. *Your strategy consists of hundreds of everyday decisions.*

It can be really tempting to take the short-term payouts life offers, by prioritising things with immediate gratification over those rewards that may take years to come to fruition. Remember though that neglecting personal health and relationships along the way can have detrimental, irreversible effects.

There is magic in the mundane, right in front of you, in the everyday tasks. Being entrepreneurial is quite simply recognising opportunity when it is presented to you. Being focused on one particular outcome means that you miss opportunities for growth, for adventure, for experiments, for chaotic creativity and transformation. Sometimes the snakes and ladders of life can catapult you to places you had no idea existed. Better than you ever could have imagined.

DELIBERATE STRATEGY KEEPS YOU FOCUSED. EMERGENT STRATEGY PROVIDES BEAUTIFUL UNCERTAINTY.

Most of the time being, without rushing, is what produces results.

'TO PAY ATTENTION WITH A HEART AND MIND AT EASE IS
WHAT PRODUCES RESULTS. IT IS ALSO — AND THIS IS ALMOST
IMPOSSIBLE TO REMEMBER — WHAT PRODUCES TIME.'
— NANCY KLINE[113]

Having it all is about balance. Balance is not easy. It really involves calling yourself on your shit and it requires structure and breath.

It really is in the pauses of life that the magic exists. At first, though, the pauses can be really uncomfortable. Yoga changed everything for me in this regard. When I was working in the film industry, Savasana (corpse pose) – the one where you lie on the floor and relax – was THE most stressful of the postures for me. It was SO hard. My mind would not shut up. I was restless and fidgety and I hated it as much as I hate running. I spent the entirety of the relaxation period wishing it would hurry up. Too much of a people-pleaser to be one of the people who got up and left, but too monkey-minded to relax into FIVE MINUTES!! Now, I love the time out. It is only five minutes. You can pick everything up again afterwards. All of your stresses can wait five minutes. You'll be amazed what resources you might discover in those five minutes of letting everything go. I am sharing that I fucking hated it when I first started practising because some of you will now be sighing relief and feeling normal. Stick at it. Allow yourself to recharge. Think of savasana as a docking station for your mind and body.

Do you know what drishti is?

Drishti is a Sanskrit word and is used in yoga for getting you to focus your gaze. It is a means for developing concentrated intention. It is used as a practice of gazing on a specific point to rest the eyes and become steady and present in the moment. When the body becomes wobbly on the mat, settling the gaze on one point can bring balance and stability to the pose, and like most things learned on the mat, the same applies to life off the mat. When life becomes busy and scattered and overwhelming, bringing awareness to the moment brings peace.

---

113. Nancy Kline's *Time to Think* is one of my all-time favourite books.

Drishti is about focus.

Deliberate strategy provides focus, having a plan is SO helpful – exploring context, knowing why you want to achieve the end goal, understanding the steps you need to take to get where you want to be is CRUCIAL.

However, being so focused that you neglect to smell the roses, or play with your children, or feel joy isn't the life you want for yourself. Allowing the flow of uncertainty into your life allows you to learn, experiment, feel, play, explore. *It is the JOURNEY that we are here for. It is the EXPERIENCES of our life that we remember way after the goals have been achieved.*

- *How can you make the experiences part of the journey?*

- *How can you factor deliberate and emergent strategies into your business and your life plans?*

Awareness and Acceptance are a great start, but they are not enough. Acceptance will not bring what you want closer to you by itself - you must take action. Doing without knowing why or for what purpose is demoralising. However, doing or taking action which is in line with your beliefs serves a purpose and is fulfilling.

Setting goals that are not in line with your values and your beliefs will lead to procrastination and resentment.

If you have goals but never seem to realise them, there is a really good reason: you are not motivated to do so. Maybe they are not the right goals, maybe there is a belief that is in direct conflict with the goal, maybe there is a fear sitting unchecked. Getting your values, beliefs and goals in line will make taking inspired action easy. When you are truly inspired to take action, it is easy, fun or rewarding. When you have the right goal, you take actions that really make a difference, that move you closer to what you want. These actions come from a place of inspiration. Inspired action is action that involves a commitment, is probably a little outside of your comfort zone but is rewarding.

'Opportunity looks a lot like hard work.'[114]

Not everything will be truly inspiring and fun all of the time. It's true...

Sometimes we do things in a relationship for our partner or friend or child or client that isn't YEY!! and unicorns for us, BUT the reward is having them know we care and being in the relationship.

Sometimes I have to do spreadsheets or sit at a computer all day and write. Sometimes I have to lift weights while doing squats. The process of these tasks isn't 'yey and unicorns' for me, but the results of the actions are, or they lead to something that is.

All the mood boards, affirmations and visualisations in the world are not going to get you your desires if you don't take some action. You will need to do something. Doing nothing will get you nowhere, but doing something for the sake of looking busy will make you believe that your efforts are in vain and then you'll have evidence that proves it's all futile. Don't set yourself up like that.

Set yourself up to win. When your list of tasks are in line with your values and you know that taking them will move you towards your goals then these are good actions.

Chunking down goals into manageable tasks creates an action plan that will bring you one step at a time closer to your bigger goal. Reminding yourself how this action links back to your overall goal will create motivation. This is the best way to achieve what you want in a way that is not setting yourself up for failure. Support yourself, encourage yourself, and explain to yourself why you're doing what you're doing.

Mapping it out will help you work out what resources you need. Exploring the context around the goal will help you stay on track and remain accountable. Working out exactly how you intend to measure your progress turns your dream into a reality.

---

114. Ashton Kutcher, *Teen Choice Awards 2013*

EXERCISES: FROM INERTIA TO ACTION

Ready to have a go?

EXERCISE 1: HOW ARE YOU SPENDING YOUR TIME?

For one day, pay attention to where your time is spent.

- Make a note in your notebook of how long things actually take.

- What tasks are you spending your time on?

- What do you enjoy?

- What are you avoiding?

- Why are you avoiding it?

Be clear about how you are actually spending your time, for just one day out of your life, be aware and make a note of how long you spend answering emails, doing research, making calls, or whatever it is that you are doing.

_____

_____

_____

_____

_____

_____

When you have a clear, realistic picture of how long tasks take, then you can:

- Allow enough time for them

- Be accountable and do what you need to do to focus on the tasks at hand.

After one day look at how you have been spending your time:

- Are you spending your time in a way that is congruent with your goals?

- Are you putting off the important but not urgent stuff?

- Rate your tasks using the Urgent / Important Matrix below.

- How are you processing everything that needs your attention and action?

URGENCY

High   Low

	1 Urgent **and** important Do it now	**2** Important **not** urgent Decide when to do it
IMPORTANCE	**4** Urgent **not** important Delegate it	**3** **Not** important **not** urgent Dump it

Low

Stephen Covey popularised Eisenhower's Decision Principle in his book, The 7 Habits of Highly Effective People.

Armed with your three words ▲[115] (the triad that remind you simply and powerfully of your peak experiences), you have a weapon against the onslaught of demands on your time. Using your 'YES' and your 'NO', you have the ability to choose how you spend your time.

Demands will always keep coming and so will stress, but you are filling your toolbox with tools, you now have more and more ways to make discerning choices. The process of moving from ARGH to AHHH is one of growing your container larger than your issues. When you have a tool for anything that comes your way you no longer feel ARGH!

Here are a few more tools and techniques to help you with moving from Apathy to Action, but do not be fooled, the biggest motivator is always your WHY[116]. Get really clear on why you are doing the things you are doing, particularly if the actions are dull or uninteresting to you. In moments when you feel like quitting, remind yourself why you started and what this action is leading to. When you have your *why*, then work on *how* and finally *what*. Most people start with *what*, then *how* and lastly – or maybe not even at all – *why*. This is again the outside-in misunderstanding at play. Starting with WHY is starting from your inside. Your core. HOW is determined by your values and the results you want. WHAT is the outside piece. It's what shows up when you've done the work, and it will be easier and of much greater value if you work from your inside, out.

When I feel
like quitting,
I remind myself
WHY I started.

——×——

---

115. From *Step 1*
116. Simon Sinek's work *Start with the Why* is SO good and so important:
https://www.youtube.com/watch?t=168&v=qp0HIF3Sfl4

THE FIVE DS: DO, DUMP, DELEGATE, DEFER, DISCUSS.

The 5 Ds reduce stress because they give you control over what you do. Used correctly, you should then be able to add a sixth – 'de-stress'.[117]

When something needs action either DO it right now or…

DUMP it. Quite simple, hit delete, throw it in the trash, unsubscribe and mentally let go of it, it's gone.

If you can't make an instant decision on it:

DELEGATE it. Do YOU need to do this? Who else can do it? How can you pass this on to someone else? Having delegated, are you still micro-managing or have you mentally passed it on, is it now gone?

DEFER. Let's have a word about defer, this means ONCE. If everything is going in the defer pile and staying there you need to have an honest word with yourself – why is this a defer? What has to happen in order for it to happen? or in order for it to be a priority? If you have a good answer then ACE! Be honest.

DISCUSS it. Use your coach, your team, your dad, mentor, teacher, friend – who can you talk this over with and how will that help you move forward?

There are many reasons why we delay doing the important but not urgent stuff:

- The project is so big you don't know where to start.

- The project isn't interesting.

- You have too long to do the task.

- You don't like the task you need to do.

- We put off the majority of important tasks because they are too overwhelming. They are too complex or time consuming for us to handle.

---

117. Dr Roger Henderson, author of *Stress Beaters: 100 Proven Ways to Manage Stress.*

POKE HOLES IN THE CHEESE[118]

Lakein's technique gets you to pick a small task related to the main project and do it. Then, follow this task with another small, easy and instant task and do that. Keep at it. Find the next little piece and do it. This process is dubbed 'poking holes in the cheese'. Eventually the cheese gets filled with holes, you get more and more involved in the project, and it becomes much easier. Don't try and bite the same hole out of the cheese twice. If you tried one task and it didn't lead to involvement, just try another task. Use this technique for all the tasks you don't like – do little five-minute bites and then do something else.

While I was writing this book a good friend of mine texted me:

How do you eat an elephant?? Bite size chunks! :)

and it's SO TRUE!

From elephants to frogs…

EAT THE BIG FROG FIRST

'EAT A LIVE FROG FIRST THING IN THE MORNING AND NOTHING
WORSE WILL HAPPEN TO YOU THE REST OF THE DAY.'
– MARK TWAIN

Mark Twain is said to have asked, 'Suppose tomorrow morning the first thing that you do, is catch a live frog, stuff it into your mouth, munch it down and swallow it all up. Once you did that, the day couldn't get much worse now, could it?'

---

118. Alan Lakein author of *How to Get Control of Your Time and Your Life*.

His point was that every morning you find the ugliest, most repulsive task that you have on your to-do list (your frog) and knock that off before getting on to doing anything else. Once you've gotten that done then everything else would feel so much easier.

Brian Tracy takes the analogy further. He says 'If you have to eat a live frog at all, it doesn't pay to sit and look at it for very long. When you've got two frogs, eat the ugliest one first. You cannot eat every tadpole and frog in the pond, but you can eat the biggest and ugliest one.'[119]

How do you eat your biggest, ugliest frog?

The answer is the same as an elephant; one bite at a time.

Break the ugly task down into specific step-by-step activities and then start on the first one.

'Never be distracted by a tadpole when a big frog is sitting there waiting to be eaten.'

USE TIMERS OR TIME / TASK MANAGEMENT APPS

Some of my favourite apps include SelfControlApp – this stops me from using specific sites (OK, Facebook) whilst I am trying to write. Or stops me from looking at email whist I have other tasks to do. You can choose which URLs to be locked out of for a specific amount of time. The more old-school, less tech way of doing this is to set a timer or stopwatch for 15 minutes. Works just as well, depends if you need to be online while tasking.

Do your task for 15 minutes and then have a break. Focus on it completely for a full 15 minutes and then stop and see how much you've actually achieved.

Along the same lines is an app called 30/30, which allows you to input tasks and assign time slots for each. I love this, I have it on my phone and use it when I am trying to juggle lots of things, or want to break up a long stretch on one thing.

---

119. *Eat That Frog! 21 Great Ways to Stop Procrastinating and Get More Done in Less Time*

USE AFFIRMATIONS

One of my favourite affirmations is:

'I EMBRACE AND SURRENDER TO UNCERTAINTY.'

Anyone who has worked with me will have heard me use it. I invite you to say it to yourself liberally. Whenever you are feeling overwhelmed, when ARGH is getting the better of you. *The other I still use all the time, usually muttered under my breath, is:*

'DEAR GOD, I AM WILLING TO SEE THIS DIFFERENTLY.'

I am always surprised by what happens. It's pretty magic what you get when you ask for it!

Lastly, if you're up for it, when your mind is chattering away, when you find yourself over-thinking and aren't sure what action to take, ask your heart what it thinks.

Sit quietly, relax and focus on your breath. Get the fluidity even and consistent. Make it so that you can hear your breath, like a seashell.

Now ask your heart the question.

Rather than asking with your head and trying to bring your energy down from your head into your heart (which I find keeps me in my head) – visualise lifting the energy in your heart up towards the energy in your head and asking with your heart.

If that's too 'woo woo' for you, try this: with a pen and paper, using your usual writing hand, write the question:

- What should I do next? (or whatever your question is)

- Then with your other hand (so your left hand if you are right-handed), write the answer.

- You may be surprised with what comes.

_____

_____

_____

_____

_____

<u>EXERCISE 2</u>: EXPLORING CONTEXT

Looking at a list of things you want to achieve:

- What have you done so far? Well done!

- What have you not done yet?

- Why?

List the reasons...

_____

_____

_____

_____

_____

_____

- Are there things on the list that feel too big to do in one go?

- If so, can you break those things down into smaller, more manageable tasks?

- Is there anything that you can do right now?

- Is there anything you can delegate?

- Write down when you are going to do each thing on the list.

- If you aren't actually going to do it cross it off.

- If it is not you who is going to take action, have you delegated it to the right person?

- Do they know what is expected of them, and by when?

Now pick one thing to explore a little further.

Journey forward in your mind to a time when this goal is realised...

- How do you know that you've achieved it?

- What is happening?

- Who is there?

- What do you feel / see / hear / believe?

- What results can you measure?

- Describe your day-to-day activities and relationships

Now come back to the present:

- What is your motivation for achieving this goal?

- How will you measure success?

- How much control do you have? To start? To maintain momentum?

- What impact will achieving this outcome have on your life?

- What are the costs of going for it?

- What is the key benefit of going for it?

- Are you committed?

- What inner qualities or resources will you need to demonstrate?

- Who can stop you from achieving your outcome?

- Who will be affected by you achieving your outcome?

- What physical resources do you need to achieve your outcome?

- How will you know when you are 25%, 50%, 75% of the way there?

- What are the next steps?

_____

_____

_____

_____

_____

_____

STEP 5: FROM BLAME TO ACCOUNTABILITY

BLAME: TO FEEL OR DECLARE THAT SOMEONE OR SOMETHING IS RESPONSIBLE FOR A SITUATION. TO FIND FAULT WITH. TO HOLD RESPONSIBLE. TO ASSIGN RESPONSIBILITY FOR A BAD OR UNFORTUNATE SITUATION OR PHENOMENON TO (SOMEONE OR SOMETHING).

I need you to be honest with yourself.

Are you blaming someone or something for the life you are not living?

In the film industry it was often referred to as having Teflon shoulders – nothing sticks. How much responsibility for your life and your actions and circumstances are you willing to take?

Conversely, are you blaming yourself?

ACCOUNTABILITY: AN OBLIGATION OR WILLINGNESS TO ACCEPT RESPONSIBILITY OR TO ACCOUNT FOR ONE'S ACTIONS.

For so long I felt responsible for the whole world, well, not the whole world, but everyone in it that I knew. Their feelings: my responsibility. Their problems; my responsibility. Their judgments; my responsibility. I know it doesn't make sense logically. But I honestly felt somehow that it was all my responsibility and that not only could I fix them, but I should. Especially if I wanted to be loved or liked by them, which I did.

The truth is twofold:

> **One** – *most other people are not my responsibility. Not to the extent that I was making them so.*

> **Two** – *not everyone will like me and it is not my responsibility to convince them. The only person I need to worry about liking me, is me!*

I had my hierarchy[120] all wrong. I was taking my learned co-dependant behaviour out into every relationship I had, personal and professional. It took a small claims court and giving half my business to someone who didn't really want it for me to feel the resentment needed to address what was really going on. Resentment is your friend. It's trying to show you that something isn't working. Blaming is a sign, but it will not help you.

> 'TELL EVERYONE YOU KNOW: "MY HAPPINESS DEPENDS ON ME, SO YOU'RE OFF THE HOOK." AND THEN DEMONSTRATE IT. BE HAPPY, NO MATTER WHAT THEY'RE DOING. PRACTISE FEELING GOOD, NO MATTER WHAT. AND BEFORE YOU KNOW IT, YOU WILL NOT GIVE ANYONE ELSE RESPONSIBILITY FOR THE WAY YOU FEEL – AND THEN, YOU'LL LOVE THEM ALL. BECAUSE THE ONLY REASON YOU DON'T LOVE THEM, IS BECAUSE YOU'RE USING THEM AS YOUR EXCUSE TO NOT FEEL GOOD.'
> – ABRAHAM HICKS

When I tell my clients that they are not responsible for my feelings I see relief wash across their faces and their energy change. Suddenly they realise this really is all about them. Then I tell them that there is a caveat:

---

120. Lots of people talk about this kind of thing, self before others not being selfish; in this instance I am talking about something Mastin Kipp refers to – the 'correct hierarchy'. Your hierarchy should always be 1. Self, 2. God, 3. Others. You must look after yourself first, then your relationship to something greater than yourself – whatever you believe that to be or whatever name you give it, and then others.

'You *are* responsible for *your* feelings. If you're feeling angry, sad, resentful, unheard – it's not my fault. Especially if you don't share it with me. So please share it with me and then we can address it.'

If you want a life of AHHH, if you truly want to move out of ARGH, then you need to take responsibility for your life and that includes the way you feel. Nobody else is to blame for how you feel. That might be controversial for some of you. Other people may act as a mirror, or trigger stuff for you, or even be cruel, but they don't control your feelings, you do.

You ARE responsible for YOU. You get to choose how you respond.

Oh fuck.

Right?!

No one else is responsible for your happiness…

But there is a glorious thing that comes beyond the fear and vulnerability of sharing how you really feel: all the extra energy you are saving not worrying about being responsible for everyone else's feelings. All the extra energy you're not using in anger or resentment. Now you have enough to communicate and cultivate intimate, honest, grown-up, powerfully life-affirming relationships. And when you do, you'll then find that you have a whole load more energy to give because you'll be fuelled by new oxygenated energy rather than old stored and stale energy. It's all prana.[121]

LIE: IT'S NOT MY FAULT.

It's not even about fault.

TRUTH: LIFE IS HAPPENING FOR YOU, NOT TO YOU…

The belief that responsibility is bad is just wrong. The belief that you are a product of your circumstances is a lie. Here's the actual truth of it: you are exactly who you decide to be.

You are asking the wrong question. 'Why me?' is a rubbish question.

---

121. Prana is the Sanskrit word for 'life force.'

'What am I learning here?' produces much more interesting answers. Life is not a chore to endure, it is a wonderful experiential blessing. You get one life as you, in this body and this time that we know of: how are you going to use it? What do you want to learn and experience. What will your legacy be?

About two years ago when I first started planning this book, I was talking about what I meant by legacy and the person I was talking to said:

'Don't talk about legacy in the book, it reminds me of death and dying – why would I want to think about that?'

Well, here's the thing, As far as I can tell there are only three certainties:

> *Birth.*

> *Death.*

> *Change.*

You were born. Nothing can be done to undo that. How you feel about it, how the circumstances of your arrival affect and influence your life is up to you.

You will die. That is certain. *I cannot tell you how you will feel about dying, or the life you have lived, but the biggest regret of most people before dying is:*

> *'I wish I'd had the courage to live a life true to myself, not the life others expected of me.'*[122]

When I talk about legacy I am talking about what is left after you are gone. It's important. As far as I'm concerned it's what you're here for.

Your purpose, legacy, lifetime is made up of moments, days, thoughts and actions. If you have a million ideas but don't ever do anything about any of them, what will you leave behind? What sense of accomplishment or pride will you feel? Fulfilment is a feeling of connection to self and something larger.[123] You want to feel fulfilled, right? That's what AHHH is all about underneath it all.

---

122. Bronnie Ware, *The Top Five Regrets Of The Dying: A Life Transformed By The Dearly Departing.*
123. Mastin Kipp shared that definition with me.

Change is constant. Change is inevitable. Change is life. One change after the next: an inhalation, an exhalation, and a pause in continuous loop.

Change will happen.

The seasons will pass.

Life and death in continuous cyclical motion are constant, all around us.

Progress however is not certain, that bit is up to you. Life is a given, but being Alive is up to you. *Living a life on purpose, with purpose, is the key to being happy, because knowing why you are here, what the bigger picture of your life is about and living your truth will give you space to actually feel alive.*

- So what do you want your legacy to be?

- What do you want people to say after you are gone about you and your life?

- What small mark in history do you want to leave behind?

These things don't have to be huge. I'm not saying invent something ground-breaking, or scale a mountain or bring peace to the world (although if you want to, then please go ahead…).

Right now, start small, think of how you would like to be described:

Rich. Generous. Pragmatic. Reliable. Inspiring. Adventurous. Stable. Creative. Scientific. Influential. Dogmatic. Realistic. Inventive. Caring. Right. Beautiful. Important.

Each of has an inherited legacy, a system of values and belief that determine how we think about ourselves. We have the choice, however, with awareness to take what belongs to us and leave the rest. *I invite you to think of the thing that you gift to life, that you will leave behind, that would not, will not, be here without you.*

- What is your service to or gift to the world?

- What is it right now?

- What would you like it to be?

SELF GOVERNANCE

This step is also about being a grown up; developing accountability, being responsible whilst having FUN!

Every grown up I've ever spoken to has told me that they aren't really sure when they became one. When I was younger I remember thinking that I became a grown up very early on, but I also thought I knew everything about everything when I was 14. Now I am really clear that I don't. I also quite regularly have days when I can't quite believe that I am a grown up.

Being a grown up has nothing to do with age, to me it is all about self-governance,

Self-governance is listening to the little voice you have inside of you. It's the voice that knows. The voice of the riddle. The voice that is your emotional guidance system and your gut instinct. When you are nurturing your inner wisdom, your body wisdom, your emotional intelligence, your moral intelligence you are whole and you trust yourself. Self-goverance is living in authentic integrity – guided by your sense of self.

It's about being responsible, respectful and kind; to yourself first and foremost and then to others.

- To whom are you accountable?

- Who is responsible for your choices, and your actions?

Unless you are a child, I sincerely hope you said 'ME!'

Good, just checking.

That doesn't mean that you have to do it alone: having a support team is vital to staying accountable. Whether it is your work team, your family, your coach, teacher or peers who keep you accountable, finding some support is a responsible way of keeping yourself on track.

Having some spiritual belief and/or practice has been helpful to me for staying accountable. Being part of a Mastermind group helps me to stay accountable. Working with a manager or mentor can keep you accountable. Writing a blog and telling your readers what you are going to do, telling your friend on Facebook, linking your goal to a charity event, these are all ways of taking your dream, your vision out of your mind's eye and out into reality where you will be held accountable.

- Who or what do you need to put in place for you to keep accountable?

EXERCISES: FROM BLAME TO ACCOUNTABILITY

So, are you ready to do some work?

EXERCISE I: SEEKING OUT ACCOUNTABILITY

Do some research; find a group either offline or online that is right for you to be a part of a network, a community and help others while helping yourself.

Or…

Find one friend, and promise to set aside time once a week or once a month to hold each other accountable and offer support.

If you don't achieve what you intended, don't criticise each other, instead listen and ask, what happened? What was learned? What is the plan now?

Celebrate each other's successes and help each other to appreciate the progress each of you is making.

This is one of the key benefits of being a part of such a group; having a space where others can help you appreciate the progress you are making and the work you are accomplishing, and being part of a community of appreciation.

Or…

Join *Misfit to Maven in 80 days*

And

Become part of our *Mastermind group.*

<u>EXERCISE 2</u>: LEGACY

Answer these questions:

- What do you want people to say after you are gone about you and your life?

- How you would like to be described?

- Who are you accountable to or who are you seeking permission from?

- What is your service or gift to the world? What is it right now? What would you like it to be?

- What might you regret if you don't take some action? What is regret?

- Who are you accountable to?

- Who or what do you blame for things not being as you would like?

- What is currently impossible/difficult/limiting to you right now, such that if it were possible/easier/accessible everything would change?

- What are you putting up with at the moment?

- What does peace look like for you? What threatens your peace?

- What's missing from your life? What would make it more fulfilling?

- What accomplishments must, in your opinion, occur during your lifetime so that you will consider your life to have been satisfying and well lived, a life of few or no regrets?

- What would you like your epitaph to read?

_____

_____

_____

_____

_____

_____

_____

_____

_____

_____

_____

Look at what you have written.

- What have you learned about yourself?
- How can you use these insights?

_____

_____

_____

_____

_____

EXERCISE 3: THE PERMISSION PIECE

Sometimes the reason that we are not living our best life, or feeling ARGH rather than AHHH about who we are and what we are being, doing or having in our life, is because we are waiting for someone to give us permission. Given what we have learnt so far, this is your moment to gift yourself permission.

I want you to write a letter, from whomever you are seeking permission to yourself. Imagine you are able to tell yourself everything you need to hear from that person.

Take a moment to centre yourself. Take a few deep breaths in and out. Make your breath fluid, and audible to yourself like the sound you hear in a seashell.

Spend a minute or two just breathing and then, when you are fully focused and present, begin. *Using the other hand than the one you usually write with (so if you are right handed, your left) write yourself a letter. Don't think about it too much, just start:*

Dear [your name]...

and watch what happens.

Dear:

_____

_____

_____

_____

_____

_____

_____

_____

_____

_____

_____

_____

_____

_____

_____

_____

_____

_____

_____

_____

_____

_____

_____

_____

_____

_____

_____

_____

STEP 6: FROM IGNOR-ANCE TO ACKNOWLEDGEMENT

IGNOR-ANCE: TO REFUSE TO TAKE NOTICE OF OR ACKNOWLEDGE. TO DISREGARD. TO BE OBLIVIOUS TO. TO DENY ATTENTION.

How many times have you forgotten to acknowledge or disregarded your progress only to look back maybe years later and see what you achieved?

For such a long time, I had an idea of something I wanted to achieve. I took action on it, completed my task and swiftly moved on to the next thing.

Again and again and again.

And wondered why I was not motivated, or proud of myself and my accomplishments. This is what I mean by ignor-ance. Ignorance of your own or others' accomplishments. Often not on purpose, it's just how we were raised. Achieving what we set out to achieve and moving straight onto the next thing without a second thought.

Taking time to acknowledge or reflect or celebrate the successes, however small, is an incredibly important part of the process.

ACKNOWLEDGEMENT: TO ADMIT THE EXISTENCE, REALITY, OR TRUTH OF. TO RECOGNISE AS BEING VALID OR HAVING FORCE OR POWER. TO EXPRESS RECOGNITION OF. TO EXPRESS THANKS OR GRATITUDE FOR.

The connotations are that being self-interested is a bad thing. Being self-less is virtuous. I think it's just a simple misunderstanding, really. I think of it as Self-lessness vs Self-fullness.

LIE: PRAISE AND ACKNOWLEDGEMENT FROM OTHERS MEANS I HAVE MADE IT.

In a way this lie comes back to the belief that other people have got it all figured out and that you are a fraud, an imposter, a blagger. I'd like for you to understand the truth and then reframe this belief.

TRUTH: THE MORE YOU LOVE YOUR DECISIONS THE LESS YOU NEED OTHERS TO LOVE THEM.

The truth is that no-one has a fucking clue what they are doing. Everyone is just making it up. The more creative and in touch with your feminine energy you are,[124] the more you are making it up. How wonderful is that? How would the species evolve without femininity, without creativity – innovation and creation?

This step is about valuing what you have got, having self-respect, learning self-love. The truth is, taking responsibility is empowering. Nobody can look after you like you can. No one else knows exactly how to acknowledge you, in a way that will be received.

When you are looked after, when your needs are met, you have MORE to give the world and you can be selfless.

However let's be brutally honest here, if you are not looked after, what have you got to give? If your well is empty there is no water to share! Your basic needs must be met before you can serve others. Get your needs met, and then reach out. The more you look after you, the more you have to give to others.

---

124. Not femininity, but feminine energy, Shakti or Kali energy.

Here's the real crux of it - no one else can look after you the way you need to be looked after. *They can support you, they can give you what you ask of them or model to them, but expecting others to take care of your needs is selfish, whereas looking after yourself is not.*

- *Selfish isn't leaving your job to do something you love. Doing a job you resent is selfish.*

- *Leaving the relationship you are in because you aren't happy isn't selfish. Staying with that person and not giving them the opportunity to meet the person who truly lights their fire is selfish.*

- *Negotiating a business deal or joint venture that looks after your needs is not selfish. Not asking for what you need or want and then being resentful or not giving your all when you don't feel well compensated is selfish.*

Being self-interested AND acting from a place of compassion and service to others is the way forward. Being self-responsible and acting from a place of gratitude is integral to a life of AHHH.

Cultivating this SELF-FULLNESS is achieved by acknowledging ourselves.

How often do you move the goal posts without acknowledging what you have achieved?

Success breeds success. As T. Harv Eker says 'success is a habit, just like failure or mediocrity'.[125] In order to create a habit of success we must do what we do with all habitual behaviour: normalise it. Not only will taking the time to consciously praise yourself for having achieved your desired outcome motivate you to do more and give you a realistic sense of what you are capable of, it will make 'success' normal for you. It is vital that you take the time to acknowledge when you reach your targets and find ways to reward yourself. Celebrate the small wins!

---

125. T. Harv Eker is an author, businessman and motivational speaker known for his theories on wealth and motivation. He is the author of the book *Secrets of the Millionaire Mind* published by HarperCollins.

I take myself to a yoga class, or take some time out and go and see a friend for coffee, or go and hang out with my friends and their kids.

- Find your own ways to recognise your achievements – this will also stop you from seeking external approval.

Ultimately the most important person to impress is you! Keeping yourself motivated and being realistic about what you can and cannot achieve is really important. If you don't hit a deadline you have set yourself, rather than seeing it as a failure, why not move the deadline and acknowledge the feedback, learning for next time to give yourself more time, or refine the resources available? Then celebrate your ability to recognise feedback and adjust. The key is in the reframing and choosing how to acknowledge the evidence.

> 'YOU CANNOT GET SICK ENOUGH TO HELP SICK PEOPLE GET BETTER. YOU CANNOT GET POOR ENOUGH TO HELP POOR PEOPLE THRIVE. IT IS ONLY IN YOUR THRIVING THAT YOU HAVE ANYTHING TO OFFER ANYONE. IF YOU'RE WANTING TO BE OF AN ADVANTAGE TO OTHERS, BE AS TAPPED IN, TURNED IN, TURNED ON AS YOU CAN POSSIBLY BE.'
>
> – ESTHER ABRAHAM-HICKS

It is your duty to be of service, it is your duty to practise compassion, empathy and kindness. Not just to others, but to yourself too. This step is about *self-responsibility, it is about learning to value what you have got, having self-respect, learning radical self-love.*[126] *Taking responsibility is empowering.* When you are looked after, when your needs are met, you have MORE to give the world. From this place you can be truly selfless and of service. You can be so much more kind, generous and giving when your cup overfloweth. If you are not looked after first you are scraping the barrel and that which you give often gets tainted by resentment. Trust me when I tell you that it is easier to help someone from a solid foundation than it is from a wobbly one.

---

126. Coined by Gala Darling, *http://galadarling.com/getting-started-with-radical-self-love/.*

Mother yourself, father yourself. Love yourself. Appreciate yourself. Practise being nonjudgmental of yourself. Don't rescue, empower.

Give yourself what you need, rather than seeking it from others.

Treat others as you would wish to be treated. Treat yourself this way too.

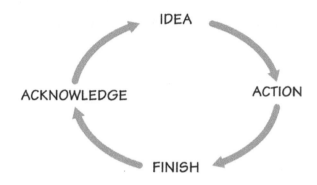

Acknowledgement Loop or the Cycle of Completion.

How can you use this loop?

EXERCISES: FROM IGNOR-ANCE TO ACKNOWLEDGEMENT

Are you ready to have a go?

EXERCISE 1: WRITE A PERSONAL MANIFESTO

MANIFESTO: A PUBLIC DECLARATION OF INTENTIONS, OPINIONS, OBJECTIVES OR MOTIVES AS ISSUED BY A GOVERNMENT, SOVEREIGN, OR ORGANIZATION. FROM THE ITALIAN WORD MANIFESTARE: TO MANIFEST.

This is your chance as your own governing body and as your own sovereign to manifest your future. Lay out your intentions. Start this as a journaling exercise – just write what comes, you can tidy it up later if you decide you want to.

1. *Think about at least one person who has had (knowingly or unknowingly) a positive influence on your life. What are the qualities you most admire in this person? What qualities did you gain from this person?*

    _____

    _____

    _____

    _____

    _____

    _____

2. *Who do you want to become? Go back the 'Exit Interview' and the 'Legacy' exercise you did. What qualities do you want to be associated with and remembered for?*

    _____

    _____

    _____

    _____

    _____

    _____

3.   *What is important to you? What 10 things are the most rewarding to you today? What do you live for and love in life? What triad of words do you now use to filter the world?*

_____

_____

_____

_____

_____

_____

4.   *Take a breather, leave your writing where it is and go for a walk or a cup of tea.*

5.   *Review what you have written and circle key ideas, words or phrases that you would like to include in your personal manifesto.*

6.   *Write a rough draft. Carry it with you for a week or so, make amends to it as you live with it. This is an on-going exercise, it is something you can refer to, alter, and it is for you. You can share it with your family, or partner, or keep it entirely to yourself. You can write it as a bulleted list, or as a paragraph, include quotes or pictures, or draw. Whatever works for you.*

_____

_____

_____

_____

_____

_____

7. *At the end of the week, write up a final draft of your manifesto and find somewhere permanent to keep it. Somewhere you can refer to it. Periodically, check in with yourself – does it invoke direction, challenge, purpose, and motivation when you read it?*

_____

_____

_____

_____

_____

_____

EXERCISE 2: 'BE' TIME

Go to your calendar or whatever you use to schedule time. You are now going to schedule in some play time, me time, pyjama time. I don't mind what you do with it, but I want you to find a way to just BE. This is time to integrate, play, think, stop and just BE.

STEP 7: FROM CRITICISM TO APPRECIATION

CRITICISM: THE EXPRESSION AND NOTING OF DISAPPROVAL OF SOMEONE OR SOMETHING ON THE BASIS OF PERCEIVED FAULTS OR MISTAKES.

Criticism can often be an exercise in noticing the differences or mistakes in ourselves, others and situations. Not really promoting feelings of AHHH, eh? How about actively noticing the similarities over the differences? – By this point all that is needed is a perception shift or a reframing. Choose to notice what has worked, what you have learned, what you are grateful for – when things aren't as you want them to be, it doesn't necessarily mean that there isn't something even better happening. Remember to ask yourself, 'What if life were happening for me not to me?' Remember that being open-minded doesn't mean that your brain will fall out.

APPRECIATION: RECOGNITION OF THE QUALITY, VALUE, SIGNIFICANCE, OR MAGNITUDE OF PEOPLE AND THINGS. A JUDGMENT OR OPINION, ESPECIALLY A FAVOURABLE ONE. AN EXPRESSION OF GRATITUDE. AWARENESS OR DELICATE PERCEPTION, ESPECIALLY OF AESTHETIC QUALITIES OR VALUES. A RISE IN VALUE OR PRICE, ESPECIALLY OVER TIME.

People who cultivate a positive mind-set perform better in the face of challenge. In fact the research shows that our brains, in positive, perform 31% better in a positive state than they do in negative, neutral or stressed states. Dopamine is released when we are happy in the present. Dopamine not only makes you happier, but it turns on all the learning centres in your brain, allowing you to adapt to the world in a different way. Much of the current research on neuroplasticity—the ability of the brain to change even in adulthood—reveals that as you develop new habits, you rewire the brain. As I said earlier, just like exercising muscles at the gym, we can build new strong neural pathways, and create an environment of positivity in our brains.

> 'OUR CHARACTER IS BASICALLY A COMPOSITE OF OUR HABITS.
> BECAUSE THEY ARE CONSISTENT, OFTEN UNCONSCIOUS PATTERNS,
> THEY CONSTANTLY, DAILY, EXPRESS OUR CHARACTER.'
> – STEPHEN COVEY

Appreciation in my experience is what happens as a result of being Aware, Aspiring, Accepting, taking Action, being Accountable, and Acknowledging. Doing these things means that you are switched on, engaged and in your element. Living in this way is a choice, an attitude, an adventure, an experience. Life is short, precious, and can be as meaningful and as deliberate as you choose to make it. Appreciation can be cultivated in other ways too:

> '90% OF YOUR HAPPINESS IS NOT PREDICTED
> BY YOUR EXTERNAL WORLD, BUT BY HOW
> YOUR BRAIN PROCESSES THE WORLD.'
> – SHAWN ACHOR

Shawn Achor's research shows that a whopping 90% of your happiness is based on how you process the world.[127] 'Happiness fuels success, not the other way around.' Achor teaches five scientifically proven strategies of happiness that will not only increase your levels of optimism but will

---

127. *http://www.ted.com/talks/shawn_achor_the_happy_secret_to_better_work.html*

help you live longer, feel better, lose weight, reduce stress, increase creativity, make better financial decisions, become more successful at work or school – the list goes on and on. Achor claims that 75% of our job success is predicted not by intelligence, but by our optimism, social support network and by our ability to manage energy and stress in a positive way.

The misconception is that success precedes happiness. 'Once I get a promotion, I'll be happy,' or, 'Once I lose weight, I'll feel great.' But because success is a moving target—as soon as we hit that target, we raise it again—the happiness that results from success is fleeting. The truth is that it in fact it works the other way around: people who cultivate a positive mindset perform better in the face of challenge. In fact the research shows that our brains, in a positive state, perform 31% better than they do in negative, neutral or stressed states. Dopamine is released when we are happy in the present. 'Dopamine not only makes you happier, but it turns on all the learning centres in your brain, allowing you to adapt to the world in a different way.' Achor calls this the 'Happiness Advantage'[128]—every outcome shows improvement when the brain is thinking positively. And his research is not in isolation; Sonja Lyubomirsky, Laura King, and Ed Diener[129] found strong evidence of directional causality between life satisfaction and successful business outcomes.

Another common misconception is that our genetics, our environment, or a combination of the two is able to determine how happy we are. Whilst it is true that both factors have an impact, our general sense of wellbeing is surprisingly malleable. The habits we cultivate, the way we interact with others, our attitude towards stress—all these can be managed.

Engaging in one brief positive exercise every day for as little as three weeks can have a lasting impact. In December 2008, just before the worst tax season in decades, Achor worked with tax managers at KPMG in New York and New Jersey to see if he could help them become happier. *He asked them to choose one of five activities that correlate with positive change:*

- Jot down three things they were grateful for.

---

128. *http://goodthinkinc.com/the-happiness-advantage/*
129. *The Benefits of Frequent Positive Affect: Does Happiness Lead to Success?* by Sonja Lyubomirsky, Ed Diener, and Laura King.

- Write a positive message to someone in their social support network.

- Meditate at their desk for two minutes.

- Exercise for 10 minutes.

- Take two minutes to describe in a journal the most meaningful experience of the past 24 hours.

The participants performed their activity every day for three weeks. Several days after the training concluded, he evaluated both the participants and a control group to determine their general sense of wellbeing. How engaged were they? Were they depressed? On every metric, the experimental group's scores were significantly higher than the control group's. AND, when he tested both groups again, four months later, the experimental group still showed significantly higher scores in optimism and life satisfaction. In fact, participants' mean score on the life satisfaction scale—a metric widely accepted to be one of the greatest predictors of productivity and happiness at work—moved from 22.96 on a 35-point scale before the training to 27.23 four months later, a significant increase. Just one quick exercise a day kept these tax managers happier for months after the training program had ended. Happiness had become habitual.

This is great news; it means that we can train our brains to become more positive. The difficultly is that permanent change takes consistency, persistence, and repetition. The brain's neural pathways must change so that the beliefs, thoughts, and perceptions we want become the easiest thoughts. For some people it will take 21 days, for others up to 35, suggesting that a month is a good amount of time to continuously practise something, and for that new idea or behaviour to have become normalised.[130]

There is some evidence that our brains are naturally wired to focus on the negative, which can make us feel stressed and unhappy even though there are a lot of positive things in our lives. Dr Rick Hanson[131] suggests that

---

130. Slater's Upside Down Glasses experiment in the 1930s and many more since, in *New Research on Consciousness*, Jason T. Locks.
131. Dr Rick Hanson Neuropsychologist, member of U.C. Berkeley's Greater Good Science Center's advisory board, and author of the book *Hardwiring Happiness: The New Brain Science of Contentment, Calm, and Confidence.*

whilst this is a natural tendency, training our brains to appreciate positive experiences when we do have them is as simple as taking the time to focus on them as they happen to install the experience in the brain and convert the neural structure.

'It's really important to have positive experiences of these things that we want to grow, and then really help them sink in, because if we don't help them sink in, they don't become neural structure very effectively... taking the extra 10, 20, 30 seconds to enable everyday experiences to convert to neural structure so that increasingly, you have these strengths with you wherever you go.'[132]

This reiterates Hebb's Law:[133] 'Neurons that fire together, wire together.'

Repeated patterns of mental activity build neural structure. The problem is that the brain is very good at building brain structure from negative experience. We learn immediately from pain; 'once burned, twice shy.' Unfortunately, the brain is not as quick at turning positive experiences into emotional learning neural structures. As Hanson explains:

'Unfortunately, we have brains that are incentivized toward seeing the negative tiles, so if anything, deliberately looking for the positive tiles just kind of levels the playing field.'

This is why we need to consciously take the time to acknowledge positive experience or thoughts. Developing feelings of calm, of safety, and of resourcefulness increases our ability to recreate these feelings at will.

If all this research isn't enough to motivate you, neuroscience research led by Mark Beeman at Northwestern University demonstrates that individuals are more likely to solve complex problems when they are in a positive mood, as measured by signature activity in the brain's cingulate cortex.[134] In one study, for example, college students who watched a short video of a comedy routine by Robin Williams were much more likely to

---

132. Dr Rick Hanson Interviewed by Julie Beck.
http://www.theatlantic.com/health/archive/2013/10/how-to-build-a-happier-brain/280752/

133. Donald Olding Hebb, 1904–85, was a Canadian psychologist who was influential in the area of neuropsychology, best known for his theory of Hebbian learning, which he introduced in his classic 1949 work *The Organization of Behavior: A Neuropsychological Theory*, (New York: Wiley and Sons).

134. John Kounios and Mark Beeman, 'The Aha! Moment: The cognitive Neuroscience of Insight.' *Current Directions In Psychological Science* 18, no. 4 (August 2009): From Tina Seelig's book: *InGenius: A crash Course in Creativity*: 210-16 *Chapter 9: Move Fast Break Things*

solve a word-association puzzle, a proxy for creativity, than those who had watched a scary or boring video beforehand.

Being in a good mood, really does make you more intelligent.

EXERCISES: FROM CRITICISM TO APPRECIATION

Are you ready to have a go?

EXERCISE I: ROUTES TO HAPPINESS

Choose one or more, there is no harm in doing all, but do them every day for 21 days in a row.

Journal: write down 3 new things each day that you are grateful for. *Journaling the positive experience relives the experience, lighting up your neurology and activating the new desired pathways.*

Move your body: There are so many benefits to having a physical practice. I don't care if you run, dance, yoga, lift, swim or do star jumps. *Exercise teaches your brain that your behaviour matters. It also released dopamine. It pulls you out of your head, and back into your body. It enables you to see physical progress. There are SO many reasons why you need to have some kind of physical practice.*

Meditate. Whatever this means for you. I don't recommend anything more than sitting quietly, without any distractions and allowing your thoughts to wash over you, without trying to push them aside, or stop them, nor allowing your brain to get involved in a thought process. I am a particularly visual person, so I like to think of my thoughts as clouds in a vast blue sky; as they enter my mind I let them cross the sky and leave again. The cultural ADHD we have created by doing multiple things at once is alleviated as we practise focusing on one thing at a time.

Perform random acts of kindness. Say one kind thing to someone every day. Or pay for someone's parking. Or send someone a note to say that you appreciate them. Whatever takes your fancy. Random acts of kindness are conscious acts of kindness. By practising kindness you not only bring someone joy, but in so doing you elevate your own levels of joy and by practising these expressions ourselves we learn to recognise them and open our hearts to the receipt of them ourselves.

STEP 8: AD INFINITUM

IN CONTEXT, AD INFINITUM USUALLY MEANS 'CONTINUE FOREVER, WITHOUT LIMIT' AND THUS CAN BE USED TO DESCRIBE A NON-TERMINATING PROCESS, A NON-TERMINATING REPEATING PROCESS, OR A SET OF INSTRUCTIONS TO BE REPEATED 'FOREVER'.

This has just been your first trip through the principles. Here's the thing: don't be fooled into thinking you're a master of life now.

LIE: I'VE DONE IT ONCE, NOW I KNOW IT.

Remember that bit where we talked about 3 things being true – birth, death, and change? The following is also true:

TRUTH: LIFE MASTERY IS A PROCESS OF PRACTISING WHAT WE THINK WE KNOW AND WATCHING IT CHANGE.

Once you get to Step 7: Appreciation, something happens – a kind of levelling up. It's a bit like in a computer game when you reach the end of a level; there's a giant celebration and you think you're done, but then you're suddenly dropped into a new level, which looks exactly like the last level, except it's more complex. For a moment you feel defeated and ready to give up, but then you remember everything that you have learned – you now know which things to jump on and which things to avoid. You know when to go for it and when to conserve your lives. You now have new

301

skills, you get a chance to try them out in new circumstances and laugh at what used to take you three or four goes now being a cinch!

Step 8 is the pause between your inhale and your exhale. It's the realisation that it goes on and on. It's making a commitment to stay aware and to use the principles.

Mystery, Mastery, Mystery.

Step 8 is your step into mastery. Into life. Into freedom. Freedom for me is about making decisions based on my values rather than survival.

> 'WISDOM COMES ONLY WHEN YOU STOP LOOKING FOR IT AND
> START LIVING THE LIFE THE CREATOR INTENDED FOR YOU.'
> – HOPI PROVERB

USE THE STEPS.... IT'S A PROCESS, LESS LATERAL - MORE CYCLICAL, A LOOP WHICH CAN BE USED FOR ANY ISSUE OR GOAL!

1. AWARENESS

2. ASPIRATION

3. ACCEPTANCE

4. ACTION

5. ACCOUNTABILITY

6. ACKNOWLEDGEMENT

7. APPRECIATION

8. AD INFINITUM

Do the internal work first – then the external. Otherwise it has nowhere to land. You'll have it, but you won't receive it. Make as many mistakes as you can. Making mistakes means you are living rather than just thinking, theorising or fantasising about life – GO LIVE!

FIN

IF YOU WANT MORE, HEAD TO WWW.ENTREPRENEURENABLER.COM.